The Inner Journey

Other titles in the
Women's Edge Health Enhancement Guide
series:

Busy Woman's Cookbook
Fight Fat
Food Smart
Foolproof Weight Loss
Get Well, Stay Well
Growing Younger
Herbs That Heal
Natural Remedies
Total Body Toning

Women's Edge
HEALTH ENHANCEMENT GUIDE™

The Inner Journey

Pathways to Emotional Health

By Alison Rice, Judith Springer Riddle, and the Editors of

Psychological Consultant: **Jerry L. Murphy**, Psy.D., assistant clinical professor in the department of community health and aging at Temple University and licensed clinical psychologist in private practice in Philadelphia

RODALE

NOTICE

This book is intended as a reference volume only, not as a medical manual. The information given here is designed to help you make informed decisions about your health. It is not intended as a substitute for any treatment that may have been prescribed by your doctor. If you suspect that you have a medical problem, we urge you to seek competent medical help.

Library of Congress Cataloging-in-Publication Data

Rice, Alison.
    The inner journey : pathways to emotional health / Alison Rice,
Judith Springer Riddle, and the editors of Prevention Health Books for
Women.
       p.   cm. — (Women's edge health enhancement guide)
    Includes index.
    ISBN 1–57954–324–3 hardcover
    1. Women—Mental health. 2. Women—Psychology. 3. Stress management
for women.   I. Riddle, Judith Springer. II. Prevention Health Books for
Women.   III. Title. IV. Series.
RC451.4.W6 R53 2001
616.89'0082—dc21   00–010980

Distributed to the book trade by St. Martin's Press

2 4 6 8 10 9 7 5 3 1 hardcover

Visit us on the Web at www.rodalebooks.com, or call us toll-free at (800) 848-4735.

RODALE

WE **INSPIRE** AND **ENABLE** PEOPLE TO IMPROVE
THEIR LIVES AND THE WORLD AROUND THEM

Contents

Introduction

When I read the outline for this book, I was immediately struck by the fact that it describes my life to a T. With three kids, a husband who travels, a full-time job, a 30-minute commute, and a dog and cat (who hate each other), I didn't need anyone to tell me about the emotional damage inherent in trying to be Superwoman. What I could never figure out was how to avoid it.

Now, I can. The women who wrote this book made it a personal mission to go a step beyond the typical. We all know we need to slow down, take time for ourselves, and learn to say no. What we don't know is *how* to do these things. This book shows us how.

Like all of the books in the Women's Edge series, this one will not only entertain and educate you, but will provide clear, actionable suggestions for ways you can bring your life into emotional balance. For instance, you'll learn how to manage your anger by keeping an anger journal. How to recognize whether you have a fear of intimacy, and what to do about it. Not only will you learn how to cope with depression, anger, fear, and a host of other emotional land mines, but you'll also see how you can transform those negative feelings into positive forces that feed creativity, pleasure, satisfaction, and effectiveness.

In writing this book, we talked not only to the usual suspects—psychologists, social workers, therapists, and psychiatrists—but to dozens of real women, too. One woman, for instance, shares with you the ways she learned to cope with her own serious illness. Because the stories throughout the book are so personal, in most instances the women's names have been changed.

In addition to educating you, we wanted to make you laugh. That's why we included the cartoons throughout the book that succinctly portray the sometimes-irrational elements of our lives. And, so you'll never be at a loss for words at the next cocktail party, we added small biographies of the pioneers in the psychology field.

By the time I finished working on this book, I felt I had completed my own inner journey. Reading the advice and suggestions throughout the book taught me the importance of emotional balance and ways to achieve it. I've started an anger journal and learned to turn to my girlfriends for support more often, and now I understand that when I work on my cross-stitch, it's not only creative, but therapeutic. I've learned that finding time for myself is not selfish, but a critical step in maintaining my emotional balance. I hope you have similar experiences. Enjoy!

Debra L. Gordon
Women's Edge Editor

PART ONE

Know
Thyself

Woman and Superwoman

Back in the 1970s, when feminism was still in its infancy, the airwaves featured a little ditty for Enjoli perfume in which a raven-haired beauty scrambles eggs while wearing a tight-fitting sheath dress, delivering a beguiling message that women could not only bring home the bacon, but fry it up in a pan and still remember how to make her man feel like, well, a man. Translation: You can have it all.

A fulfilling career. A satisfying marriage and sex life. A happy, harmonious home. Kids who don't whine.

Yeah, right.

What the Superwoman in the ad *didn't* sing about was that having it all costs us big time. "The Superwoman hasn't changed much since the 1970s," says Kaye V. Cook, Ph.D., chair of psychology at Gordon College in Wenham, Massachusetts. "We're still expected to bring home a paycheck, take care of the kids, look attractive, entertain, and keep a beautiful home."

Listen up, ladies—it just ain't working anymore.

"Women can't do it all, and they shouldn't believe that they have to," says Leah J. Dickstein, M.D., director of the division of attitudinal and behavioral medicine at the University of Louisville School of Medicine in Kentucky. "There is no such real-life person as Superwoman or Superman."

So instead of desperately clinging to our tattered, jelly-smeared capes, we need a new role model—a *new* Superwoman.

One who brings home the bacon, but isn't above serving takeout. Who realizes that with so many roles to juggle, she's bound to drop a ball once in a while. Who brings the best of herself to all of the roles she plays, but understands that she won't be able to please all of the people all of the time.

This is the true Superwoman. You don't have to emulate her; you *are* her—you just don't know it. But being a superhero is a tough job. Which is why, to save our health and sanity, we need to strive for balance. That is, devoting our time and energy to the most important areas of our lives in ways that make us feel fulfilled, energized, and whole—and letting the rest go.

And while we can't have it all (yes, it's time to break down and admit it), we can have a lot. Peace. Energy. Contentment. A rich, rewarding (if often chaotic) life.

Welcome to the Grind

We rise at dawn to get ourselves dressed for work and the kids ready for school. We give them a bag of Cheerios to eat in the car (since we don't have time to cook breakfast), the dirty coffeepot gets left in the sink, and then it's into the car for the commute to work, where deadlines, performance reviews, and unceasing demands await.

Eight (or 10) hours later, we head home to start the second shift: dinner, homework, baths, laundry, bedtime stories. If we're lucky, we'll sit down around 9:00 P.M. for an hour before exhaustion drives us to bed—only to repeat the grind the next day.

This schedule can deplete even the most energetic woman and turn us into seething cauldrons of stress. If we boil over (as we usually do), physical and emotional illness results. Stress can weaken our immune systems and lead to stomach problems, back pain, menstrual irregularities, migraine headaches, high blood pressure, and even heart disease. It's a primary player in depression and anxiety disorders, and it can throw us into an emotional tailspin faster than you can read to the end of this sentence.

Think of it as your body's way of sending up a white flag. At the root of this emotional and physical stress

WOMEN ASK WHY

Why won't my husband just listen to me rather than always try to offer solutions?

Generally speaking, men are more inclined to assume the take-charge role of Mr. Fix-It because they're raised to deal with life's issues head-on without letting their feelings get in the way. By contrast, women are raised to express their emotions first and handle problems second. Of course, there are women who focus on solving problems and men who want to express their emotions.

It sounds as if your husband's way of helping is to offer you solutions. He hears news about a fire and, without thinking, rushes to put it out. It's painful for him to see you upset, so he figures he has to help you.

There's nothing wrong with that. But if you're the type of person who likes to get whatever it is off her chest without advice, talking to your mate will often be frustrating.

Take heart. What you're dealing with is simply a difference in communication styles. You want to be heard. Your husband wants to save the world.

Here's one way to smooth out the situation. In a quiet, relaxed moment, tell your husband, "When I'm upset, it's really helpful for me to express how I'm feeling. I need some time to talk about my feelings. So it would really help me if you would listen and empathize with me—without offering advice."

If you can do this, you'll communicate better, increasing the chance that your needs—and your husband's—will be met. You'll feel satisfied knowing that each of you is being listened to, and he will no longer feel that you're incapable of handling your dilemmas.

Expert consulted
Amy Halberstadt, Ph.D.
Professor of psychology
North Carolina State University
Raleigh

REAL-LIFE SCENARIO

She Can't Say No to Her Boss

Sharon, 41, is the executive assistant to the president of a software manufacturing company. Her boss puts in marathon 16-hour days and expects Sharon to do the same. To get the work done, Sharon skips lunch, stays late, and works weekends. Yet Sharon, who is married and has three children, is afraid to let her boss know she's sinking under her workload. It's no surprise that her marriage is beginning to suffer, her oldest son is having problems in school, and she's having trouble sleeping. What should she do?

Like many women juggling a career and family responsibilities, Sharon is overextended, overrun, and overwhelmed. The number of hours her boss expects her to work—given the fact that she has a family—is not acceptable.

Sharon needs to take a hard look at her life. She should set aside some quiet time for herself and write down what her priorities are, what's important to her, how many hours she'd like to work, and how much time she wants to spend with her family. Sharon should also ask her husband for suggestions on how they can get their family life back on track.

Next, Sharon should develop a plan to put her wish list into action. She needs to talk to her boss about reducing her workload. She should tell her how many hours she's currently working and how many she's willing to work. Sharon should also be prepared to offer her boss suggestions on how to get the extra work done. For example, she might suggest delegating the work to other colleagues.

Sharon should understand that asserting herself in this way is a risk. But it's a risk worth taking. Her boss may respect her for standing up for herself and agree to try one of her suggestions, or she may tell Sharon it's her way or the highway. If the latter wins out, Sharon should begin looking for another job pronto, or resign if she can afford it financially.

For Sharon, the bottom line here is self-preservation.

Expert consulted
Susan M. Seidman, Ph.D.
Associate professor of psychology
Fordham University
New York City

is the fact that we simply take on too many roles. At home, we're domestic goddesses, mothers, and lovers. At work, we're hard-driving professionals.

Do we ever stop to think how difficult juggling all these roles can be? Not likely. We're just too darn busy. But take a closer look at some of our more common roles and the demands each one places on our shoulders.

Mother. We're nurse, disciplinarian, good listener, chauffeur, scheduler, and nurturer, all wrapped into one. "Switching from one role to the next, in split-second intervals, can be overwhelming," says Dr. Cook.

Being on call 24 hours a day, 7 days a week is tough even for psychologists. "I work from 9:00 A.M. to 11:00 P.M., and I'm up at 6:30 in the morning," says Dr. Cook. "It takes its toll." Our marriages, our kids, our health, and even our physical environment (who has time to clean?) suffer as a result.

Career woman. "The average career woman who is also a wife and mother works 78 to 81 hours a week, at work and at home," says Roberta Nutt, Ph.D., professor of psychology and director of the counseling psychology doctorate program at Texas Woman's University in Denton. And the strain shows. In a study of 152 working women with families, those who reported high levels of job strain also scored high for depression, anxiety, and hostility.

"Working women also have to deal with being passed over for promotions, being asked to perform tasks they're overqualified for, and being left out of meetings where decisions are made," says Dr. Dickstein.

Wife. After the kids are in bed, it's time for the third shift: lover. He wants to make love, you want to hit the pillow and start snoring. "You almost have to schedule time for sex," says Dr. Cook. Which doesn't exactly make you feel, well, hot.

"Sex falls by the wayside in a marriage because you're too tired. But couples need to find time to spend with each other. The kids will move away and the jobs will change, but the marital relationship will remain," says Dr. Nutt.

Friend. Our girlfriends keep us sane. We laugh, gossip, listen to problems, and even cry together. But to reap the benefits of our friends' love and concern, we have to give them our time and energy. Which, as we know, is in short supply. The result? Guilt.

Social planner. "Most women are superorganized," says Dr. Dickstein. Which is why we usually get the job of events coordinator—planning vacations and birthday parties, reserving tickets, making doctor's appointments, and hosting family gatherings and holiday parties. It's just one more drain on our energy.

We didn't audition for any of these roles, but they landed in our laps anyway. And no matter how much we have on our plate, the people we love don't seem to realize that there are limits to our time, energy, and strength.

THE SIGNS OF CAREGIVER BURNOUT

According to a survey conducted by the National Family Caregivers Association, 70 percent of its member caregivers are between the ages of 36 and 65, and 82 percent are women. If you're caring for mom, dad, an ill or disabled husband, or a child with special needs, take heed of these warning signs of burnout, and seek professional help.

1. Depression. You're constantly unhappy, have trouble sleeping, experience crying spells, or take little or no interest in activities you once enjoyed.

2. Isolation. Your caregiving duties are consuming you to the point where you virtually lose touch with the outside world. You stop returning phone calls and visiting friends. You feel as if you have no downtime to relax, unwind, and stay in touch with the outside world.

3. Anxiety. You wake with a sick feeling in the pit of your stomach and go to bed with it, too. You constantly worry about making ends meet, administering medications, and monitoring at-home nursing-care equipment.

4. Irritability and anger. You blow up over trivial matters and are continually crabby, short-tempered, frustrated, and impatient. You're always on the edge of your temper.

Participating in a support group can help you manage stress and give you an opportunity to talk with others who understand what you're going through. For more information, contact the National Caregiving Foundation, 801 North Pitt Street, Suite 116, Alexandria, VA, 22314, or visit its Web site at www.caregivingfoundation.org. To request a free caregiver's support kit, call (800) 930-1357.

When we don't live up to everyone's expectations, we can feel like failures. "We even feel irresponsible and less of a woman," says Dr. Nutt.

Who Cares? We Do

Every role we play, however, has one thing in common: They all involve taking care of others' needs.

ALL IN THE GENES?

What is maternal instinct?

Biologically speaking, it's a woman's prepro-grammed readiness to respond to an infant's hunger or distress. Perhaps that's why many of us believe we're supposed to "just know" what to do as soon as our child is born.

True maternal instinct stops within a child's first year of life. But we tend to confuse that biological readiness to meet a child's basic needs with the developmental process of becoming a mother.

And that process takes time. With time, we *learn* to become good mothers. Our relationships with our children develop as we form connections with them and discover who they are as people. We tune in to their psyche and know intuitively what is in their best interests, even if they don't.

At times, even the most loving mothers can temporarily lose that keen sense of awareness. Our lives are so hectic, or our own issues so pressing, that our antennae fail to pick up the subtle cues that tell us when our kids are hurt, upset, or frightened.

But after all, we're not imbued with special powers when we give birth. Despite our expectations, mothers are, in the end, mere mortals who make mistakes. All we can do is our best.

And make time in our busy schedules for talking, laughing, and pillow fights. "We need to make it a priority to enjoy time with our kids at least a couple times a week." After all, staying close emotionally will keep our mothering skills sharp.

Expert consulted
Diane G. Sanford, Ph.D.
President, Women's Healthcare Partnership
St. Louis
Author of Postpartum Survival Guide

"Caregiving is so much of what we do," says Carole R. Rothman, Ph.D., professor of psychology at Lehman College in New York City and coauthor of *I'll Take Care of You: A Practical Guide for Family Caregivers.* "We were raised to care for others."

But this all-care, all-the-time credo can be draining. When we're always on call, there's never time to take care of ourselves, says Dr. Rothman. And if we stifle our feelings, we end up angry. Then we feel guilty about our rage.

We also become less competent as fatigue and frustration get the best of us. For example, if we care for an aging parent, the film of fatigue may result in administering the wrong medication or forgetting a doctor's appointment. If we're on call all the time for the kids, we might come to resemble a raving lunatic more than a loving mom.

Perpetual caregiving can lead to depression, when "nothing is much fun, and you stop seeing friends and doing what you enjoy," says Dr. Rothman. "Difficulty sleeping and fatigue are also signs of depression that you may not be aware of."

A Question of Balance

If you're currently living barely ahead of the eight ball day after day, you may not even be able to imagine how to attain peace, joy, and a sense of purpose in your life.

Experts have one word for you: balance.

"Balance is about preserving your mental and physical health. And you achieve that by making time for yourself," says Dr. Dickstein.

The first step is to spend time reflecting on your priorities and pinpointing those you've let slip by the wayside. "Women have to take the time—*make* the time—to examine their lives and figure out what's most important to them," says Dr. Nutt.

Set aside a block of time (tell your family the mom-machine is closed) and make a list of everything you do each day. For each item, ask yourself if it is absolutely necessary to the functioning of your life. For instance, how much television do you watch? What else could you be doing during that time? Is it absolutely necessary that you try to sell Girl Scout cookies at work for your daughter?

You'll inevitably find several things you can cross off your to-do list.

"These are the things that constantly make women feel guilty. We say, 'I'm not doing enough. I shoulda, coulda, woulda,'" says Dr. Dickstein. "But nobody's perfect. I advise women to tell their friends or family members, 'I can't do it at this time. I'll get back to you. Thanks for asking. And please ask again.'"

You also need to ask for help, both at work and at home, and to start building a support system. Can a neighbor drive your son to soccer while you start dinner? Can you turn over floor washing to your husband? Can you ask your secretary to screen your e-mail? Can you ask your gourmet-cook-of-a-mother to double her recipes when you visit so you have leftovers?

And every time you take on a new responsibility or role, evaluate the impact on other areas of your

INNER-SPACE EXPLORERS
Who was Sigmund Freud?

In the 1890s and early 1900s, Austrian neurologist Sigmund Freud laid the foundation for modern psychology with his revolutionary theories. He is perhaps best known for introducing psychoanalysis and popularizing psychotherapy in the Western world.

Freud's male-dominant view of psychology that is centered around sex has often been criticized. He said that our sexual urges, or libido, are our strongest drives from infancy through adulthood. By "sex," Freud meant anything we find pleasurable to our touch. He said that the primary sexual urge of an infant, for example, is to suckle its mother's breast. Freud held that young girls experience "penis envy" when they discover they don't have a penis like their brothers. He believed that this was something women never quite resolved, and as a result, women were psychologically inferior to men. He also theorized that anxiety stems from sexual energy that has been repressed in our unconscious from childhood.

While Freud's ideas were not kind to women, they very much reflected the culture of Victorian Vienna, says Ellyn Kaschak, Ph.D., professor of psychology at San Jose State University in California. He lived in a time when sexuality was taboo. *Leg* was a suggestive word and even piano legs were covered with a skirt for fear they were too suggestive.

In addition to his sex-centered theories, Freud was especially interested in the unconscious mind, which he believed originates in the "id." He said that all of our wishes—including our sexual urges, our basic need for food, and our creative ideas—come from our unconscious. Freud explored this mysterious part of the mind through his patients' free associations and slips of the tongue (Freudian slips).

Freud also relied heavily on interpreting dreams, which he felt held symbolic clues to the wishes that are locked in our unconscious. His dream analysis marked the real beginnings of scientific research into the mind and led to better understanding and treatment of mental health problems.

Freud's ideas are very influential even today.

life. Are you thinking of joining a women's Bible-study group? Maybe it meets only once a month, but that's one night you can't cook dinner or drive the kids to the library. Are you willing to get takeout and put the chauffeuring responsibilities on your husband that night? If not, don't join.

Finally, set aside quiet time to just be. To do what you want to do. To dream many great dreams, and to achieve a few of them. When researchers asked 16 working mothers what the word *well-being* meant to them, finding solitude and inner peace topped the list.

"Ask yourself, 'When I'm old and gray, what are some of the things that I will wish I had done?'" says Dr. Nutt. "And make sure you do them."

To start, read on. The rest of this book is brimming with ways to plumb the depths of your hidden emotions, set priorities, shed those damaging negative feelings, and find your own definition of well-being.

From Clan Woman to Career Woman

Our female friends are more than just people to lunch or shop with.

They're the ones who agree with us when we say our husbands are pigs—and when we say our husbands are so wonderful that we don't deserve them. Who ply us with wine and chocolate when we're laid off, break up, or realize that our favorite pair of jeans, the ones worn in just the right places, are now ready for the trash heap. Our husbands want to solve things; our girlfriends let us beat a problem into the ground without caring about the outcome.

We need our girlfriends more than ever, given the crazy pace of our lives and the complexity of issues we face today.

"Women chatting over coffee are not just sharing news," writes author Terri Apter, Ph.D., in her book *Best Friends: The Pleasures and Perils of Girls' and Women's Friendships*. "Instead, they are involved in intricate patternings of love and conflict that inexorably shape and change who they are."

And while your husband may be a "best friend," it's a rare man who can provide the level of intimacy that another woman can.

"Talking with women offers a special understanding that we often don't get with men, however close we are to them in other ways," says Dr. Apter, who tutors in psychology at the University of Cambridge in England. "Men simply cannot understand a lot of the things we as women go through. There's a deep understanding that comes through suffering and experience."

The Women's Room

Connecting with our own gender in a frank, meaningful way is more important to us than it is to men, says Jean Baker Miller, M.D., director of the Jean Baker Miller Training Institute at Wellesley College in Massachusetts. As women, we put special value on relationships of all kinds because, in a way, that's our job. Men, however, adhere to a societal ideal that independence is best.

Perhaps that's why a man can play basketball with another man for a decade and still not

ALL IN THE GENES?

Do women everywhere talk in a singsong voice to their babies?

The higher-pitched, singsong tone is what we call infant-directed speech—and many societies do some version of it. We don't have enough research yet, however, to say that this is a universal pattern.

What we do know is that changing the rhythm and pitch of our speech says to a baby, "This talk is for you." And it isn't just women who make this adjustment: Men do it, and so do children.

Babies are magnets for us, so using infant-directed speech is reinforced because it gets their attention. We quickly learn that if we use a normal voice, a baby will ignore us. But if we talk in a higher register and use exaggerated sounds and a singsong rhythm, a baby responds.

Different cultures demonstrate this trait in different ways. In the United States, we exaggerate the pitch and rhythm to the extreme. The speech modifications made by Japanese people are within a narrower band than ours. Chinese-speaking people adjust the sound and even the meaning of their tonal language when addressing babies. There's also evidence that among a certain tribe of Peruvian Indians, infant-directed speech is centered around volume: They whisper to their tiny ones.

We can't seem to help talking "baby talk" even when it isn't spoken. Research indicates that deaf parents of a deaf baby will modify their signing and facial expressions when communicating with the infant.

So while the singsong rhythm and high pitch may not be universal, it seems that most humans do alter their speech when talking to babies. We don't yet know exactly why, but we do know that it works.

Expert consulted
Roberta M. Golinkoff, Ph.D.
Director, Infant Language Laboratory
University of Delaware
Newark

know how many kids he has, while two women can sit down on a park bench as strangers and stand up an hour later having shared their childbirth stories. Women want to talk and men want to accomplish things, like playing basketball. Men are like filing cabinets: They can't mix up conversation and sports and family. Women, on the other hand, are like soup kettles: When one thing turns sour, everything else is affected.

And our women friends understand that.

"We tell a friend of our experiences and we feel they're shared," says Dr. Apter. "But it isn't only sympathy we get from a friend; it's also humor. Many women speak of the sassy thrill they get from talking to a girlfriend. Problems become funny, and that helps us feel stronger."

But all too often, we let the very stress of our lives separate us from our friends. Having a girlfriend seems selfish, so we give her up to meet the demands of career and family. That can be dangerous, since our friendships not only help us manage stress, but actually improve our health.

In one study, researchers at Carnegie Mellon University in Pittsburgh found that the more social relationships participants had, the fewer colds they got. Overall, their immune function operated at a 20 percent higher level than that of more introverted people.

A study of people with atherosclerosis showed that those without a close friend or confidant were more than twice as likely to die within 5 years as those who had such sustaining relationships. Close relationships also lower our risk for heart disease, alcoholism, and depression.

The challenge, then, is to find and nurture those friendships.

Friendship through the Ages

It used to be pretty easy. From the forced intimacy of a cave or tribal village to close-knit farm communities, women have always had each other.

"When we lived in caves, our 'village' was right there with us," says Susan M. Ice, M.D., medical director of the Renfrew Center in Philadelphia, which specializes in women's mental health. "We didn't have to work hard to find women to talk with."

As we moved from hunter-gatherer societies into agricultural ones, communal activities such as sewing circles, quilting bees, and church services took the place of meals around the fire, becoming regular sources of conversation and sharing for women, she says. Even into the middle of this century, when most women stayed home, there was an entire neighborhood of potential friends to choose from, not to mention mothers, sisters, and aunts who would have probably lived nearby.

But once we headed out into the

A DAY IN THE LIFE OF A TRIBAL WOMAN

Support groups aren't new; they were part of life for women in tribal cultures. Anthropologist Barbara Feezor Buttes, Ph.D., assistant professor of American studies at Arizona State University West in Phoenix, sketches a day in 1800 for a Sioux woman in the northern plains.

The rising sun is her call to prayer with her children. Her husband or other family member starts the day's fire, on which the women will cook and warm food all day. No three-meal structure binds them. There is always something ready to satisfy hunger: turnips, carrots, berries, or fresh or dried deer or rabbit meat.

The extended family gathers to eat and talk, maybe to plan what food will be gathered and hunted today from their land, later to be called the Black Hills of South Dakota. The men will hunt or fish; the elder women will care for the young children, telling them stories, instructing them in the ways of the Creator and their Sioux Nation. It's up to the women to keep the blood pure through marriage, and to carry on the oral traditions of the tribe.

The mother sets off to gather roots and wild oats with her sister-in-law. They talk about the cradleboard they're making for the new baby, the buffalo hides to be smoked and scraped that afternoon, the baseball-like game with sticks and bones that the whole family played yesterday.

The mother and sister-in-law return home to eat, to play with the young ones, to join all the able-bodied women working the hides to be fashioned into tepees. This is work they like: While hands are busy, much socializing and visiting goes on.

Toward dusk, the mother may go off alone for a private spiritual ceremony; otherwise, she is almost always surrounded by the company and caring of her communal family. She's an important part of her community: She is a teacher, wife, mother, homemaker, medicine woman, tanner, horticulturist, artist, and spiritual anchor.

At night, she and a few other women stoke the fire and carry in more water to keep the food pot full. The whole family eats together, then shares singing, stories, and news from neighboring tribes.

A DAY IN THE LIFE
OF A FARMER'S WIFE

Next time life leaves you drained, consider the lot of a farmer's wife around 1900 in midwestern America. Anthropologist Jane H. Adams, Ph.D., author of The Transformation of Rural Life: Southern Illinois 1890–1990, *traces a typical day.*

Up before the sun, this mother of at least six stokes the kitchen stove fire to start breakfast: biscuits from scratch, coffee, fried meat, and eggs. She serves up the morning meal to as many as 15 or more: kids, husband, a couple of hired hands, an elderly relative or two, and an unmarried brother or sister.

After breakfast, the girls help clean up, while Mom and children dash out to milk the cows, feed the chickens, collect eggs, and if needed, clean the henhouse.

The kids are packed off to school, leaving a grandmother or aunt to help with the next task: baking bread. This takes the rest of the morning, filled with hours of hard, steady kneading. But during the kneading and baking, she and her relatives talk . . . speculate . . . dream.

By midday, it's time to prepare dinner, the day's biggest meal. Again, the table is set for some dozen people to fuel up.

And again, Mom and any other females in the house wash the dishes with water hauled in from the well, then sweep out the house and tackle some ironing. For them, this entails handling heavy cast-iron devices heated on the stove and could take all afternoon, giving them hours to talk about their world and their lives.

If there's enough time before supper, Mom may churn cream for butter . . . make braided rugs . . . sew clothing for the whole family. In season, she might sit with relatives and neighbors on a shady porch, shelling peas and trading stories.

The last round of kitchen activities has her back in the kitchen preparing the evening meal, supervising cleanup, and then relaxing with the family. Mom lights the kerosene lamps while the kids make taffy. When everyone else retires, she returns to the kitchen one last time to organize things for the next morning's breakfast.

workplace, leaving our neighborhoods veritable ghost towns, the opportunities for closeness became harder to find.

"The one who is crunched the worst is the woman who has a paying job outside the home as well as school-age kids," says Bonnie Jacobson, Ph.D., adjunct psychology professor at New York University. "She's really neither here nor there—she can't go out to socialize with her coworkers after hours, and she can't spend much time with stay-at-home mothers."

That can be dangerous. "When we don't have groups of peers to share with, joke with, complain with, it leads to depression," says Dr. Jacobson.

A researcher with Wellesley College's Stone Center counseling services studied depression in new mothers to determine who was less depressed: women with paying jobs, or those without. Significantly, the research showed that work status didn't matter much; the key factor was female support.

And the strength of that support mattered more than the number of friends. Frequent, face-to-face contact is desirable for strong connections, but regular phone calls and even e-mail can fit the bill.

The quantity isn't nearly as important as the quality. "There's no simple rule about how many friends a woman needs. It's a matter of choice or personality," says Dr. Apter. "But most women need *at least* one very good friend."

A Friend Is . . .

Not every woman you meet is going to become your next friend. Recognizing the elements of a true friendship early on in the relationship can help you avoid making mistakes and wasting valuable time. Here are some clues.

- Self-revelation. You feel that you can be yourself and say what you think, and you feel confident that she won't criticize you in her mind or talk badly about you to other people.
- Support. A true friend won't ditch you when you're having a hard time, as if your misfortune might rub off on her. She anticipates what you might need without asking (as when she brings that critical gallon of ice cream after the boss rips apart your proposal), but she isn't afraid to push you when necessary (as when she nags you to redo said proposal).
- Service. She does things for you simply because she's your friend. Taking you to the airport. Picking up the kids from soccer. If someone does something for you, it helps to cement the relationship.
- Honesty. You can speak your mind with her, even if you disagree, and she will still be your friend.
- Forgiveness. A strong friendship will withstand the little betrayals and failures of life.

A DAY IN THE LIFE OF A MODERN HOMEMAKER

For Colleen P. Crossen, 35, being a stay-at-home mother of four is more than a full-time job: it's her life, round the clock. At her Allentown, Pennsylvania, house, here's how a typical day fills up.

Colleen's 6:00 A.M. wake-up call is her 6-month-old baby, who wants to be changed and nursed. After tending to the baby, Colleen heads downstairs to make coffee and turn on the television. The morning revs up then: breakfast for three other children, ages 7, 5, and 3, making sure the oldest is dressed, bookbag ready, and out the door to school. Husband Paul, an electrical engineer, is off to start his day.

Baby in tow, Colleen starts a round of housework and laundry (two loads each day, minimum) while keeping a watchful eye on the two children still with her. Around 10:30 A.M., hunger pangs remind her that she hasn't eaten, so she has some cereal. While the two preschoolers play with molding clay or building blocks, Colleen minds the baby. If there's time, she'll shower and dress while the baby naps.

By noon, she has to get the kids dressed and fed so she can take the 5-year-old to preschool. Back home, she'll continue doing laundry, making beds, picking up toys, and doing dishes. Simultaneously, she'll be on the phone with a member of her MOMS Club (Mothers Offering Mothers Support), to get some adult conversation with her close circle of other stay-at-home mothers. "It's like a lifeline; these women know exactly what my day and my problems are like," she says.

At 2:30 P.M., there's another car trip to preschool to pick up her son, and by 4:00, when all the children are back together, it's "complete chaos." Running around, yelling, discharging kid energy, they demand all of Colleen's attention—plus snacks. When Paul returns home at 5:00, he shepherds the brood into another room so Colleen can make dinner. After the family is fed, the three older children play in their rooms while Paul does the dishes, Colleen nurses the baby, and the two of them catch up on the events of the day.

Between 8:00 and 9:00 P.M., all the kids are put to bed; Colleen and Paul are usually asleep by 10:00. "This is the hardest job I've ever had . . . and I love it," says Colleen.

Negative People

Sometimes, friends turn toxic and all you hear from them is "It won't work. It never did. It never will. If you think it might, you're kidding yourself." What makes some people so negative?

"Life. Biochemistry. Childhood problems. Unresolved issues. Constantly being defeated. Not having a lot of success. Not being acknowledged or respected. Not being appreciated. Not feeling they have what they want in life or in a relationship," says Lillian Glass, Ph.D., communications consultant in New York City and author of nine books, including *Toxic People*.

Sometimes it's easy to deal with negative people—you just ignore them. But what do you do about friends, relatives, or coworkers who have a tendency to see the proverbial glass as half empty? For starters, don't try to change them.

"You always hope the person will change. You hope you can do something to make her not act that way," says Dr. Glass. The problem is, you can't change another person. (Didn't you try that with a boyfriend or two?) But you can change your own behavior and attitude and the interaction between the two of you.

The next time you encounter a negative friend, try these tactics.

❧ Every time she says something negative, say, "Smile," "Say something nice," or "Let's not go there." Don't scold her—that only adds fuel to the fire.

❧ Cut her off kindly, letting her

GIFT-GIVING ANGST

Twenty or so Novembers ago, Charles Langham of Charlottesville, Virginia, and his coworkers were making plans for the upcoming holidays. Like most of us, they expected to receive a lot of gifts they didn't ask for and to spend money on gifts other people didn't want. So they formed SCROOGE: the Society to Curtail Ridiculous, Outrageous, and Ostentatious Gift Exchanges.

SCROOGE publishes an annual newsletter before Christmas, but its message of keeping presents simple and affordable can apply to gift giving throughout the year. Here's how.

In General

Think homemade. If you have a talent for crafts, artwork, or making other goodies, give them as gifts. Your friends may remember these longer than they would store-bought presents, Langham says.

Think quality, not quantity. If you have a certain amount of money to spend for a gift, buy something that's small yet nice as opposed to an object that's sizable but cheap-looking, recommends Maria Everding, founder of the Etiquette Institute in St. Louis and author of *Panache That Pays*.

Pay attention to presentation. Always wrap your gift nicely, even if the store puts it in an attractive bag. "Otherwise, you're saying, 'Hey, I don't think too much of you—here's a bag with a gift inside,'" says Everding.

Pay with cash. Don't use your credit cards to buy gifts. That way, you're apt to think a little longer about the money you're about to spend, and you won't be as stunned when the bills arrive.

Don't bow to pressure. Send a wedding gift only if you attend the wedding. Otherwise, you shouldn't feel obligated to send a present, Everding says.

For the Holidays

Set guidelines and stick to them. Whether gift giving involves your family, friends, or coworkers, setting ground rules is a good way to avoid awkward situations, suggests Everding.

Set a dollar limit. SCROOGE suggests 1 percent of your gross annual pay be spent on all your holiday gifts. If you make $30,000 a year, for example, consider limiting yourself to $300 of gift-wrapped cheer.

Draw names. If you exchange gifts with your extended family, do what many large families traditionally do: Draw names so that each person buys a gift for one person instead of for everyone, Everding suggests.

Give to charity. Instead of gifts, make a donation to the person's favorite charity.

At Work

Consider consequences. Rarely, if ever, give your boss an individual gift. It may make your coworkers think you're trying to curry favor, and it can make your relationship with the boss awkward.

Collaborate. If you must give a gift, several employees should contribute to it, Everding says. Make a donation to a charity in your boss's name or take her out to lunch.

Forget employees. If you're a supervisor, refrain from giving gifts to employees. If gifts to staff are customary in your workplace, stick with something impersonal, such as a gift certificate to a restaurant or the movies.

Celebrate collectively. To stanch the stream of dollars that you spend on coworkers' birthdays, suggest that your office hold a simple monthly party for everyone whose birthday falls in that month.

Helpful Hint

If you're invited to someone's home, you should bring a small gift, such as a bottle of wine or box of chocolates, for your host or hostess. It's not intended to be opened and consumed while you're there. If your host or hostess doesn't drink or needs to avoid sweets, flowers or other fancy foods, such as gourmet olive oil, are safe choices.

know you don't want to deal with it. Say to her, "Let's not talk about this. It upsets both of us."

❧ Agree with her. Say to her, "You're right. It won't work. Not even you could find a way to make it work." Continue with this kind of response to every negative comment until the only way she can contradict you is to switch to a positive position and argue that yes, she can make it work, says Rick Kirschner, N.D., a naturopathic physician in Ashland, Oregon, and coauthor of *Dealing with People You Can't Stand*.

❧ Really listen to her. "When someone is discouraged, they don't need others to tell them exactly what they think they should do. That only makes them uncomfortable and may make them dig deeper into the hole," says Michele Novotni, Ph.D., assistant professor of counseling at Eastern College in St. Davids, Pennsylvania. Instead, simply let the negative person express what she is feeling. By encouraging a person to identify the problem area causing the discouragement, we help them keep it in perspective. It's one problem, not her whole life.

❧ Suggest that at the end of each day, she make a list of positive things that happened, both little and big. This will help her look for goodness in her life.

❧ Insist on respect in a positive way. Say to her, "When you put me down, it doesn't do good things for our relationship. I'm on your side." You may find this technique valuable when your

ALL IN THE GENES?

How is it that women's periods get into sync when they're together a lot?

In the research lab and in the world at large—on female basketball teams, among women on kibbutzes in Israel, and in just about any large office building—the phenomenon of menstrual cycles coming into synchrony has been observed over and over.

It appears to stem from what we call a primer pheromone—an odorless chemical "messenger" in the underarm secretions of women that influences hormones and cycles. In our lab, we made an extract of such secretions from one group of women, and exposed another group of women to the extract. The cycles of the recipients shifted to coincide with the cycles of the donors.

The evolutionary reason for this? We don't know. The phenomenon may have served an important purpose hundreds of thousands of years ago, but its purpose now is unclear.

What is clear, though, is how significant this area of research is. Imagine: Someday, you may be able to both regulate your cycle and know when you're most fertile just by exposing yourself to a compound in a primer pheromone. As an organic chemist, my task is to isolate and identify the compounds responsible.

These pheromones are *not* the "sex scent" ingredients that some cologne manufacturers tout as making you irresistible to the opposite sex. There is zero evidence to support these claims for humans. Males aren't out of the picture, though, when it comes to primer pheromones. We conducted a study of women with histories of abnormal-length cycles. After male underarm extract was rubbed under their noses, the women's cycles all moved closer to the normal length of 29½ days.

Expert consulted
George Preti, Ph.D.
Member, Monell Chemical Senses Center
Philadelphia

friend misdirects her frustrations and anger at you. Be assertive to keep the direction of the conversation positive. Respond with, "I really want to be helpful, but you're making it hard for me. Let's refocus on your situation and see if there's something we can come up with that would help," says Robert D. Kerns, Ph.D., associate professor of psychiatry, neurology, and psychology at Yale University and chief of psychology service at VA Connecticut Healthcare System in West Haven, Connecticut.

➤ Focus on your own attitude instead of your friend's. Instead of trying to change her mind and ultimately feeling negative yourself, maintain your own sense of well-being by taking whatever she says and telling yourself the opposite. "If she says, 'You'll never get it to work,' tell yourself, 'I'll find a way to make it work.'" If this isn't enough, "take a deep breath and think of something relaxing, peaceful, and distracting," says Dr. Kerns. Your goal should be to relax and respond to her in a rational and reasonable manner instead of becoming unnecessarily angry.

Chronic negativity can be a sign of deep disappointment—perhaps she wants to protect you from the same thing. If she feels the need to keep warning you of things, simply say, "I don't want anything to go wrong either." This should help relieve some negative people of the responsibility they feel to announce disaster or constantly point out harmful things to you, says Dr. Kirschner. It can, however, also be a sign of serious depression. If her attitude is seriously interfering with her life in any way, encourage her to get help.

Old-Fashioned Community

There are still close-knit communities of women; you just have to know where to look.

Anthropologist Jill Florence Lackey, Ph.D., an instructor at Marquette University in Milwaukee, was stunned when she found one such traditional population of full-time homemakers in a corner of Pennsylvania's Lehigh Valley.

"Every day, once their families were fed and out the door, these women worked together to provide almost all their town's social services," says Dr. Lackey. From food banks to women's clubs, supervising after-school playgrounds to staffing the volunteer fire company, the women she studied had a tightly woven social network. "They *were* the community, and the community was them," she says.

Thanks to this strong network, the women had a keen sense of belonging, purpose, and value. "These were very powerful women," says Dr. Lackey. "They controlled their town; they felt secure and important because they were."

Maybe we don't have that kind of neighborhood, but there are ways to

WOMAN TO WOMAN

Divorced from Her Sunday Support Network, She Built a New One

After her divorce in 1996, Elena Y. Rohweder of Dallas missed family Sundays. That's when she and her husband used to get together with his close-knit family. With no relatives of her own in town, Sundays just seemed "wrong" to the 37-year-old public relations executive. So she created her own "family."

I wanted to have some special time on Sundays, and a lot of my girlfriends felt the same. Some, like me, had no family in the Dallas area; others were stay-at-home moms, and every other day revolved around other people. So I called seven women I was comfortable with and suggested that we all meet at my place on Sunday.

That first meeting was a little awkward: we looked at each other and said, "So what are we doing, exactly?" We made it up as we went along. Some days we go out for brunch or a movie, or do some shopping. Some days, we sit and talk about what's bothering us. One of us will say, "Help! I'm so frustrated with my child or my husband," and we'll be a sounding board for that person. Someone might be having trouble with a coworker, and we might suggest a different way of saying something that can put a new spin on a situation.

We call our special Sundays Goddess Days. One of our founding members is Lynette Miller, a jewelry designer who has pieces based on ancient figures, and we liked that imagery; in fact, many of us have some of her "goddess" earrings—they're like a tribal badge.

We get together every couple of Sundays; in between, some of us get together for an outing or activity. We welcome women who can be supportive, nonjudgmental, and noncompetitive. Our ages range from 20 to 60, and we are in all kinds of occupations and family situations. I just wish I had started Goddess Days earlier; it would have helped a lot when I was getting divorced.

If I ever have a daughter, I hope she can grow up with my Goddess group as a set of alternative adults to turn to; it's kind of *tribal*. We just don't have much like it in our culture now.

INNER-SPACE EXPLORERS

Who was Alfred Adler?

Austrian psychiatrist Alfred Adler broke away from colleague Sigmund Freud's circle in the early 1900s. After becoming openly critical of Freud, Adler and a group of followers developed a new system of psychology called individual psychology. This system holds that our main drive is to reach self-actualization or, in other words, our full potential. (Adler actually used the term *superiority*, which today has an altogether different meaning.) Feelings of inferiority or inadequacy can get in the way of reaching self-actualization, Adler said. Unsuccessful attempts to compensate for our inferior feelings may lead to mental disorders. Adler also suggested that we have a second drive, which he called social interest. This innate urge leads us toward working with others for the common good.

Still widely used today, Adler's form of psychotherapy helps the patient recognize and change her misdirected behavior in favor of building self-esteem, setting realistic goals, and playing a useful role in her community.

nurture our existing relationships and develop new ones even in the midst of our no-time-for-me lives.

Start a book club. They're not just for Oprah. Book clubs today are what sewing circles were 100 years ago. And because they typically meet once a month in the evening, they don't require an enormous time commitment. Yet the certainty that you will see this group of friends at least once a month is an anchoring thought. Today, there are more than a quarter of a million such groups in this country. Not into reading? One group of women meets to knit together. Another to play the dice game Bunco. Still another just does dinner and drinks at a nice restaurant each month. To start, invite three friends and ask each of them to invite three friends.

Multitask. Never wash the dishes, fold the laundry, or dust the house without the phone sheltered in the crook of your neck, your best friend on the other end of the line.

Use e-mail. It's enabled one woman to stay close with her best friend despite two 3,000-mile moves in 2 years. The two e-mail each other several times a week about the most mundane details of their lives—what they did over the weekend, what they had for dinner, if their kids were sick—and so have maintained nearly the same degree of closeness as when they lived three blocks away.

Wander the neighborhood. If you're a stay-at-home mom and don't know many women in your neighborhood, design a flyer inviting other stay-at-home moms to a play group (depending on the age of your kids) or informal lunch at your house one afternoon. Make sure to have them RSVP first so you don't get overwhelmed. You'll be amazed by how many other lonely women are lurking behind those picture windows.

Run errands together. Do your Saturday morning grocery–dry cleaner–Wal-Mart run with your best friend, add in lunch, and just watch how much catching up you can do.

Walk. Do you have a neighbor you'd like to get to know better but you both work? Start walking together for half an hour after dinner. You'll improve your fitness along with your friendship.

The Storm of Stress

Now, here, you see, it takes all the running you can do, to keep in the same place. If you want to get somewhere else, you must run at least twice as fast as that!" said the Queen of Hearts in Lewis Carroll's *Alice's Adventures in Wonderland*.

She should have checked out *our* kingdom. With our lives an endless procession of chauffeuring kids, meeting deadlines, cooking, cleaning, planning, accounting, consoling, and managing, no one knows better than we do about running frantically just to keep in place.

And what do we get from our sped-up pace? Too often, some of life's decidedly less pleasant paybacks: stomach problems, colds, headaches, and heart trouble, just to name a few. And that's just the physical side: Our nonstop lives can also open the door to depression, anxiety, difficulty concentrating, and other mental woes.

Why is it that the work deadline, the kid's bad report card, or your husband's third business trip in a month has this amazing ability to soak into your body, where it percolates and finally bubbles out as this mélange of maladies?

Let's journey inward and take a closer look.

The Way We Were—And Are

Way back when, long before family sedans, washing machines, or even soccer practice, our bodies already had an exquisite mechanism for handling threatening situations.

When a furry predator announced its presence in the cave, our long-ago ancestor immediately dropped into fight-or-flight mode. Her hypothalamus, a grape-size structure in the brain that serves as the stage where the mind and body do their dancing, sounded an alarm that rallied her nervous system and other internal workings into action.

A cascade of hormones surged throughout her body. The hypothalamus pumped out corticotropin-releasing hormone (CRH), and the adrenal glands atop her kidneys produced adrenaline. The CRH signaled the pituitary gland in her brain to produce the even-longer-named adrenocorticotropic hormone (ACTH), which

TAKE THE STRESS TEST

In this test, created by Sheldon Cohen, Ph.D., professor of psychology at Carnegie Mellon University in Pittsburgh, write down the number corresponding to your answer and add them up at the end.

In the last month, how often have you felt:	Never	Almost never	Sometimes	Fairly often	Very often
Upset because something happened unexpectedly?	0	1	2	3	4
Unable to control the important things in your life?	0	1	2	3	4
Nervous and "stressed"?	0	1	2	3	4
Unable to cope with all the things you had to do?	0	1	2	3	4
Angered because of things that were beyond your control?	0	1	2	3	4
That difficulties were piling up so high you could not overcome them?	0	1	2	3	4
Confident about your abilities to handle your personal problems?	4	3	2	1	0
That things were going your way?	4	3	2	1	0
Able to control irritations in your life?	4	3	2	1	0
That you were on top of things?	4	3	2	1	0

Total score: _____

The higher your total score, the higher your stress level. The average score for women is 14.

caused her adrenal glands to make the stress hormone cortisol.

This hormonal flood caused her body to burst into a flurry of activity, boosting all the systems required to stay alive and halting the ones that weren't needed at the moment.

So as she hoisted a club to smack the predator in the head, or grabbed little Og-Og and bolted for the door, her pupils dilated to help her see better, her blood turned stickier in case she got cut, easy-to-use fuel swirled into her bloodstream for quick energy, and her digestion slowed to divert blood and fuel elsewhere.

With her inner warrior released, she quickly dealt with the problem and her system returned to normal. Her body's adaptive techniques had just helped her live another day.

Fast-forward several millennia to the world of the Internet, cell phones, and pagers. Yes, we may still face situations where our physical safety is threatened, but more often the wolf at the door is a figure of speech and not a real, hungry creature. Unfortunately, our bodies aren't very good at telling the difference.

"That protective mechanism is certainly something that we want and need," says Linda

Welcome Home!

Luecken, Ph.D., research assistant professor in the department of psychology at the University of Vermont in Burlington. "Even in modern days, it's what allows you to react quickly if someone jumps out at you in a dark alley. It's a good thing."

At least, it's good when used for the occasional real threats—not for the stress of daily life.

But try telling that to your body. As far as it's concerned, the drama of being an 8-minute drive away from a meeting that starts in 1 minute poses the same sort of risk to your life as a saber-toothed tiger. Of course, no one's actually going to kill you if you're late. But while your mind knows that, your body doesn't.

So deep in the darkness of your inner workings, hormones start squirting as your body prepares for a fight or an escape. This can happen over and over again in the course of a day. Add enough of these reactions together and don't cope with them properly, and this system that once protected us begins to harm us, says Dr. Luecken.

Breaking It Down

The job of a hormone is to regulate activities throughout our body, in both nearby and far-flung locations. With all the hormones involved in stress, it's no wonder that prolonged exposure to them can cause some serious problems.

Stress affects everyone differently; one woman's headache is another woman's urgent sprint to the bathroom or vending machine. Here are some of the areas in which stress can harm you.

Heart. The stress reaction raises heart rate and blood pressure. This increases your chance of stroke, causes the arteries around your heart to tighten, and strains your heart. And when the platelets in your blood become stickier, they can clog your arteries, increasing your chance of a heart attack.

She Can't Eat, Can't Sleep, and Doesn't Know Why

Carin, 45, thought she was doing great. After a messy divorce, she and her two boys moved across the country so she could take a new job with a start-up Internet company. She is making more money than ever, has more responsibility, and loves her new job. She bought a house and found great schools for her boys, one with a special program for the younger, who has attention deficit disorder.

But lately, she's been waking up in the middle of the night and is unable to fall back to sleep for hours. She feels so tense she's afraid she's going to explode. And she's popping antacids like they're jelly beans. Yet she insists she's happy. What's going on?

Between her job, her kids, her mortgage, and the recent changes in her life, Carin has stress nipping at her heels like a puppy she can't shake.

For starters, her stress is triggering a lot of anxiety. And even though she's not in a sad or blue mood, she may still be suffering from depression, which can be caused by too much stress. One symptom of depression is waking up in the middle of the night—and she definitely has that problem.

To begin de-stressing herself, Carin should immediately start claiming some rest and relaxation time.

First, she should ensure that she goes to bed and wakes up at the same time every day. She should also avoid stressful situations right before bedtime, such as paying bills and arguing with the kids; stay away from stimulants such as nicotine and caffeine; and abstain from using alcohol to help her drift off, since it can disrupt her sleep cycle.

Second, she should manage her time so that she can exercise every day. And while she's at it, she should remember to make room in her schedule for relaxing activities, such as meditation and sharing time with friends.

Expert consulted
Pamela Edwards, M.D.
Director, adult psychiatry clinic
Oregon Health Sciences University
Portland

Body shape. The more stressed we are, the more likely we are to gain weight around our tummies, resulting in a body shaped like an apple, rather than the more typical womanly pear shape. The reason? Stress increases levels of the hormone cortisol, which seems to direct fat to our tummies. This apple won't keep the doctor away. Instead, it's associated with an increased risk of heart disease.

Digestive system. You know the butterflies you feel just before a roller-coaster ride begins or after a fender bender? Those are benign compared with the digestive problems that constant stress produces. Even though doctors no longer think stress causes ulcers (thank the bacteria *Helicobacter pylori* for that), stress can make them worse. When we're stressed, our bodies may bump up the production of stomach acid while reducing production of the mucous lining that protects our stomach. The end result is an even more debilitating ulcer.

Then there's irritable bowel syndrome. With this affliction, the small and large intestines, which normally work in a coordinated cadence, start behaving erratically. Depending on which area reacts to the stress, you may experience diarrhea or constipation, cramping, and bloating.

Endocrine system. During times of stress, our body starts pumping easy-to-use fuel, such as glucose and fatty acids, into our bloodstream to prepare us for that tooth-and-nail fight or quick-footed flight. This causes our body to deliver more insulin, a hormone designed to siphon the glucose *out* of our bloodstream. If too much insulin is produced, our cells may eventually lose their ability to respond to the hormone, one cause of a condition called insulin resistance, which is a a risk factor for diabetes.

Immune system. Our bodies' natural defense systems constantly protect us from invaders such as viruses that cause the common cold. But stress weakens this shield, making us more susceptible to disease.

Muscles. If we're going to fight or flee, we need ready muscles, which is why our necks and backs tense up when we're hit with stressors. If those muscles don't eventually loosen, we're left with sore backs, shoulders, and necks, and a headache that pounds hard enough to wake the neighbors.

Emotions. Stress can lower the levels of chemical transmitters in our brains, making us more prone to depression. If we're already depressed, it darkens our already gray lives. Lower levels of these transmitters also play havoc with our memory, which may be why the little details in life, such as whether or not you turned the coffeepot off, become so difficult to remember.

Longevity. In addition to everything else, too much stress can simply age us faster and make us die younger. It makes our brain cells die sooner, particularly in the areas of learning and concentration. And since highly stressed people tend to have poor health habits, this just feeds into and

WOMEN ASK WHY

Why do I always feel better after I cry?

Because you're confronting the stressful problem, the vexing predicament that's got you all wound up and upset inside, and you're taking the time to let it pour out of you.

After you release these troublesome emotions in a flow of salt water and sniffles, and mend the water damage with a handful of Kleenex and a bag of makeup, then you can get back to your life feeling lighter and happier. It's like a ponderous black cloud purging itself with a soothing rain and perhaps a bit of thunder for dramatic effect.

But if you're crying frequently and still feel awful, or you just can't stop crying, chances are that you're suffering from depression or another serious emotional problem and should get some professional treatment. The sooner you figure out what's causing the crying, the sooner you'll return to a more peaceful state.

Expert consulted
Pamela Edwards, M.D.
Director, adult psychiatry clinic
Oregon Health Sciences University
Portland

compounds the other physical and mental effects of stress.

So if the negative health effects of unceasing stress are so well-known, why is nearly every woman you know so stressed? One word: life.

Where It Comes From

Here's what stress *isn't:* It's not a flat tire, a pile of work, a sick child, or any of the other situations that drive us to distraction. Those are stressors. Stress is the way we perceive and react to those situations.

And if you've seen one woman react to a

stressor, you've seen one woman react to a stressor. For instance, you may get high on public speaking, while the thought makes your friend recoil in horror. Or you thrive in a madcap work environment while she loves her quiet library job. Switch jobs, and you'd both be miserable.

The two of you have something in common, however. Studies show that women feel more stressed than men. But then, we're probably not telling you anything you don't already know through first-person research.

The question is why.

For the answer, say experts, look to our families, our society, and ourselves.

We attach great importance and high expectations to so many roles in our lives: mom, wife, employee, friend. But these roles don't always mesh smoothly, says Joan Robison, Ph.D., a clinical psychologist and associate professor at West Virginia University. "And you carry those roles around and you say to yourself, 'I should be this, I should be that, I'm not, and I'm failing.' Then you put a tremendous amount of stress on yourself based on the belief systems you carry around," she says.

So when we come home from a tough day at work, where we tend to get paid less than men, have less control over our jobs, and face more harassment (can you say "stressor"?), we often feel that we should flow right into our after-hours duties as meal provider, housekeeper, and tutor. That's what our mothers and their mothers did, and that's the message we're still getting from society. Men, on the other hand, may come home and feel perfectly fine just resting in front

MYTHS ABOUT STRESS RELIEF
Don't Believe Everything You Hear

Heard the one about armpit sniffing as a cure for stress? Turns out that in a study at Rutgers University in New Brunswick, New Jersey, college students who sniffed gauze pads that had been strapped onto people's armpits felt their spirits lift when they smelled a pad that had been on an elderly woman.

Obviously, we can't go around sniffing older women's armpits. So this idea just doesn't cut it as a remedy for stress relief. We can toss it onto the pile with the other theories about stress relief that turn out to be unworkable.

Myth: Alcohol is a good way to relieve stress.

Actually, "treating stress with alcohol is ineffective and unhealthy over the long haul," says Pamela Edwards, M.D., director of the adult psychiatry clinic at the Oregon Health Sciences University in Portland. "When used regularly, it acts as a depressant and alters your sleep cycle."

Unfortunately, women who drink may increase their consumption of alcohol during stressful times, leaving them less able to handle stress, thus triggering a vicious cycle.

"It's a no-win scenario," she says. We're better off eradicating what's bothering us or learning to cope with the situation instead of bringing on more trouble by drinking.

Myth: Taking big breaths will relieve stress.

"People say 'Take a deep breath . . . like a big sigh . . . and go ahhhhhh-hahhhhhhh,'" says Suzanne Segerstrom, Ph.D., assistant professor in the psychology department at the University of Kentucky. "That is not a relaxing technique. That actually contributes to hyperventilation." As a result, it

of the television, because that's what their fathers did.

Dr. Luecken has researched the effects of our home environments on our stress levels, finding that those of us with children at home produce more cortisol—the stress hormone—than women without children.

will probably add to the fight-or-flight reaction in your body.

On the other hand, diaphragmatic breathing, done properly, can be a great stress reliever. With this relaxation technique, you take deep, slow breaths that feel as if they're heading to the bottom of your abdomen.

To do it, find a comfortable spot and relax your whole body. Place one hand on your chest and the other on your belly. Now breathe, concentrating on making your stomach, not your chest, expand with each breath. If you're doing it right, the hand on your belly will rise. Do this for 15 minutes once or twice a day.

Myth: Stress management can cure cancer.

We know that our immune systems work better when we're relaxed than stressed, allowing our bodies to cope better with threats. While we don't think stress management can cure cancer, lowering stress levels and learning to relax can help us cope with the illness and side effects of treatments. And studies have shown that cancer survivors with a good support network tend to live longer.

"People shouldn't feel guilty if they have cancer that they've either done something to cause it or didn't prevent it or didn't help themselves cure it," says Carol Goldberg, Ph.D., a clinical psychologist and president of Getting Ahead Programs, a New York–based corporation that specializes in workshops on stress management, health, and wellness.

The extra pressure to practice stress management vigorously, Dr. Edwards says, may be stressful in and of itself.

Instead, if you do face cancer, do what you can to stay relaxed and emotionally strong, knowing that you're creating an environment for healing to occur, but not necessarily curing yourself.

Additionally, while men's stress hormone levels decline in the evening when they get home from work (there's that television watching again), ours often stay elevated because we're still working, she says. The same thing can happen to our blood pressures, compared with our husbands'. "For a lot of women, coming home after work is just a second shift," says Dr. Luecken.

We're also conditioned to believe that we should take care of everyone else first, with our needs going to the end of the line, says Dr. Robison. So we don't do the things that would help us through difficult times, such as exercising, eating right, and getting enough rest, because we're always caring for someone else. In fact, we may take up bad habits we'd normally avoid, such as drinking and smoking. Thus, our health suffers and we're less able to withstand the physical damage of stress.

"By the time you get to a point where you say, 'I deserve some time to myself,' you're probably sick, stress-wise," says Dr. Robison.

Then, there's our perspective on life.

"If your boss decides that your job is coming to an end, you can say, 'This is a great opportunity for me. It was a difficult place to work anyway, and I can make this into an interesting phase in my life,'" says Dr. Robison. "Or you can say, 'My life is over, I'll never find another job, and everyone will think I'm a bum for having lost my job.'"

Which do you think is more stressful?

Plus, unlike men, we tend to internalize problems. If you lose your job, you're likely to say, "It's my fault. I didn't work hard enough." Your husband, however, would probably point the finger outward, saying, "My boss is a jerk," according to Dr. Robison.

Many times, when we fall prey to stress in our lives, we get caught in a vicious cycle, says Pamela Edwards, M.D., director of the adult

WOMEN ASK WHY

Why do I have such a hard time saying no to my kids?

Many women are people pleasers. We don't want others to be angry with us, including our children. And nothing ticks a kid off more than your standing between him and that new CD player.

If saying a firm "no" makes you anxious that you're a bad parent, soothe your worries with the thought that you're actually giving your child a useful lesson and helping yourself be a better mom.

Children who learn that they can browbeat their parents to get everything they want may not learn that there are limits and frustrations in life that must be dealt with constructively. They need to learn this in order to grow into decent, pleasant adults.

That doesn't give you free rein to deny your child's every desire, but when you need to shake your head no, do it firmly, stick with your answer, and don't feel guilty.

Expert consulted
Pamela Edwards, M.D.
Director, adult psychiatry clinic
Oregon Health Sciences University
Portland

psychiatry clinic at the Oregon Health Sciences University in Portland. The stress may lead to depression, which may hamper our short-term memory and concentration, making it harder for us to come up with solutions to what's stressing us in the first place.

Check Your Levels

If only we had some way to tell when the pressure's getting to us. Unfortunately, scientists have yet to invent a pop-up timer that tells us when, figuratively speaking, our turkey is cooked. But if we pay attention to our moods and our bodies, we can catch the early signs of stress overload and take action.

Here's where being a woman pays off. Since we've learned from an early age to stay attuned to our body's cycles and anticipate monthly changes, we're well-prepared to monitor our stress changes, says Dr. Robison. The trick is to use our skills of observation.

So if our shoulders hurt, we need to recognize that it's more than just a physical pain, she says. "It's a cue that stressful things are going on and you need to change the way you're doing things."

Keep track of changes in your body, your thought processes, and your habits for clues that your stress levels are climbing. Specifically, watch for the following things.

Muscle tension. You may feel tension anywhere in your body, but especially in your shoulders, back, neck, legs, and abdomen, which can translate into stiffness, pain, or trouble sleeping, Dr. Luecken says. Also, the muscle tension in your neck may be what's causing that headache.

Changes in appetite. You may lose your appetite because of an upset stomach, or, conversely, you may crave fattening foods as a way to seek comfort.

Negative thoughts. You start feeling hopeless, that things will never get better, or that you'll never succeed.

Bad habits. Take note if you're drinking or smoking more than usual, or avoiding exercise.

Release Your Pressure

So you're aware that your chronic headaches, sore neck, and acid-filled stomach are the result of more than just a wild night. You're stressed. Now what?

Work Out your worries. At least five times a week, go for a walk or do some other gentle form of exercise. If you can, bring along a friend for some stress-relieving social interaction along the way. "Just walking 30 to 45 minutes every day is an immensely effective stress reducer and mood enhancer," Dr. Robison says. When you exercise, you release muscle tension, take your mind off your worries, and break your cycle of stress.

Write your worries. Keep a stress journal, in which you track the worries you have and how they make you feel. Write every time you're feeling stressed, says Dr. Robison. "You don't have to write a lot, just a little bit, and write where you are, what's happening in your body, how stressful it is, and what you're thinking at the time."

You may discover that what's actually bothering you is not the immediate stressor at hand, but a more distant problem at home, at work, or with your parents or in-laws.

Put yourself first. Remember the advice flight attendants give passengers about oxygen masks before the jet takes off? Don your own mask *before* you help your child with hers. "What sort of mother does

WOMEN ASK WHY

Why do I get a stomachache every time I get into a confrontation with someone?

When you go toe-to-toe with your boss, tell off your mother-in-law, or argue with your spouse about wearing *that* shirt again, your body's alarm system leaps to duty like an Amazon warrior.

Of course, you're not facing a real physical threat (though you never know with some mothers-in-law), but your body alters itself just in case, boosting the systems you need right away and halting the ones you don't.

During this reaction, stress hormones essentially shut down systems not needed for emergency response, such as digestion, which may make your stomach hurt. Also, muscles tense up all through your body. And since your stomach and abdomen are home to an abundance of muscles, you could be getting pain in any muscle in that area.

One reason we seem to dislike confrontation more than men may be that we have less testosterone, the hormone believed to be related to aggression, than men. Another reason could be societal pressures: Men fight and play sports; women swallow their feelings and play nice.

Instead of letting a confrontation work you into a stomachache, examine why you're getting worked up, and think of possible solutions. Do tailgaters have you pounding the steering wheel? Maybe you'd find fewer if you stuck to the right-hand lane. Is your boss being unreasonable? Perhaps you could discuss it with a human resources representative at your company, or even find another job.

Expert consulted
Carol Goldberg, Ph.D.
Clinical psychologist
President, Getting Ahead Programs
New York City

INNER-SPACE EXPLORERS

Who was Carl Jung?

Swiss founder of analytic psychology Carl Gustav Jung emphasized the unconscious even more than psychoanalyst Sigmund Freud did. But Jung parted from Freud in stressing that it was more important to examine a patient's present conflicts than her childhood issues. Their formal break occurred in 1913 after Jung's publication of a major article that emphasized the role of symbolism in the unconscious.

Jung met Freud in Vienna in 1907. Reportedly, on the day they met, Freud canceled all of his appointments for the day and talked to Jung for 13 hours. Jung soon became Freud's close collaborator, a relationship that lasted for 5 years until Jung disagreed with Freud's theory that there was a sexual basis for neurosis. The split led to Jung's resignation from the International Psychoanalytic Society.

In 1912, he published *Psychology of the Unconscious*, which directly challenged Freud's views. In Jung's theory of the unconscious, we have both a personal and a collective unconscious. He also said creativity comes from the collective unconscious. Scientists have criticized Jung's theory because, since it is unconscious, it's impossible to prove.

Jung's most-liked theory explains our personalities as either introverted or extroverted. Introverts focus on inner thoughts, feelings, and dreams and tend to be quiet and shy. Extroverts focus on the outside world of people, seek out activities, and tend to be more sociable. Once we know whether we're an introvert or extrovert, we can then look at our degree of four other functions: sensing, thinking, intuiting, and feeling. Jung said our goal should be to develop all four functions.

In the 1940s, Katharine Briggs and her daughter Isabel Briggs Myers created the Myers-Briggs Type Indicator, a personality test based on Jung's theory. It's one of the most popular personality tests today.

that?" you think. A smart one. If you don't take care of yourself now, you may be unable to help your child later, and then you'll both be in trouble. It works the same way in your day-to-day life. If you aren't ensuring that your own needs are met—recreation, meditation, nutrition, rest, and exercise—as you're taking care of those around you, you may burn yourself out to the point where you can't take care of anyone.

"Schedule an hour a day for yourself and use that time to relax," says Carol Goldberg, Ph.D., a clinical psychologist and president of Getting Ahead Programs, a New York–based corporation that specializes in workshops on stress management, health, and wellness. "When I say that to women, they look at me like, 'What's wrong with you?' But everyone has the same number of hours in a day. It's a matter of time management."

Ask yourself a question. Instead of feeling the anxiety of a stressful yet vaguely defined situation, ask yourself exactly what about the problem bothers you, Dr. Robison advises. One way to do that is to use the "worst-case scenario."

Say you don't complete an assignment at work perfectly. What's the worst thing that could happen? The boss might get mad. Then your job might be on the line. Then you might get fired. Then you might never get another job. Then you might end up a destitute bag lady on the street.

Write down the possibilities, and

you'll soon see how silly most of them are.

Accept your limitations. Until the day you get the power to fly and see through walls, enjoy the fact that you're not Superwoman and can't be responsible for everything and everyone in your life. Remember the Serenity Prayer, Dr. Luecken suggests: "God grant me the serenity to accept the things that I can't change, the courage to change the things that I can, and the wisdom to know the difference."

Stay healthy. When we're feeling the pinch of stress, we often run right into the arms of seductive rogues that bring more trouble: sleep deprivation, poor eating habits, too many cigarettes, too much caffeine or alcohol. Getting sucked into their world will just make our bodies weaker and less able to handle the effects of stress. It's important to eat healthy foods, get enough sleep, and watch the use of harmful substances, says Dr. Robison.

Use relaxation techniques. Find a method of relaxing that you enjoy, such as meditation, yoga, deep breathing, or progressive muscle relaxation, and do it at least daily to interrupt your stressful reactions and gain control over your body.

Dr. Robison often teaches her patients muscle relaxation, where they progressively tense muscles throughout their body, then let them go slack.

Listen to tunes. For centuries, philosophers and poets have celebrated the healing power of music. Researchers are now jumping on the bandwagon as well. Increasingly, studies find that music offers wide-ranging therapeutic ben-

---

WOMEN ASK WHY

Why does my sex drive plummet when I'm stressed?

If you're stressed and feel your sex drive declining, there often is an underlying depression that may be creating this problem. When you're depressed, you often physically and mentally just don't feel like making love. When you consider how you feel when you're depressed—your energy is low and you just don't feel good about yourself—it's not surprising that this is hardly the mood that encourages a lively romp in the sheets. In fact, a decreased interest in sex is one of the symptoms mental health experts use to diagnose depression. If you find yourself in this situation, you should talk to a doctor or therapist.

Expert consulted
Elizabeth Arnold, Ph.D., R.N.
Associate professor and coordinator of the
*   behavioral health track*
University of Maryland School of Nursing
Baltimore

---

efits. A serenade, for instance, can help alleviate stress, insomnia, and depression. To find the right music for you, start with a piece of music that you like. Before listening to it, jot down the name of the selection, your pulse rate, and your breathing rate in a notebook. Also make a note of whether your muscles are tense or relaxed. Then listen to the music for 20 minutes, allowing your body to respond. Write down your feelings, then use that information to help you use music to relax.

Talk it out. If you have more to do than you can realistically handle or too little control over your schedule to get things done, speak up, says Deborah Belle, Ed.D., associate professor of psychology at Boston University. At work, talk to your boss. At home, talk to your spouse.

"If nothing else, you'll feel less powerless having spoken up—and that sense of control can significantly reduce the negative impact of stress," says Susan Heitler, Ph.D., a clinical psychologist in Denver and author of the audiotape *Anxiety: Friend or Foe?*

Take minibreaks. Stress is most damaging if it's unrelenting. Even a few moments of relaxation can help considerably, says Dr. Heitler. "If you're at work and start feeling stressed, get up and stretch or talk to a coworker for a couple of minutes." If you're at home, take a break in a quiet room.

Give yourself a longer break at least once every day, recommends Sharon Greenburg, Ph.D., a clinical psychologist in Chicago. "If you have children, set aside some time for yourself to read a magazine, watch television, or simply do nothing at all." That time can be when the kids are napping, at school, or playing by themselves, she says.

Stay connected. Women are more oriented toward personal relationships than men; make sure you use yours to keep yourself healthy, Dr. Goldberg advises. When you have a strong social support network for sharing troubles and solutions, you become stronger and more resilient during stressful times, she says.

The Picture of Health

Remember the day you learned to ride a bike? Your parents promised they wouldn't let go as you pedaled. So you rode along confidently . . . until you realized they *had* let go. Then you panicked, swerved, and hit the pavement. But you kept at it, and pretty soon, you were zooming around the neighborhood, perfectly balanced on two wheels without any help at all.

Unfortunately, emotional balance is not a milestone we can reach in the same way as learning to ride a bike. In fact, it's doubtful there even *is* such a thing as perfect balance in our crazy lives.

The goal, then, is to find a way to keep the scales tipped more or less in our favor. To hang onto the handlebars of life and stay upright as we career through our days.

The Look of Emotional Balance

Although extremely rare, there have been reported sightings of the emotionally balanced woman (usually around spas and Caribbean resorts). From these reports, we've gathered the following data about this elusive creature.

She's in emotional homeostasis. Emotional systems are much like our physical bodies in that all parts—thoughts, actions, and physical reactions—must work harmoniously before balance occurs. So that great promotion you just got at work isn't going to change the fact that you and your husband are having problems. Whether you realize it or not, your marital problems will seep into other areas of your life, throwing off your emotional balance and potentially jeopardizing your performance at work.

"Ultimately, everything gets integrated, so we need to work on *all* areas of our lives," says Judith Kessler, Psy.D., a behavioral psychologist and professor in the mind-body medicine department of the National College of Naturopathic Medicine in Portland, Oregon.

She communicates. Balanced women clearly state what they want, respect the opinions of others, and successfully work out solutions to conflicts, says Tina B. Tessina, Ph.D.,

WOMEN ASK WHY

Why do I feel so tired on the first day of my period?

If a woman bleeds very heavily, her fatigue *could* be due to the anemia caused by the sudden loss of blood. But since most of us feel tired before much bleeding has occurred, this explanation doesn't always work.

So look to our hormones. There are certain substances (called pro-inflammatory prostaglandins, but that's more than you need to know) secreted in our uteruses when our periods begin. These substances are part of our defense system against foreign invaders, such as bacteria, viruses, and fungi. They stimulate our immune systems and may make us feel slightly flulike. In other words, tired.

Additionally, both hormones that are active just before our periods—estrogen and progestin—cause us to retain fluid and become bloated. So we feel lethargic because it takes more energy to propel our swollen bodies.

Finally, estrogen and progestin drop very suddenly just before our periods begin. Since estrogen usually acts to enhance our energy, this sudden drop may leave us listless and tired.

To combat first-day period fatigue, exercise, steer clear of sweets, which cause blood insulin levels to spike and then fall, leaving us even more tired, and get enough sleep.

Expert consulted
Lila A. Wallis, M.D., M.A.C.P.
Clinical professor of medicine
Weill Medical College of Cornell University
New York City
Author of The Whole Woman: Take Charge
   of Your Health in Every Phase of Your Life

emotionally balanced response would be to acknowledge and discuss his arguments the first few times, then ask if the two of you can address the rest of his comments after the meeting, so as not to take up too much of everyone's time. You're giving his opinions respect and, at the same time, appeasing your annoyed coworkers who want to keep the meeting short.

She's creative. When our emotions are in equilibrium, we make stained-glass windows, knit, write short stories—because our creative juices are flowing. "We tend to report being most happy when we become totally immersed in an activity, losing our sense of time and even our sense of self," says Kristina M. DeNeve, Ph.D., assistant professor in the department of psychology and neuroscience at Baylor University in Waco, Texas. Creativity also helps us enjoy time by ourselves. Many of us spend so little time alone that when we finally *do* get a few precious moments to ourselves, we're paralyzed and don't know what to do. But when we're emotionally balanced, we can brainstorm interesting ways to spend a half-hour, 3 hours, or even a whole day.

She's flexible. Emotionally balanced women can deal with change calmly and rationally. "When we're emotionally balanced, we react to what's really going on instead of what we *think* is going on," says Dr. Tessina. For example, you come home and find your teenage son and his

a psychotherapist in Long Beach, California, and author of *The 10 Smartest Decisions a Woman Can Make before 40.* Say you're leading an important meeting at work for the first time and a rude colleague continuously interrupts, challenging you on every point. The

girlfriend alone in the house (which he knows shouldn't happen). Your son is on the couch and she's in the bathroom. "She must have run in there to put her clothes on," you might think at first. But instead of jumping to conclusions, the emotionally balanced woman calmly asks what's going on. "Julie got locked out of her house," your son says—an understandable reason for breaking the rule. Instead of creating a scene, you first gathered information.

She's satisfied. Crucial to emotional balance is a sense of happiness and well-being that comes from *inside*. Emotionally healthy women don't look to external stimuli such as winning a lottery prize, losing a few pounds, or buying new shoes to make them happy.

She's nutritionally balanced. When it comes to emotional health, diet is a major factor. When we're out of balance, the voice inside us crying out, "Chips! Chips!" drowns out the whispers calling for broccoli. So we go for the chips. "But a craving is a sign of unbalance," says Dr. Kessler. Balance means allowing ourselves the occasional indulgence, but not relying on a daily dose of chocolate to launch us out of our depression.

She's well-rested. "If a woman is sleeping well—not too much or too little—in all likelihood, she's in balance," says Alice Domar, Ph.D., director of the Mind/Body Center for Women's Health at the Beth Israel Deaconess Medical Center in Boston.

Sleep is a basic need that keeps us

WOMEN ASK WHY

Why am I attracted to men who are no good for me?

There's something called preparatory set. This occurs when you want something so you begin noticing it everywhere. Maybe you want a new Volkswagen. Suddenly, the streets seem filled with Volkswagens and the television crammed with Volkswagen ads.

Preparatory set also works in our relationships. When you look for a partner, you have a preprogrammed vision of what a man should be. That idea may come from your father, your brother, or even your softball coach. If you grew up in a dysfunctional family, that vision may include an alcoholic or someone who is always criticizing you. So you pick the alcoholics or critical guys from across the room, even though you don't know at first that's how they are. And you think they're your type.

Additionally, you could be confusing attraction with anxiety. You meet with the "wrong guy," your heart beats rapidly, your palms sweat: You're excited. And you confuse this anxious excitement with the excitement that results from falling in love. In addition, this anxiety feels familiar, so you think it's good.

To break out of your preparatory set, you need to reprogram it. Analyze what you want in a man and create a mental picture of him. He may be a great listener, have a great sense of humor, and treat you with kindness. Picture yourself spending the rest of your life with him. Soon, you'll start noticing the guys who fit your new and improved mental picture. Once you've reprogrammed your preparatory set, you'll no longer be attracted to men who aren't good for you.

Expert consulted
Tina B. Tessina, Ph.D.
Psychotherapist
Long Beach, California
Author of The Unofficial Guide to
    Dating Again

REAL-LIFE SCENARIO
She Laughed at Pollyanna Optimists

Marie, 42, has always gone through life with her eyes wide open. She knows that life isn't fair and that bad things *do* happen to good people. One of her three children was born with a learning disability that requires special tutoring; her husband is currently unemployed; and last year, the IRS audited them. That's why Marie has little patience with the women in her office who are always telling her to "look on the bright side." Yet lately, she's been feeling depressed.

Marie is feeling depressed because she feels powerless. In order to lift her depression, Marie can do a few things.

First, she can sit down, close her eyes, and say, "If I were angry at something, what would it be?" The vision that comes to her mind will help her pinpoint what she's really angry about. So if Marie sees her unemployed husband on the couch watching TV when she closes her eyes, then she's begun the process.

The second test of whether she's correctly pinpointed the situation is to ask herself who looks bigger and more powerful in her vision. If she sees her husband as big and herself as small and powerless, she's correctly identified the problem. Then she should ask herself, "What do I want?" Maybe she wants her husband to get a job.

The next step is to puff herself up really big in her vision. Once she's big, she can look at the situation more objectively. She may see that her husband is terrified of going out into the world again. From that big place, she can begin to see him with more understanding and compassion, and think, "What can I do to help him?" By picturing herself as bigger and able to gather more information, Marie will gain more control over the situation.

Expert consulted
Susan Heitler, Ph.D.
Clinical psychologist
Denver
Author of the audiotape Depression:
    A Disorder of Power

in physical, mental, and emotional balance. "A lot of women report that when they're stressed, they can't fall asleep, they get up in the middle of the night, or they wake up early in the morning," Dr. Domar says. And without enough sleep, we're more likely to get tense, edgy, and emotionally distressed.

She's in good shape. We've all heard it before, but exercise is a truly wonderful way to stay balanced. "Exercise increases feelings of well-being on both a physical and a psychological level," says Dr. Kessler. Movement releases chemicals that enhance mood and boost energy. And the commitment and achievement of something positive that comes from exercise is also likely to help. The emotionally balanced woman knows this, and turns on the radio and dances, gardens, runs, or just throws rocks at a tree—anything to help her physically release some of her emotional tension.

She's selfish. She knows that in today's busy world, effective time management is a crucial step in her journey toward emotional balance. Like the emergency room nurse who decides which patients are the most critical, she prioritizes the elements of her life. She won't stay on the phone for an hour with that not-so-great friend who doesn't say much. Instead, she'll politely extract herself so she can spend that time with her child. "Save time for what's meaningful to you—your relationship, your kids, your career, and yourself—to help keep you in balance," Dr. Tessina says.

She makes dates with herself. Instead of just reading about luxurious bubble baths and then tossing the magazine to go make lunch for the whole Brownie troop, the emotionally balanced woman actually buys the bath oils, runs the tub, and spends an hour steaming away, says Dr. Kessler. She knows that if she doesn't make time for herself, her physical and emotional self will shut down.

She recognizes her weaknesses. She knows she's not perfect; that she is the total of her parts, both good and bad. So she's learned to balance her quick temper with her equally quick wit.

She mingles. Emotionally balanced women thrive on social support, says Dr. Domar. And some of that support has to come from outside of our marriages and romantic relationships. So the emotionally balanced woman makes time for girls-only lunches or dinners, for afternoons spent antiquing with her best friend, and for nightly walks with the next-door neighbor.

She escapes. The emotionally balanced woman understands that a productive method of channeling stress is an important part of balance. If she's feeling stressed or angry, she plants some flowers or rides her bike. She may not eliminate the source of her anger, but she knows that by channeling her stress in a positive direction, she'll keep those negative emotions from tipping the scales too heavily.

She stops. Our society tends to live for tomorrow and yesterday at the expense of what's happening today, says Dr. Domar. "Look at kids and dogs—they are so in the moment, and they get so much more out of life than we do," she says. So does that elusive emotionally balanced woman. When she takes the kids to the park for the afternoon, she doesn't bring a book. She watches them play, or plays with them. She observes the quirky movements of the squirrels, listens to the babbling brook and the chirping birds, breathes the fresh air, feels the sunshine on her face, and smells the freshly cut grass.

She's optimistic. She's a glass-half-full kind

WOMEN ASK WHY

Why do females mature faster than males?

It relates to the socialization process of girls and boys in virtually all Western, Asian, Latin, and Middle Eastern cultures. Boys are often born into a privileged status simply because of their gender. So less is expected of them in terms of being helpful, nurturing, and giving. In many cultures, males never learn how to do the most basic of household chores, such as cooking, cleaning, and babysitting, because these tasks are "women's work."

Girls, on the other hand, are often recruited at a young age to help out around the house. In some cultures, girls are groomed to be the caretakers of aging parents. Girls are also taught that emotions such as anger are inappropriate for their sex: Nice girls don't get angry. So we end up with young women who have much more emotional discipline than young men. And emotional discipline is considered a major factor in the early development of maturity in females.

From a medical standpoint, the short answer to why females physically mature faster than males is that their production of sex hormones, estrogen and progesterone, begins earlier than males'; we really don't know why. These hormones jump-start the development of their reproductive systems: breast development, menstruation, and body hair.

Experts consulted
Patricia McWhorter, Ph.D.
Psychologist
Palm Harbor, Florida
Author of Cry of Our Native Soul: Our Instinct for Creation-Centered Spirituality

Mary Lake Polan, M.D., Ph.D.
Professor and chair of the department of gynecology and obstetrics
Stanford University School of Medicine
California

of woman, without being a sickeningly sweet Pollyanna. She realizes that if she can find a way to look on the bright side, to view things in a positive rather than negative light, then even the curveballs life throws her won't hit too far afield. So when she's invited to yet another happy-hour event after work, instead of whining about inconsiderate co-workers who don't realize she has to pick up her kids at day care, she views the outing as a welcome excuse for a break. She asks (or tells) her husband to pick up the kids, and enjoys a glass of wine with her work friends.

Balancing the Emotional Scale

To approach anything resembling the "B" word is to identify what emotional balance means to us. That means looking deep within ourselves and understanding why we react the way we do to the things we do.

Becoming more aware of our personality traits is one way to reach this self-knowledge. We can use several traits that the psychology world has identified as key in tipping our emotional scales one way or the other. To understand the differences between them, let's watch a group of women at a party.

Extroverted versus Introverted. The extroverted woman mingles and talks to everyone, introduces people to one another, and starts the conga

SELF-EVALUATION QUIZ

Still not sure if your emotional scale is tipping? Take this self-evaluation quiz to get a better idea of how your weight is distributed.

Answer each question based on the following criteria:

5 = Always	2 = Rarely
4 = Usually	1 = Never
3 = Sometimes	

__I view change as a challenge and a door to opportunity, not as a setback.

__I look at situations realistically.

__I respect others' opinions.

__I feel equipped to handle challenges that come my way at work, at home, and in my relationships.

__I do not feel lonely.

__I'm not afraid to say no.

__I feel grateful to be alive.

__When I'm angry, I feel it coming on before I erupt.

__When I'm faced with a mountain of work, either on the job or at home, I do not panic. I approach the tasks in a relaxed yet efficient way.

__I often take part in meaningful conversations with others.

__I compliment others.

__I laugh a lot.

__I know when my mood has changed.

__I cooperate well with others at work.

__I cooperate well with my family members at home.

__I congratulate myself.

__I live for the moment.

__When I feel stressed, I use the stress positively to motivate me.

__When I'm angry, I am good at quickly calming myself down and looking at the situation rationally.

__I often use "self-talk" to analyze my feelings.

__When I feel like I'm being attacked by others, I can stay calm and discuss the situation with them.

__The conflicts I have with others are easily resolved.

__When I've made a mistake, I learn from it and quickly move on.

__I am good at managing my time.

__I am aware of how I feel.

__I recognize when my thoughts are becoming too negative, and I make an effort to think more positively.

__I am satisfied with my life.

__I feel happy.

__I creatively express myself.

__I make time to spend by myself, and I enjoy it.

__I get enough sleep.

__I eat a healthful, balanced diet.

__I exercise.

Scoring:

149–165: You're so emotionally balanced, you should try out for tightrope walker at the circus.

133–148: You're doing pretty well on the tightrope, but you can't stay on without a balancing pole.

115–132: Your balance is a bit unsteady, even with the pole.

99–114: You've fallen 9 out of the last 10 tightrope walks.

66–98: You're having trouble just climbing the rope ladder to get to the tightrope.

Under 66: You're so off balance they won't let you in the ring.

Continue journeying through this book for the keys to better emotional balance.

line. In balance, she's popular, happy, and outgoing, calling on her friends for support when she needs it. But the unbalanced extrovert values quantity over quality in her friendships, is unable to resolve problems on her own without sharing them with the world, and looks to others to "fix" her.

Her alter ego, the introvert, has just as much fun watching the people at the party from the sidelines. She resists being pulled into the conga line and is quite content to clap along with the music rather than dance to it. After a few hours, she becomes overwhelmed by the social stimulation and goes home to a good book. If the introvert is out of balance, however, she may become passive and unable to stand up for herself, viewing confrontation and rejections as a threat. Then she'd leave the party just a few minutes after her arrival, running the risk of isolating herself socially.

Agreeable versus Headstrong. The agreeable woman arrives at the party late because she was tutoring an illiterate man, and she leaves early because she has to get up early for her job as a psychiatric nurse. She loves helping people. Her friend tells her about a recent setback at work because she listens with compassion and attentiveness. She finds no one at the party too brash or irritating, and waves to her husband without feeling jealous as he talks with a young blond model. But if she tips too far into agreeableness, the agreeable woman risks subjugating herself and her own needs to everyone else's, leading to emotional exhaustion and depression.

On the opposite pole from her is the head-

SPENDING TIME ALONE

Once in a great while, we find ourselves with 30 minutes, an hour, or even—oh, joy of joys—a whole day to ourselves. Too often, we spend it the way we spend the rest of our life: doing for others. But what if we just spent the time on ourselves? What would we do? We polled a group of women who work outside their homes about this, and here's what they told us.

Half an hour:

- "While waiting for my son's guitar lesson to finish, I sleep in the car."
- "I love to climb into bed and do something mindless, like look at a catalog."
- "I organize my baby's pictures. That way I can still look at her and have some time to myself."
- "I give myself a manicure or a pedicure."
- "I sing."
- "I get a cappuccino at a coffee shop."

An hour:

- "I buy the *New York Times* and read in luscious silence for an hour."
- "I go to the gym."
- "I grab a grown-up book, put on a favorite grown-up CD, and curl up on the couch."
- "I run while listening to my favorite tunes on my Walkman."

---

strong woman who comes across as strong and confident when in balance. Out of balance, however, she may view loss of control as a threat and handle it with confrontation. *She's* not likely to wave merrily at her husband when he's flirting with another woman.

Conscientious versus Distractible. The conscientious woman brings a dish to the party that she knows none of the guests are allergic to—she did her research. She runs back out to her

❧ "I light the candles, put on a slow jazz CD, fill the tub with soothing bath salts, and take a long, hot soak."

❧ "I park myself on a bench in the mall and do some heavy-duty people-watching."

❧ "I reread old love letters."

Anything more than an hour:

❧ "I took a drumming workshop and found it to be an intensely physical and spiritual experience. I recommend it as a great creative outlet for everyday stress."

❧ "I went berry picking by myself one afternoon with my Walkman and a book on tape. I came home with 8 pounds of blueberries."

❧ "I get a massage."

❧ "I plant and garden in the yard."

❧ "I go to a movie or rent a movie."

❧ "I cook."

❧ "Believe it or not, I find grocery shopping by myself to be great fun."

❧ "I drive somewhere I've never been and just wander around."

❧ "I spend an evening alone with some prime chick-flick movies and a big bowl of popcorn."

❧ "I take myself out for lunch."

❧ "I stay home and veg: I read and sleep on and off all day."

car to get gifts for each of her friends who have birthdays that month. And she finished her project at work 3 days early so that she could enjoy the party without having a deadline looming over her shoulders. If her conscientiousness tips out of balance, however, she may venture into perfectionistic territory. A tip-off: When pulled into the conga line, she can't relax and have fun because she's too worried that her rhythm is off.

Her personality opposite is the distractible woman who lacks the skills to get organized and disciplined, and who is threatened by excessive structure. She shows up late to the party because she never wears a watch, and creates a conga traffic jam by abruptly stopping to chat with the woman behind her.

Open versus Rigid. The woman who is open to experience comes to the party straight from her pottery class. She talks to her friends about how she stenciled her kids' bedroom walls, and bungee jumped with her husband to celebrate their 15th anniversary. She's very interested in hearing about her friend's African safari, and eagerly takes down the travel agent's phone number. When pulled into the conga line, she breaks away, leading it through the hall, into the kitchen, and out the door into the yard. Too great a need for adventure, however, could endanger her physically. And a constant need for new stimulation may result in her job- or man-hopping, leading to a lack of satisfaction and contentment in her life.

At the other end of this personality pole is the rigid woman who views change, uncertainty, and disorder as a threat. She is probably disturbed by the chaos of the conga line and uncomfortable with its unpredictability.

Neurotic. The neurotic woman picks a fight with her husband because she feels he's ignoring her at the party, then feels guilty about the rift and convinces herself he's going to leave her because of her outburst. She thinks the hostess's best friend has taken an instant dislike to her, so

INNER-SPACE EXPLORERS
Who was William James?

Anger makes us clench our fists, right? Wrong, according to American psychologist William James. The 19th century psychologist says it's the other way around: Our emotions stem from our physiological responses to an event.

A friend makes us mad, our heart rate increases, we tremble, we clench our fists, *then* we feel angry. So, conversely, if we smile at someone who usually makes us mad, we won't feel the anger.

Because Danish physiologist Carl Lange, working separately from James, said the same thing about emotion, the theory is called the James-Lange theory.

Some people argue with this theory, saying we can't read our internal organs because they're too slow and not sensitive enough, and that similar internal changes happen for a variety of reasons. For instance, when scientists change a body function by increasing a person's heart rate, no emotional change results.

But other research bears out James' theory. People who have spinal cord injuries, in which their brains don't receive every message from their bodies, feel less intense emotions. Also, when people are told to move their facial muscles into expressions of anger, surprise, happiness, or sadness without knowing which emotion they're mimicking, they experience physiological changes, such as an increased heart rate for anger.

James is also known for a unique (for his time) therapeutic approach called functionalism, in which he asked his patients to be introspective—to analyze their own thoughts and actions—while he observed their behavior. He concluded that our identity comes from two factors: our own beliefs and the way we think other people perceive us.

line and thinks about how ridiculous everyone looks. When pulled in, she dances, but thinks she looks clumsy and regrets having that last drink. She spends the rest of the night wondering who in the room thinks she's a bad dancer who drinks too much.

The personality traits that allow us to be in balance are considered emotionally stable ones. "Neuroticism is negatively correlated with the other personality traits," says Susan Mohammed, Ph.D., assistant professor in the department of psychology at Pennsylvania State University in University Park. In other words, if we're agreeable or extroverted, as long as we're in balance, we tend not to be neurotic. And while most of us have elements of all of these traits in our personality, it's the degree to which we display them that makes them stand out.

To balance our personality traits and thus our emotions, we must first be aware that we have them. "We are all reacting creatures; it's the extent to which we react emotionally and how often that matters," says Dr. Kessler. Think about your reactions to situations. How often are you irritable? How often do you laugh? How often do you feel guilty? How often do you feel in control of your emotional reactions?

Say your husband forgot about the ballet and got basketball tickets for the same night. How do you react? If you hurl things at him and screech out of the driveway

she gives the woman the cold shoulder. She has unrealistic ideas, she's easily angered, and she often feels guilty and sad. She watches the conga

dateless, only to spend the entire performance feeling guilty about your outburst, you may have neurotic tendencies. If you calmly express how important the ballet is to you and suggest that your husband may be able to sell the basketball tickets at the last minute, you're probably pretty agreeable.

If you think that you have the tendency to be neurotic or that even though most of your personality traits are more positive, they are tipping out of balance, the best thing to do is to observe others who are in balance. "Put yourself in a situation where you are around more people, and observe how they react," says Dr. Mohammed.

If you're tipped too far into introvertedness, spend more time around extroverts, she says. "It may help balance you out."

So if you feel yourself losing control after your husband shows you the basketball tickets, think of your agreeable friend at work, and picture yourself reacting as she would: calmly and rationally. Then try to let that reaction carry over into your emotions. If you don't react by immediately throwing your shoe at your husband, you won't become as uncontrollably angry, and you'll be better able to handle the impending discussion over whether or not he will join you at the ballet.

Belle of the Masquerade Ball

There are quantities of human beings, but there are many more faces, for each person has several.
—Rainer Maria Rilke

As kids, we waited all year for Halloween. For a brief time, our faces hidden behind plastic masks, we ceased to be ourselves and were transformed into Cinderellas, Batgirls, or witches.

As adults, we still wear masks. They're invisible, of course. But like the masks of Halloweens past, they transform us into the women we want to be or want others to see.

These masks are called personas, from the Latin word for mask. The term refers to the elaborate masks of ancient Roman and Greek drama, worn not only to hide the actors' true identities, but to define their on-stage roles.

Thousands of years later, the psychologist Carl G. Jung borrowed the word to describe the self that we present to the world. This public self includes our social roles (such as "mother," "wife," or "career woman"), our image, and the way we speak and dress. These things serve to protect us, to shelter us, to make our interactions with the outside world smoother and more pre-

dictable. In effect, we wear masks to play ourselves in the drama of our lives.

At the office, for instance, we don our "manager" or "employee" mask at the stroke of nine and hang up the "Mom" mask until the workday is over. If we teach, we're likely to dress and behave in a way that helps our students know what to expect from us. And we all feel more comfortable with a pediatrician who sports a white coat rather than an armload of tattoos.

But our masks can also serve to delude us. The trouble starts when we confuse our false faces with our true selves. When we come to believe that we *are* the roles we play.

When we're always on stage, we lose touch with our true selves. There's an emptiness inside that eats away at our spontaneity, creativity, and fulfillment. We appear one-dimensional; others might describe us as shallow, phony, or cold.

Most important, we can't connect with or express the intimacy locked in our real selves. As practical as they are, masks keep others at a safe distance.

"When you don't let others know who the real you is, you can never be truly loved," says Polly

Young-Eisendrath, Ph.D., clinical associate professor of psychiatry in the medical college at the University of Vermont in Burlington and author of *Women and Desire: Beyond Wanting to Be Wanted.*

Women in the Iron Masks

According to Dr. Young-Eisendrath, we wear masks because we would rather be wanted than known. "Wanting to be wanted is about finding power in an image rather than in our own actions," she says.

"We find ourselves always wanting to be seen in a positive light: the perfect mother, the ideal girlfriend, the seductive lover, the slender or athletic body, the kind neighbor, the competent boss."

So we expect others—our partners, kids, employers, men on the street—to provide our own feelings of worth.

But even as we reap the rewards of being wanted, we cheat ourselves. When we act for others, instead of for ourselves, we can feel resentful, frustrated, and powerless. We've shirked our responsibility for our own lives, and betrayed our own needs and desires.

Our desire to be desired forms very early, says Dr. Young-Eisendrath. As kids, we "learned the rules." Not just the rules of society, but the more subtle and often confusing rules and attitudes that governed our homes. (Crying is for babies. Children should be

WOMEN ASK WHY

Why do women seem to cry more often than men?

Quite simply, because women are raised to believe that it's okay to cry. From a very early age, however, men are taught that crying is for sissies.

But research suggests that hormonal differences between men and women may also account for a man's decreased frequency of shedding tears of emotion (which are chemically different from tears that serve to lubricate the eye or flush away irritants).

We've known for a long time that a woman's tear glands are anatomically different from those of a man. These structural differences may have to do with gender differences in blood levels of a hormone called prolactin.

Prolactin is the sex hormone that, in females, stimulates breast development and milk production. But prolactin is also found in our tear glands, and it probably stimulates the development of tear glands and the production of tears.

It's interesting that boys and girls under the age of 12 cry equally as often and have the same blood levels of prolactin. But as girls enter adolescence, their blood levels of prolactin rise, while those of adolescent boys drop. By the time girls are 18, their prolactin blood levels are 50 to 60 percent higher than men's. What's more, by age 18, women cry four times as often as men, averaging 5.3 crying episodes a month to men's 1.4 episodes.

Expert consulted
William H. Frey II, Ph.D.
Director
HealthPartners Dry Eye and Tear Research
  Center
Regions Hospital
St. Paul, Minnesota

seen and not heard. We don't fight in this house.) If we broke the rules, we encountered shouting, punishment, or ridicule.

Or, if our parents continually told us, "You're

the prettiest, smartest little girl in the world," we may have believed that being perfect was the way to our parents' love and approval.

"Little girls learn quickly that being pretty, popular, and nice gets them positive attention," says Dr. Young-Eisendrath.

Either way, these lessons taught us that our authentic selves weren't always acceptable. So we drove them underground. We learned to act, rather than be. We played the roles that would win us approval, and hid "unacceptable" feelings and behavior.

Sadly, "the masks that served us well in our families often do not serve us as adults," says Elaine Waldman, a certified psychotherapist in New York City.

If we grew up with a critical parent, we may have become a Perfectionist. If we received praise for our blond curls and sweet faces, we may have emerged as a Seductress. And those of us who grew up believing that our feelings didn't count, or who feared that expressing them would cost us love, may have become Doormats.

Our masks feel like protection, but they function as a prison. Often, it's a crisis, such as finding out that our partner is involved in an affair or not getting that big promotion at work, that rudely rips off our protective masks, forcing us to confront our true selves.

The Masks We Wear to the Party

How do we know whether the masks we wear prevent us from acting on our wants, needs, and desires? From, as Dr. Young-Eisendrath would say, being the subject of our own desires, rather than the object of others' desires?

There's one surefire clue, she says: "feeling resentful when you make a decision."

Maybe the teacher in your child's class asks you to bake cookies for the class party. You hate

to bake. But good mothers bake cookies. So you oil up the cookie sheets, hissing through your teeth.

A good friend takes a trip to Hawaii and arrives home armed with slides. Would you like to come over and see them? You'd rather have your appendix out. But you paste a smile on your face and say, "Sure!" as you emit an inner groan of irritation.

In both cases, you've sacrificed your real desires to those of others.

Of such small sacrifices are thick, impenetrable masks made.

Getting clued in to this inner resentment can help us become aware of when we're stepping into a role we have no desire to play.

"There's a school of thought that believes that awareness is curative," says Les Parrott, Ph.D., codirector of the Center for Relationship Development at Seattle Pacific University and author of *High-Maintenance Relationships: How to Handle Impossible People.* "Simply being aware of what you're doing is enough to help you begin to transcend it."

But let's be real: Getting to know ourselves is a long, slow process. What's more, taking off our masks involves risk. So we need to treat ourselves gently and to seek therapy if the journey becomes too difficult to go alone.

Within the next few pages, you'll read about the nine masks we don most often. See if you can find yourself. Then read what experts suggest you can do to shed your masks and become someone you've always wanted to meet.

You.

The Bitch

Last heard saying: "Oh yeah? Well, get over it."

Remember Joan Collins on the 1980s TV drama *Dynasty*? Her character, Alexis Carrington, was the *uber*-Bitch, plotting and scheming

her way through life, and bulldozing anyone who got in her way.

Unfortunately, some of us are Alexises in training (though perhaps without the designer wardrobe and Dom Perignon).

But let's be careful here. Many of us use "bitch" to describe a woman who is strong, competent, and confident, or fiercely independent and opinionated. This is bravery rather than bitchiness, and it can be all to the good.

The Bitch *we're* describing uses her bitchiness for ill rather than good. She's rude, crude, aggressive as opposed to assertive, and, most important, cares not a fig for other people's feelings.

"She's nasty and disrespectful. She makes it clear that she doesn't care about you at all," says Patricia McWhorter, Ph.D., a psychologist in Palm Harbor, Florida, and author of *Cry of Our Native Soul: Our Instinct for Creation-Centered Spirituality.*

At work, the Bitch isn't a team player. She's abrasive or rude in meetings, gossips about others, and generally seems to relish turning the office into a living hell.

The Bitch doesn't behave any better at home,

where she may drive her partner and kids away, both emotionally and physically, with her continual carping, criticisms, and complaints.

Some Bitches are aware of how their behavior affects other people. And some actually thrive on it, says Dr. McWhorter. "They say, 'Yep, I'm a bitch. Deal with it.' They enjoy rattling other people's cages."

But underneath her unpleasant facade, the Bitch may be hiding some painful feelings, such as hurt, fear, and anxiety. She may have grown up in an emotionally abusive home, where she was regularly humiliated. Fighting back, even when there's no emotional threat, became her modus operandi.

The Bitch may also feel uncomfortable with her more vulnerable side, fearing that she may be hurt or rejected if she allows people to see it. Presenting herself as a Bitch makes her feel invulnerable, powerful, and in control, which is far preferable to confronting those genuine yet unsettling emotions.

But that chip on her shoulder repels others. And sadly, that's frequently what these women want, or think they want. "The Bitch pushes people away. She won't allow anyone to really touch her, or get to know the real her," says Dr. McWhorter.

Demasking Tip: Nurture your inner softie. No, you don't have to assume the role of Pollyanna. Instead, focus on random (and short) acts of kindness. At work, smile at a colleague as you pass her in the hall, or drop into a coworker's office for a 5-minute chat. At home, before you explode at your partner or kids, learn (and use) the anger management techniques described in Inner Fire and Brimstone on page 58. To help you get in touch with the tender, vulnerable aspects of yourself, consider seeing a therapist, who can help you confront the anger, hurt, or fear that's been buried deep inside.

The Drama Queen

Last heard saying: "You won't _believe_ what just happened to me!"

All the world's a stage—and no one knows this better than a Drama Queen.

"The Drama Queen lives her life as if it were a soap opera," says Dr. McWhorter. She broadcasts the tales of her tearful breakups (and passionate reconciliations), impending financial ruin, and various other crises to anyone who will listen.

The Drama Queen doesn't feel comfortable or appreciated unless she's the center of attention, which she often gets by creating a scene. She's likely to go into fits of theatrical sobbing at a funeral, or stalk out of a party at which an "enemy" is present.

And while she's often charming, her emotions seem shallow. They're facsimiles of emotion that

REAL-LIFE SCENARIO
She Constantly Worries That She's Not a "Good Enough" Mom

Diane, 40, was 29 before she married, and her first child wasn't born for another 5 years. Now she's got two children, a boy, 6, and a girl, 3. She works part-time and spends her days off taking the kids on outings to the children's museum, the park, the zoo, the ice-skating rink, and, in the summer, the pool and the beach. What she doesn't do is play _with_ them. When they're home, she's usually doing dishes, cleaning, folding laundry, or cooking while the kids watch videos or play in their rooms or with friends. So she's always worrying about her mothering skills, never feeling she's quite good enough. Does she have a problem?

From a psychologist's point of view, if she's worried, of course she has a problem. But the bigger question here is, _should_ she be worried?

I don't think so. Throughout most of our species' history, kids have accompanied their mothers at their work, whether moms were gathering food in the fields or pounding clothing on rocks.

The same is true today. I'm a mother myself—my girls are 4 and 9—and I consider taking them to the supermarket a kind of "play." It's obviously a chore. But there's interacting we can do as we shop that, on some level, isn't unlike playing.

Plus—and let's be real here—kids' games are boring to us. That's because we're in a different developmental stage than they are.

seem pasted onto her face, rather than generated by her heart.

The Drama Queen also tends to use her physical appearance to draw attention to herself. She may spend a lot of time, energy, and money on clothes and grooming. She may also act the part of Seductress, being inappropriately provocative at work or flirting with her daughter's boyfriends.

Sadly, the Drama Queen's theatrics prevent her from getting genuinely close to others, or

Children, especially younger children, need repetition to understand various concepts fully. Adults find repetition toxic. A child can watch *Beauty and the Beast* 49 times, and it's even better on the 50th viewing. But adults need more and different stimulation. Which is probably why it's not so much fun for a mom to play one of the Powerpuff Girls or squeeze into her kid's Buzz Lightyear tent.

I also think we need to remember that the idea of a mother being all-giving and self-sacrificing is a myth, and it doesn't help us at all to have that myth dogging us. I want my children to know that I'm a person and I don't live only for them; that I love them, but there are other things that I am besides their mother.

There are ways Diane can convey to her children that she's doing her thing, but that the children are on her mind and part of her life. Maybe just connecting with them from time to time—going into the family room to say hi, giving them a quick hug when they're watching a video or at the computer—would make them feel better. She's sustaining contact without having to orchestrate the children's play directly. She's being what mothers have always been: busy, but loving.

Expert consulted
Tomi-Ann Roberts, Ph.D.
Associate professor of psychology
Colorado College
Colorado Springs

from letting others know who she is. Her addiction to attention and her histrionics often cause others to write her off as a flake.

Her need for drama may also drive her to enter unstable relationships with unsuitable men: alcoholics, abusers, or chronic philanderers. And, of course, her turbulent life can cause her, and those around her, a boatload of emotional stress and pain.

Beneath the flash and glitter, however, the Drama Queen often feels empty, worthless, and fearful, says Dr. McWhorter. She may also have a powerful need for control, unconsciously acting out a role (such as "victim" or "princess") that allows her to control others by appearing seductive, dependent, or manipulative.

The Drama Queen seeks emotional rescue, and distracts herself from the emptiness inside by creating crises. Says Dr. McWhorter, "When I have a Drama Queen as a patient and she reels off this long list of the crises in her life and says, 'I have no control over this,' I think, 'Oh, yes you do.'"

Demasking Tip: Sit still. Think about why you have a need to stir up others and yourself. Is it because you prefer drama to the inner emptiness you may feel? Because being rescued is easier than digging yourself out of the holes you've dug? Strive to solve your own problems, rather than relying on others to rescue you. Therapy may help you quell the anxiety beneath your theatrical displays and give you the tools you need to become more emotionally self-reliant.

The Doormat

Last heard saying: "Fine by me!"

We all know what a doormat is; we wipe our shoes on one every day. Human doormats serve much the same function: They take insults or downright abuse with nary a peep.

The word *no* just isn't part of the Doormat's vocabulary. As a result, others tend to dump on her. If she does manage to say the "N" word, she feels guilty. This leaves her open for others to manipulate her into agreeing to do things *they* don't want to do.

At work, the Doormat garners praise for her hard work and long hours, but no promotion. At home, she may jump from the table to make her child a completely different meal if he doesn't like what she's prepared. She may agree to go to an action movie with a friend, even though she can't stand car chases. Or she may uncomplainingly put up with her partner's stinging barbs about her weight, intelligence, or mothering skills.

The Doormat tends to have very loose emotional boundaries, or none at all. You might say that she has no personal line in the sand. She lets others step over it again and again, violating the things that are most important to her.

The Doormat's lack of assertiveness is often fueled by low self-esteem teamed with a fear of abandonment. "She's afraid that if she says no, she'll be left or rejected," says Dr. McWhorter.

But she pays a hefty price for her need to be liked or loved. The more she puts others' desires ahead of her own, the less she connects with her own. As she violates her own moral standards, her self-esteem withers. She denies herself regular helpings of emotional nourishment, and her soul slowly starves.

But even as a Doormat submits and accepts, "she stews inside," says Dr. McWhorter. As she allows others to violate her wants, needs, and values continually, her repressed anger may turn into serious depression. "I've had some Doormat clients who, at some point, have gotten so depressed that they became suicidal," she says.

Demasking Tip: Acknowledge your feelings first. To end the Doormat syndrome, ask yourself the following questions: "What do *I* want? What do *I* need? What do *I* believe in?" At first, you may draw a blank. After all, you may have spent years putting others' interests and feelings before your own. But struggling for answers is the start of discovering your identity.

Also, consider enrolling in an assertiveness-training program or joining a group that explores issues of assertiveness. To find an assertiveness-training course in your area, check with your

DRAMA THERAPY: LIFE IMITATING ART

When drama therapists say that all the world's a stage, they really mean it. Because to them, we *are* the roles we play. And playing them better can lead us to self-awareness and emotional healing.

"The goal of drama therapy is to help people play their everyday roles in as effective and enriching a way as possible," says Robert Landy, Ph.D., professor and director of the drama therapy program at New York University and author of *Persona and Performance: The Meaning of Role in Drama, Therapy, and Everyday Life.*

Drama therapists combine the techniques of theater, such as role-playing, improvisation, and pantomime, with those of traditional talk therapy. They may also use props such as puppets, dolls, and masks.

The goal is to use the power of art to illuminate and resolve emotional hurts.

Most drama therapists tap into the creative power of storytelling. Dr. Landy often asks his patients to tell him a story, starting with the classic fairy-tale line "Once upon a time . . ."

"I get more insight into their lives from that story than if I had spent an hour asking about their childhood," says Dr. Landy.

Role-playing can also be therapeutic, he says. "Being" someone else, such as your mother or your partner, can reveal much about the nature of your conflicts with them.

Say you have issues with your mother. Rather than saying, "So tell me about your mother," Dr. Landy is more likely to ask you to *become* her.

"I might say, 'Sit in the chair the way your mother does. Show me how she holds her coffee cup.'" Then, he'd talk to your mom. "I might ask, 'What's going on between you and your daughter? What do you think of her?'"

Playing Mom allows you to tap into a huge amount of emotion, which may lead to insight into your mother's behavior as well as your own, says Dr. Landy.

Or let's say you're a Doormat (see description on page 47). A drama therapist might ask you to tell a story about a woman who wears this mask. Then, he'd explore her character with you. He'd also ask you how she's like you—the idea being that the woman in the story is you, since you made her up.

Drama therapy can be especially helpful for those of us who find it uncomfortable to talk about our feelings, says Dr. Landy. Playacting is a safe way to access troubling or threatening emotions, because they belong to the character, not you.

Drama therapists are trained in theater arts, psychology, and psychotherapy, and must be registered by the National Association for Drama Therapy (NADT). You're most likely to find a drama therapist in a large city. To see if there's a registered drama therapist in your area, visit the NADT Web site at www.nadt.org.

local mental health center. Learning to express your feelings, and to call things the way you see them respectfully without getting caught up in accommodating others, is the first step to discovering who you are—and revealing yourself to others.

The Martyr

Last heard saying: "All I do is give. And am I appreciated?"

Joan of Arc selflessly gave her life for the country she loved. But there are lots of modern-day Joans of Arc who actually *look* for opportunities to burn themselves at the stake.

The Martyr is all about self-sacrifice. At least, that's what she believes. Because she expects something in return for her self-sacrifice: your guilt and pity.

"Unlike the Doormat, the Martyr is more likely to employ guilt," says Dr. McWhorter. "Instead of putting on a happy face and saying, 'Fine, no problem, whatever you want!' like the Doormat does, she sighs and complains."

In other words, the Martyr chooses the hard way, then whines about the selfishness of those who "forced" her to make that choice. At the same time, she rarely asks for help, and will rebuff it when offered.

Overburdened with household chores, the Martyr might say, "I give and give and give, and no one cares." Struggling to meet a deadline at work, she'll refuse a helping hand, saying, "Oh, I'll be fine, don't worry about me." Exhausted from nursing a sick child all night, she'll insist on cooking a big breakfast and tackling the household chores alone, even if her partner offers help.

Martyrs carry this I'll-just-sit-in-the-dark attitude into their relationships, too. "Say a Martyr asks her husband to mow the lawn. If he doesn't do it in what she thinks is the proper time frame, she does it herself," says Dr. McWhorter. "She'll resent it, and will most certainly let him know about it in one way or another."

A Martyr's mask of self-sacrifice often hides her fear of being considered weak or dependent.

After all, not asking for help means she has it all together. As a result, the Martyr loses out on being vulnerable, the cornerstone of our ability to forge intimate relationships.

"To risk asking others to meet her needs, or to ask for or accept help, makes her feel vulnerable," says Dr. McWhorter. "She fears that if she asks for what she needs, she won't get it. So she guilts people into meeting her needs."

Demasking Tip: Learn to ask for help. Martyrs suffer from the I-have-to-do-everything-myself syndrome, partly because they fear being dependent and partly because they have a powerful need for control. But more often than not, many people would gladly give us their help if we ask for it or accept it when it's offered. So the next time you're cleaning up the kitchen after a party, allow friends and family to pitch in. If you can't make a deadline, ask a colleague to lend a hand. Learning to accept help means learning to be vulnerable—the first step toward becoming truly intimate with yourself and others.

The Mother

Last heard saying: "Oh, you poor dear!"
We've all been raised to meet the needs, emotional and otherwise, of others. But the Mother brings nurturing to new heights.

The Mother not only mothers her kids, but lavishes the same maternal attention on her husband, colleagues, and strangers on the street. Her concern knows no bounds, her selflessness no limits.

At work, she's the one who brings in the doughnuts, organizes surprise birthday parties, or says, "Turn that frown upside down!" At home, she fusses over her partner's cold, proffering magazines, orange juice, and pillow plumps every 15 minutes. At a restaurant with a friend, she wails, "You look so thin!" and urges her to clean her plate.

"The Mother can even anticipate others' needs—or thinks she can," says Dr. McWhorter.

The problem is, the Mother is so focused on meeting others' needs that she often doesn't consider her own. And she's so concerned with others' feelings that she may lose touch with her own. For example, the Mother may insist that everyone in the family go to the doctor for their annual physical, but not schedule her yearly mammogram. Or, after an argument with her partner, she may get so caught up in soothing his ruffled feelings that she doesn't confront her own. After all, keeping the relationship humming happily is *her* job.

Actually, the Mother considers the care and feeding of all relationships to be her job. Underneath that seemingly noble behavior, she's often meeting her own primary need for control.

While some folks on the receiving end of a Mother's hovering concern may enjoy basking in the warmth of her attention, others feel smothered, and more than a little resentful. "A Mother's implicit message is, 'If I don't take care of you, you'll fall apart,'" says Dr. McWhorter.

Caring for others also feeds a Mother's often-tenuous sense of self-esteem. "Mothers need others to need them," says Dr. McWhorter. "If they don't feel needed, they don't feel good about themselves."

Demasking Tip: Take some time for you. Fulfilled as you may feel in your role, you would do well to consider your own needs more, advises Dr. McWhorter. At least once a week, take time to meet friends for lunch or to pursue or learn a hobby. You may just find that you're a budding hiker, painter, or small-business owner, and begin to develop talents you never knew you possessed. What's more, you may discover that nurturing these parts of yourself is just as satisfying as nurturing others. Let adults take care of their own needs. It will give you a chance to fulfill your own.

The Passive-Aggressive

Last heard saying: "Hostile? Me?"

You're trying to lose weight. Your best friend cheers you on. Then she gives you your birthday present: a box of Godiva chocolates.

You smile and thank her, but secretly think that her gift is a little, well, hostile.

And you're right.

The Passive Aggressive's hurtful behavior is masked by goodwill and apologies. At home, she may "forget" to buy her husband's favorite breakfast cereal or shrink his favorite shirt in the dryer, or "mistakenly" offer her child's favorite toy at a yard sale. Or she may be habitually late, leaving a friend cooling her heels for a half-hour because she "just couldn't get away."

At work, she may turn in projects after deadline, or sabotage a colleague's pet project. Or she may promise to help a coworker prepare a report, then back out at the last minute, pleading deadlines of her own.

Engaging in this type of maddening behavior is a safe way for the Passive-Aggressive to avoid conflict or express negative feelings while maintaining her "nice gal" image, says Dr. McWhorter.

Most important, it allows her to express anger, which may stir up intense feelings of anxiety and guilt. "As a child, she may have learned that being angry was not acceptable: the old 'nice girls don't get angry' trip," says Dr. McWhorter. "Unconsciously, she fears that if she gets angry with someone, or is honest with

---

VIVE LA DIFFÉRENCE?

We've always known that we cope with and express our emotions differently from men. Recent psychology research confirms this "feelings gap." Here are some of the latest findings.

We think, men drink. When we feel mad, sad, or blue, we tend to dwell on our troubles, according to a University of Michigan study of 1,300 men and women. Specifically, we ruminate, which the study defines as "passively and repetitively focusing on symptoms of distress and the possible causes and consequences of those symptoms."

Men, on the other hand, tend to turn to alcohol to combat their problems, according to the study. And according to researchers, that excessive drinking may simply give *us* one more thing to worry about.

We strive for harmony; men strive for power. When it comes to expressing our emotions, our motives are based on relationships; men's are based on maintaining power and control. In a study of 314 men and women, researchers found that women expressed more "powerless" emotions, such as crying or admitting to sadness or disappointment. Men, on the other hand, were more reluctant to relinquish their power by expressing these emotions. They were also more likely to use anger to regain the upper hand.

We're hungry when we're angry. According to a recent study of more than 200 men and women, both genders tend to eat more when joyful. But when women are angry or sad, we're more likely than men to pig out.

---

her negative feelings, they will no longer like or love her."

The Passive-Aggressive also lacks the self-esteem to ask for what she needs, which can be death for an intimate relationship. Because she doesn't assert herself with her partner, she must resort to sabotage. That's why, for many women, the ultimate passive-aggressive act is embarking on an affair.

Demasking Tip: Connect your anger with your behavior. Really think about what getting angry means to you and how it makes you feel. Does expressing anger directly make you anxious? If so, is it because you fear conflict with others, or because you connect being angry with being rejected?

Getting in touch with your anger is crucial, but it can be hard to do alone. Getting into therapy can help you get in touch with your anger and explore why it's there, says Dr. Parrott.

The Perfectionist

Last heard saying: "There's the right way and the right way."

Always worried that your best isn't good enough? Continually disappointed in the people you live or work with? Chances are you're a Perfectionist. And it's a sneaky trap.

"Striving for perfection is exhausting, not to mention unrealistic," says Dr. McWhorter. "But the Perfectionist doesn't feel good enough about herself to give herself permission to be anything less than perfect."

And yet, the Perfectionist tries. Her home must be spotless, her job performance stellar, and her marriage the best on the block. Flaws, such as an unscrubbed toilet, tough times at work, or a not-exactly-perfect partnership, are evidence of her incompetence and ultimate worthlessness.

"At her core, the Perfectionist feels that she is only the sum of her achievements," says Dr. McWhorter.

What the Perfectionist fears most is lack of control, says Monica Ramirez Basco, Ph.D., clinical assistant professor of psychology at the University of Texas Southwestern Medical Center in Dallas and author of *Never Good Enough: How to Use Perfectionism to Your Advantage without Letting It Ruin Your Life.*

The Perfectionist may have experienced a chaotic childhood marked by divorce, continual moves, financial instability, illness, or alcoholism. Feeling terrified by such disorder, she controlled what small things she could. She may have kept her room and appearance excessively tidy, her grades top-notch, and her relationships with her friends, family, and boyfriends deceptively tranquil. "As an adult, she may have continued to work hard to maintain her hard-won control," says Dr. Basco.

The Perfectionist may also have had a mother or father who directly or indirectly communicated that she just didn't measure up. When she brought home Bs on her report card, her father wondered why they weren't A's. When she played at a piano recital, her mother commented only on the wrong notes.

The Perfectionist may carry this childhood experience into adulthood—and it takes a heavy toll. "I treat women who underachieve because they're so afraid of failure. They'd rather not try than fall on their faces," says Dr. Basco.

She is also vulnerable to depression, loneliness, and anger. It's likely that she has low self-esteem. She may also have a hard time taking risks or making decisions. After all, to risk or to choose may mean failure, rejection, or humiliation.

Demasking Tip: Question your quest for perfection. Dr. Basco advises pondering such questions as "Do I really *have* to be perfect? Does being perfect really gain me more love or respect? Are there truly negative consequences to not being perfect—real ones, not feared ones?" There are no right answers, according to Dr. Basco (much to our relief). "These questions are simply tools for self-exploration."

The Seductress

Last heard saying: "How do I look?"

She dons short skirts, plunging necklines, and three-inch heels, despite the fact that she was a teenager during the Nixon Administration. And her makeup looks, well, like a mask.

You've had an encounter with a Seductress: a woman who believes that the sum of her parts is greater than her whole self.

Don't mistake the Seductress for the woman who values looking attractive and youthful. Our sexuality is a valid part of our identity. Besides, today's 40- or 50-something female is hardly over the hill. Why shouldn't she strive to look as youthful as she feels?

We're talking about the woman who believes that all she has to offer is her appearance, and who finds her sense of self-worth in the T. J. Maxx Juniors section.

"I see women in middle age and older who are still dressing like 25-year-olds," says Dr. McWhorter. "It's sad." As she grows older, the Seductress's provocative clothing, heavy make-up, and flirtatious ways may make her an object of ridicule or pity—an aging Barbie doll, not to be taken seriously.

The making of a Seductress is part nature, part nurture. The nurture part? Our culture, which has always objectified women's bodies, says Tomi-Ann Roberts, Ph.D., associate professor of psychology at Colorado College in Colorado Springs. Women reap a ton of rewards for simply being young and beautiful, namely, fame, money, and admiring attention.

But the Seductress's self-esteem is often in the basement. And she can feel ashamed and worthless if she thinks she's not measuring up to social standards of desirability. There's also anxiety. She's always aware that she's on display. This self-consciousness prevents her from getting to know others or revealing her true self to others.

"She can get so consumed by how she's being seen that she loses her ability to relate to others," says Dr. Roberts.

Nor does she have much time to reflect on what she wants, what she believes in, or who she is as a person. The time she might have spent on self-reflection or creative pursuits is spent in the gym, at the tanning salon, or at the designer out-lets: places where she can quell her anxiety, pump up her shaky self-esteem, and blunt her gnawing sense of emptiness.

Demasking Tip: Indulge in an emotional makeover. To help you see that your self is more than skin deep, list all of the positive qualities you have to offer other than your outward appearance. "Your list might include such things as, 'I'm great at my job. I'm a caring mother. I'm a terrific cook,'" says Dr. McWhorter. "Carry the list in your wallet and read it until these accomplishments start sinking in." You may also want to go on yet another mall expedition. This time, try on clothing you usually leave on the racks. "You can see what feels the most like you," says Dr. McWhorter.

The Steamroller

Last heard saying: "It's my way or the highway."

More men than women fit this type. But rest assured, plenty of us are Steamrollers, although we're sure not to see it.

The hallmark of a Steamroller is her astounding insensitivity to others' feelings. She simply flattens everyone in her path with her iron will and sandpaper-like style.

At work, the Steamroller is often controlling, arrogant, and stubborn, insisting that her way is the best way. At home, she may force her child onto the baseball team even though he prefers to play chess, because she believes "it's good for him." Or she may infuriate her partner by continually scheduling events on their social calendar regardless of whether he'll enjoy the activity or the company.

It may seem as if things always go the Steamroller's way. But continually flattening others has consequences. At work, she may lose a promotion because she's not a team player. As her children grow older, they may rebel against her values. "A Steamroller is setting herself up for

INNER-SPACE EXPLORERS

Who was B. F. Skinner?

We cry because we're sorry. We tremble because we're afraid. Right? Not according to B. F. Skinner. This influential 20th-century American psychologist believed it's not our emotions that rule our behavior, but our environment.

Skinner was a vocal proponent of behavioralism. This theory of personality views all human behavior as a response to our surroundings. In fact, he went so far as to call the belief that our feelings influence our behavior a mental fiction.

As a psychology professor at Harvard, Skinner influenced a generation of psychologists. His goal was to predict and control human behavior. Using various contraptions of his own invention, Skinner trained lab animals to perform complex (at times, wondrous) acts. His hero, the Russian physiologist Ivan Pavlov, had trained dogs to salivate at the sound of a bell (hence the term *Pavlovian response*). But Skinner did even better: He got pigeons to play ping-pong by giving them food at precisely the right moment.

One of his most famous inventions was the Skinner box, in which lab animals are rewarded with food for carrying out simple tasks such as pushing buttons and levers. It's still used today to monitor animal reactions to new drugs.

His experiments with animals led him to formulate the principles of programmed learning, which he thought would work with the use of "teaching machines." When students picked the right answers, these machines would dole out reinforcements or rewards.

In his controversial book *Walden Two*, he wrote about creating a utopian society without nuclear weapons, pollution, or overpopulation—a feat accomplished by running the society on his own principles.

While Skinner attained cult status in the 1960s, his work was far from universally accepted. He was also labeled dangerous, opinionated, and a "rat lover" (because of his use of animals in his experiments). Some philosophers and political scientists (not to mention psychologists) found his views inimical to a democratic society.

some serious heartache with her kids," says Dr. Parrott.

For example, if she forced them to attend church as kids, they may reject religion altogether as teenagers and adults. If she derided them about less-than-brilliant performances in school, they may become underachievers in later life.

At the root of the Steamroller's behavior is anxiety and fear. Often, she's had an unstable or unpredictable childhood. Bending others to her will is her way of making the world safe and predictable.

"Often, Steamrollers are jellyfish with armor. They look tough on the outside but are extremely vulnerable inside," says Dr. Parrott. "Steamrolling over others allows them to manage their anxiety."

Demasking tip: Try a little empathy. Before you speak or act, try to imagine how your behavior might affect others, suggests Dr. Parrott. You just may find that stepping into someone else's shoes gives you more insight into their point of view, and less of a need to impose yours.

And yet, relinquishing that need for control can leave you feeling vulnerable and anxious. Seeing a therapist can help you confront and make peace with these scary emotions.

Saving Face: Finding the Real You

Did you recognize yourself in any of these types? (And it is possible to be more than one type.) If so, you may be in danger of losing the real you. But with lots of soul-searching and hard work, you can find her again.

Because you'll need to confront the painful feelings that led you to don your mask in the first place, the demasking process can be difficult and even frightening. So as you begin this inner journey, consider seeking the guidance of a therapist.

In the meantime, the following tips can help start you on your journey to self-discovery.

Keep a dream journal. Leave a small notebook and pen on your nightstand. When you have a dream, record it as soon as you wake up. You can even draw your dream.

After you write down your dream, pull it apart. Think about what it means to you. "The fundamental rule for dreams is that every character—even animals—represents an aspect of yourself," says Waldman. "So ask yourself, 'What character do I identify with?' That character can often tell you about those aspects of yourself you've been hiding." For example, being pregnant in your dream (if you're obviously not) may be telling you that you have creativity that's not being released.

Practice talk therapy. Break with your role as mother, career woman, or partner, and share your feelings with a close friend. "For some reason, actually saying how you feel out loud makes your feelings real," says Waldman. Don't worry if you're confused as to what your real feelings actually are. Stumble through the confusion until the issues begin to unfold.

Find your spiritual side. Knowing that you're not alone will give you the courage to continue your inner journey. "It's vital to acknowledge a loving presence who is more powerful than you are," says Waldman. As you go through this often frightening process of self-discovery, you can give your burdens over to this presence, and let it hold and support you.

Be reborn each day. If you possibly can, bathe in the morning, rather than shower, suggests Waldman. "Taking a bath in the morning allows you to experience renewal and rebirth every day," she says. Think you don't have time? Fill the tub while you're brushing your teeth and making your bed, then indulge in a 10-minute soak.

Fill your emptiness with creativity. Learn to paint. Take up needlework. Try your hand at writing poetry or cooking gourmet meals. "The creative force is an awesome power because it's an authentic expression of yourself," says Waldman. Don't worry if your creative efforts turn out less than perfect. Even if they're awful, you'll have been in touch with your authentic self. For more on the power of creativity, see When Your Inner Genius Comes Out to Play on page 135.

PART TWO

To Thine
Own Self
Be True

Inner Fire and Brimstone

What's your take on anger?

Perhaps you agree with 17th-century English clergyman Thomas Fuller, who said, "Anger is one of the sinews of the soul."

Or maybe you agree with comedienne Phyllis Diller, who said, "Never go to bed mad. Stay up and fight."

Wherever your sentiments lie, one thing's for sure: We all get angry.

It's part of the grand repertoire of human emotions. It's a natural response to assaults on our *self*—our self-worth, feelings, and values.

Anger is also a normal reaction to stress. As we juggle competing obligations to home, family, and career, life can get so impossible that throwing a tantrum can seem reasonable. (Although, of course, it's not.)

But while our anger is real and understandable, we frequently react to it in one of two unhealthy ways.

The first, suppression, turns us into human pressure cookers of frustration and resentment. We stew and simmer until, eventually, we boil over. The second, venting aggressively—screaming, shouting, throwing china—is the equivalent of emotional gunfire, as we spray innocent bystanders with verbal bullets.

But take heart. Whether anger now turns us into meek little mice or screaming banshees, we can learn to express it constructively. And once we do, we'll most likely discover that anger, once our worst enemy, can become our best friend.

When we're aware of our anger and use its energy in a healthy way, it can be a path to power. It gives us insight into our wants and needs. It lets us know when our rights or values are being trampled. It encourages us to explore new choices and improve our lives. It compels us to correct injustice and to improve the lives of others.

Our anger is our personal line in the sand: Beyond this point you shall not go.

The Myths of Anger

Despite its clear signal, anger can be a murky emotion. Perhaps that's because so many of us have fallen for the myths that obscure it—myths we learned from our parents or, as adults, in the pages of pop-psychology books.

Myth: It's good to "let it all out" by pounding a pillow or going postal on your partner or colleague.

Fact: Research shows that venting angry feelings in an aggressive way can actually increase anger.

Myth: Anger causes heart disease and high blood pressure.

Fact: Normal, everyday anger can be healthy if it's dealt with in a way that focuses on problem solving and mutual respect. It's hostile, aggressive behavior or personality as well as the repression of anger that is linked to disease.

Myth: Nice girls don't get angry.

Fact: "That's part of the old sugar-and-spice stereotype of women," says Carol Tavris, Ph.D., a social psychologist in Los Angeles and author of *Anger: The Misunderstood Emotion*. In fact, research shows that women get as angry as often and as intensely as men do. We just tend to express it differently. For instance, men are more likely to get angry in public and to express anger aggressively, whereas women are more likely to cry in anger.

Myth: Women have a hard time recognizing their anger.

Fact: "Women *do* know when they're angry—they told us about it," says Sandra Thomas, Ph.D., professor and director of the doctoral program in nursing at the University of Tennessee in Knoxville and principal investigator of the Women's Anger Study, the first

WOMEN ASK WHY
Why do I feel guilty when I get angry?

Women have been socialized to believe that it's their responsibility to maintain relationship harmony. By getting angry, we introduce disharmony, and we feel bad.

Women learn to hide their anger early on. In one long-term study of girls and anger, researchers found that 9-year-old girls spoke openly about anger. By the time they were teenagers, they had stopped. They had begun to receive strong messages about expressing anger, such as "You won't be popular if you're unpleasant or make waves" and "Girls are supposed to be nice, gentle, and pleasant."

Many of us have heeded these messages too well. In my research, we've found that even if women can express anger at, say, a salesclerk, they're still reluctant to do so in their intimate relationships, especially with men. Not only have they heeded the social message that their role is to maintain harmony in relationships, they've also heeded another powerful message: "If you show anger, you'll drive him away."

But just because a woman feels guilt about getting angry doesn't mean her anger vanishes. It can stay with her for a long time. Often, that's because she didn't get a satisfactory resolution to whatever made her angry to begin with. Whether she stuffed her anger or screamed and yelled, her needs were still not met, her values were still violated, and she wasn't able to make the other person understand how she felt.

To stop feeling guilty when we get angry, we need to believe that we have the right to get angry, the right to dignity and respect, and the right to let others know, in an assertive way, what has made us angry. When you believe in these rights, you're more likely to speak out and stick up for yourself. And that's when you stand a better chance of using your anger productively to make positive changes in your life without feeling guilty.

Expert consulted
Sandra Thomas, Ph.D.
Principal investigator, Women's Anger Study
University of Tennessee
Knoxville

large-scale, comprehensive study of everyday anger in women's lives.

To chip away at these myths, we need to understand what anger actually is, and what it is not.

Anger: A Definition

What anger is: a strong feeling of emotional distress in response to a threat, insult, or injustice. "It's an emphatic message: 'Pay attention to me. I don't like what you are doing. Restore my pride. You're in my way. Danger. Give me justice,'" says Dr. Tavris.

What anger is not: hostility, the enduring belief that the world is out to do us dirt. Hostility is more pervasive and lasts longer than anger. Nor is it frustration, the frequent response to everyday annoyances such as traffic jams or infuriatingly drawn-out voice-mail systems. "Unlike anger, frustration doesn't threaten our integrity or values," says Dr. Thomas.

Anger is also not aggression: the painful put-down, full-face slap, flung coffee mug, or vengeful deed meant to draw the emotional or physical blood of another. "Anger is the feeling; aggression its overt expression," says Dr. Tavris.

What Sets Us Off

As we all know, there are plenty of reasons to get red-in-the-face, fist-shaking pissed. Partners who pull our chains. Mouthy kids. Stupid coworkers. Bosses who screw us over. And, of course, Mother, who can make us purely apoplectic with her "helpful" criticism about the current state of our lives.

FROM ANGER TO ACTION

At 10:00 P.M. on August 14, 1971, on a road in Franklin, Tennessee, Millie Webb's life changed forever.

An alcohol-impaired driver plowed into the 1955 Chevrolet that Webb's husband, Roy, had lovingly restored. The crash ultimately killed their 4-year-old daughter, Lori, 2 weeks later, along with Webb's 19-month-old nephew, Mitchell.

Webb, 7 months pregnant, sustained burns over 75 percent of her body and spent 3 months in intensive care. As a result of the crash, her daughter, Kara, was born premature and legally blind. Roy also suffered severe burns and spent 2 months in the hospital. Their large family cared for them and Kara, and their faith gave them the strength to go on.

The driver was charged with manslaughter and put on probation for 2 years. And in the financial settlement, the Webbs received almost nothing.

You would think that Webb, now national president of Mothers Against Drunk Driving (MADD) would be enraged at the cards life had dealt her. But at that time, anger was a luxury she couldn't afford. Being in constant, excruciating pain, with a critically hurt husband, a newborn, and two dead children to grieve over, left her little physical or emotional strength for rage.

Her anger was a long time coming. But eventually, it came.

"I was angry when my child was born premature and legally blind," she says. "And again, when our attorney advised

But no one knows our hot buttons like Dr. Thomas. She's spent more than a decade researching and talking to real women about what fuels our anger and how we tend to respond. Here's what rattles our cages most.

- **Powerlessness.** "Feeling powerless—caused by being unable to get someone or something to change, or to make ourselves heard—is the most frequent anger trigger," says Dr. Thomas.
- **Injustice.** "The women in our study talked

us to settle because, as he put it, 'It doesn't matter what you look like, Mrs. Webb—you already have a husband.' And again, when, in high school, my daughter struggled with what little sight she had. And yet again, when she started college, and I saw the young sorority pledges coming out of one set of double doors, and the handicapped students, who were getting their orientation separately, coming out the other.

"I thought, 'Kara probably would have been going out a different door if that man had chosen not to drink and drive.'" (Kara is now married and has a child.)

But slowly—very slowly—Webb's mind and body healed. And 10 years after the crash, she turned her anger and grief into action. She joined MADD.

She almost didn't. "I thought that forgiving this man meant forgetting what he had done, and I didn't want to forget. Then I realized that if someone had talked to the man who caused my tragedy, my life would have been different."

To Webb, anger is a normal, natural response to tragedy—not just alcohol-related fatalities, but death, divorce, and other life-altering traumas. But she also believes that anger without action is useless. Which is why she encourages others to use her motto, "Curse it, then reverse it."

"When a tragedy happens, we can choose to become bitter or better," she says. "I can't change what happened to me. But I can do everything in my power to keep it from happening to someone else."

and coworkers who spend more time gossiping than working.

Then there's that slippery foe, stress. Like death and taxes, it seems to be one of life's certainties. In the Women's Anger Study, stress was found to be the most frequent and powerful predictor of female wrath. The more stressed we get, the more we tend to explode or lash out. (For practical stress-busting techniques, see The Storm of Stress on page 19.)

Here's the dilemma: Even when we *know* we're furious, we face some pretty stiff opposition from society, which still clings to the belief that nice women don't get angry.

So too often we muzzle ourselves. "Women are afraid of alienating their partners or friends with their anger," says Dr. Thomas. "Or they're afraid of negative consequences at work."

Some of us are so disturbed by our anger that we can't even identify it by its rightful name. "Many women have learned to say, 'I'm hurt,' or 'I'm disappointed,' rather than 'I'm furious!'" says Dr. Thomas.

The Nice-Lady Syndrome

Faced with smart-mouthed kids, insufferable colleagues, or idiot bosses, many of us repress our anger and take the "Nice Lady" route, says Harriet Lerner, Ph.D., clinical psychologist and psychotherapist at the Menninger Clinic in Topeka, Kansas, and author of *The Dance of Anger*.

The Nice Lady has society's blessing, says Dr. Lerner. She gives in, goes along, accommodates. And she avoids conflict like a crusty lasagna pan

about people lying to or betraying them," says Dr. Thomas. "They were also angry on behalf of others who were treated unjustly. For example, they might be furious at a teacher who seems to have it in for their child."

♦ **Irresponsibility.** We get angry when others don't pull their weight at home or at work. Frequent targets of our wrath: partners who blithely drop their soggy towels on the bathroom floor, kids who balk at chores,

that needs scrubbing. "Nice Ladies never say, 'This is what I believe. This is how I see it,'" she says.

That's not surprising. From time immemorial, we've been handed the job of nurturer. We're the flesh-and-blood glue that holds life together, the disseminators of clean sheets, home-cooked meals, and other hearth-and-home comforts. So it's easy to see how Nice Ladies might worry about giving voice to a feeling with the potential to disrupt the harmony of an important relationship.

Nice Ladies may also fear that giving voice to their anger may cause them to commit an act so heinous that they land themselves a spot on the 6 o'clock news.

"I've heard women say, 'If I were ever to get really angry, we'd all burst into flame,'" says Deborah Cox, Ph.D., psychologist, anger researcher, and assistant professor in the department of guidance and counseling at Southwest Missouri State University in Springfield.

But holding anger in doesn't mean we're not expressing it, says Dr. Cox. Our bodies will help us express it quite well with headaches and other physical ailments.

Or we'll vent on the easiest target: ourselves.

"Women may turn to drugs, alcohol, cigarettes, or food," says Dr. Thomas. "All of these substances temporarily mask the emotional arousal anger causes."

But even Nice Ladies eventually explode, says Christine Padesky, Ph.D., founder and director of the Center for Cognitive Therapy in Newport

CONTROL YOUR TEMPER IN ANY SITUATION

Have you ever watched a pyrotechnics-loving friend light a long string of firecrackers on the Fourth of July? The match passes the flame to the fuse, which quietly crackles for a moment as bystanders grow tense, waiting for the . . . BANG POW BANG BANG BANG that becomes an extended battery of noise.

A burst of temper can grow like that firecracker display. If you want to avoid it, learn to keep hot situations from lighting your fuse instead of trying to stop your anger after it has started, suggests Marcia J. Slattery, M.D., a psychiatrist with the Mayo Clinic.

Pay attention to your warning signals. Whether they're the type who readily vents or quietly turns anger inward, many women don't notice when they're becoming angry. The next time you're in a temper-provoking scenario, take a quick inventory of your feelings. Do you get a knot in your stomach? Or ask a trusted friend to give you her impression of how you act when you're angry. Do you start to twitch? Tap your foot? Does your voice get tense? Once you're aware of them, listen to your warning signs sooner.

Think before you act. Before you say exactly what's on your miffed mind, take a few moments to consider ways to deal with the situation without making it worse. Walk away if you have to, then come back and continue.

Chase the little aggravations away. If you allow petty annoyances to accumulate, you push your temper to its limits. Let annoyances pass, and forget about them.

Compartmentalize your life. Find a proper balance be-

Beach, California, and coauthor of *Mind over Mood*.

"It's common for a woman to be overaccommodating and hold in a simmering resentment," says Dr. Padesky. "Eventually, given enough resentment or stress or fatigue, she'll

tween all of the aspects of your life, such as your friends, family, work, exercise, and hobbies, Dr. Slattery suggests. When your life becomes focused on one narrow pursuit (work, for example), you tend to lose perspective on all of the things that are important and to react too quickly to problems that shouldn't be such a big deal.

Make a list. Write down all of the things that make your life complete, or draw them out on a pie chart. Hang it up on your office wall or put it in your purse. The next time you're in a huff, look at the piece of paper and weigh the current minor aggravation against all of the good things in your life, Dr. Slattery says.

Stop problems before they start. If your child keeps doing something that always triggers a battle, write out a contract when you're both calm that specifies what the consequences will be the next time he does it. If he breaks the agreement, don't get mad—just pull out the contract and follow the plan you've established.

Don't assume others are out to get you. If you encounter a slow cashier in the supermarket checkout line, remember that she didn't wake up that morning determined to make your life miserable. She's doing the best she can, just as you are. Instead of losing your temper and escalating the situation, treat her with a positive attitude.

Put your problems in perspective. Keep in mind that at any given time, disasters are changing people's lives all around the globe. Even though you may be exasperated when your computer freezes up, this inconvenience isn't worth getting upset over when you compare it with a real tragedy.

The Dragon-Lady Trap

While Nice Ladies experience an anger buildup that can lead to an explosion, some of us explode as a matter of course. Those of us who are Dragon Ladies blow fire at our partners, kids, or colleagues, even over trivial matters. We tell off salesclerks and rage at the guy behind the counter at the Department of Motor Vehicles. We threaten, shout, swear, bitch, and complain.

Dragon Ladies may have just cause to be angry. But the raging-bull technique just doesn't work, says Dr. Lerner. In fact, our approach to anger—expressing it loud and long—puts us squarely in the same boat with the Nice Ladies, for whom silence is golden. Our anger remains unheard (who's going to stand firm in front of an erupting volcano?), and the issues that provoked it go unsolved.

Dragon Ladies may also be using anger to cover up other, more threatening feelings such as sadness or fear. These emotions may make us feel vulnerable, while our anger makes us feel powerful. So we become Janey One-Notes, using anger to keep these disturbing emotions at bay.

Sadly, the consequences of out-of-control anger can haunt Dragon Ladies. It can harm our relationships with our partners and kids, cost us jobs or promotions, and fuel self-loathing and depression as we mourn yet again losing our temper.

Can't decide which one you are? You're probably a combination of both. The Nice Lady and the Dragon Lady can coexist within you.

explode, usually over something fairly minor. And because her anger is so extreme relative to the situation, it fuels her guilt about getting angry and her reluctance to be angry. She thinks, 'Look what anger does. It turns me into a monster.'"

Bringing Anger Aboveground

There's another quality that Nice Ladies and Dragon Ladies may share: total unawareness of how furious we really are, or where our anger should be directed.

At home, Nice Ladies may "express" their anger by using the silent treatment, a punishment dreaded by men since the dawn of time. Even worse, we may withdraw emotionally. "This passive expression of anger, classically labeled passive aggression, can cause women to withhold affection from their partners or children," says Dr. Thomas.

At work, Nice Ladies also turn passive-aggressive, expressing their displeasure by procrastinating or working *very* slowly.

And the woman who's a walking tinderbox? "She may focus all of her energy on a target that may not even be the cause of her anger," says Dr. Cox. "For example, she may be unconsciously angry at her partner, so she's vicious with her children or coworkers."

At work, a Dragon Lady may act impulsively, shouting, "That's it! I quit!" when she can ill afford to. At home, she may storm into her kid's room and scream at him to clean it up, being only dimly aware that she's feeling overwhelmed by her novel-length to-do list and lack of support on the home front.

To get to the root of our anger, and to express it without harming others, we need to first become conscious of it, says Dr. Cox. Then we have to admit to it and ask ourselves what's behind the fury.

This is a frightening prospect for those of us who learned the nice-girls-don't-get-angry message all too well. We may believe that if we let ourselves fully express our anger, we'll be consumed by it. Not true, says Dr. Cox.

"What we see is that women who allow themselves to be as angry as they fully are for as long as they need to be, and who talk about their anger honestly, grow and change," she says. "All of that buried anger becomes a catalyst for positive change and growth." For instance, many of the women she sees return to school or leave abusive relationships when they work with their anger.

Raise Anger Awareness

One way to let out our unconscious anger is to keep an anger journal, says Dr. Thomas. This detailed log of incidents that incite your wrath can "help you zero in on the real issues and identify the source of your angry feelings, which is the first step in changing your behavior," she says.

It's easy to start an anger journal. Simply buy an inexpensive notebook small enough to carry with you.

The hard part is making a commitment to write in your journal every day for at least a month. But it's a commitment worth keeping, says Dr. Thomas. "By recording your anger incidents as they occur, you will be able to identify the repetitive themes and patterns in your anger behavior."

The best time to write out your anger is while it's still fresh in your mind, but after you've calmed down enough to think logically about the incident, she says. This step-by-step strategy will help you get the most out of your anger journal.

1. Describe who or what provoked your anger. Be sure to include whether the perpetrator was male or female and whether they were above or below you in status.
2. Describe your first reaction. Was it "There he goes again!" or "Her condescending attitude drives me nuts!"
3. Describe the tactics you used to handle your anger. Did you smile and accommodate, or yell, kick the dog, and throw a potted plant? Did you pout and sulk, or employ a lot of

eye-rolling and sarcastic re-marks? Did you talk about your anger with your partner or a close friend, or keep it to yourself?

4. Think about the physical sensations or reactions that accompanied your anger. Did you cry? Get a stomachache or headache? Breathe more rapidly, get a lump in your throat, experience shakiness? Reach for a cigarette, a doughnut, or a glass of wine?

5. Record how long you stayed angry. Fifteen minutes? Three hours? All day? Longer?

6. Describe how you felt when the incident was over. Did you feel guilty, wiped out, depressed? Or proud of yourself?

7. Finally, analyze your anger. What was it that really set you off? What was most threatening or hurtful about the incident?

The longer you keep your journal, the more adept you'll become at recognizing your anger style and the situations that fuel your anger, says Dr. Thomas.

But raising our anger consciousness is only the first step. Whether we're silent seethers or fire-and-brimstone types, we need practical strategies to help us use our anger productively. Keep reading, ladies.

The Nice Ladies' Anger Cheat Sheet

For Nice Ladies to express anger in a positive way, we need to learn to communicate clearly and directly

ALL IN THE GENES?

Are women hardwired to be less violent than men?

Our society doesn't want to think of women as violent. We're the nurturers and mothers, not the armed robbers or murderers.

But my research and experience suggest that women are capable of as much violence as men.

True, men are more than twice as likely to commit acts of extreme violence as women. But I've found that the women who work with men in armed robberies or team killings are every bit as violent.

The backgrounds of extremely violent men and women are also virtually identical. For example, male and female serial killers tend to be similar in intelligence, personal achievement, and criminal motivation. And both tend to have been physically, emotionally, or sexually abused as children.

There's no doubt that serial killers are angry. Often, murder is a manifestation of extreme anger. What's interesting is that many extremely violent women, like many normal women, turn their anger on themselves before they turn it on others. Many have attempted suicide, which is the extreme of turning anger inward. Violent men have not.

In fact, the only significant differences I've found between male and female serial killers are in their methods of killing. Women tend to use more subtle methods, such as poisoning, suffocation, and lethal injection (if they work as a nurse or care for the elderly). Men tend to use guns and knives.

So no, women don't appear to be less hardwired for violence than men. But experience tells me that there is something faulty in the hardwiring of the extremely violent, regardless of their gender.

Expert consulted
Patricia L. Kirby, Ph.D.
Assistant professor in sociology and crimi-nology, College of Notre Dame of Maryland in Baltimore
Former psychological profiler in the FBI's Be-havioral Sciences Unit

what we're angry about and what we want to change, says Dr. Padesky. In other words, we need to become more assertive.

This crash course in assertive behavior can help us feel more confident about expressing our feelings, stating what we want, and standing up for ourselves.

Tune in to your body. Nice Ladies may not even be aware that they're angry, says Dr. Padesky. But your body has ways of telling you, if you listen. "Perhaps you become quieter, or your muscles get tense, or you get a headache or stomachache," she says. "They may be a signal that something about a situation is disturbing you."

Analyze your thoughts. Consciously identify thoughts that could be making you hold in your anger. This self-talk often goes something like this: "If I get angry at this person, it will hurt or upset them," or "Maybe I'm overreacting. I'll just let it go." The point: Don't let these thoughts prevent you from speaking up.

Learn another language. Using "I-messages" when you're angry can help you focus your anger and state your feelings in a clear, straightforward way, says Dr. Padesky. To give an I-message, use this simple fill-in-the-blanks template.

When you (describe the behavior) it makes me feel (describe how the behavior affects you). I want (describe the action you would like them to take).

For example, you might say to your pit-bull-of-a-mother-in-law, "When you criticize my cooking, it makes me feel hurt and unappreciated. I want you to stop."

Road Rage: Know the Feeling?

Rebekah Lynch, Ph.D., never thought of herself as an angry person—until she started studying road rage and recognized herself in her research.

"I was one of those high-anger drivers who didn't think I had a problem," admits Dr. Lynch, a research associate at Colorado State University in Fort Collins. "I thought I was justified in getting angry at drivers I felt had endangered me on the road."

Justified, maybe. Safe, no. As our highways become increasingly congested, tempers are flaring on the freeway, with life-threatening results. In California, a motorist angered by a fender bender tossed the other driver's pedigreed dog into traffic. In Alabama, one woman shot another dead when the two vied for position on a congested freeway.

These stories represent the extremes, but many of us lose our cool when driving. "People who are normally good problem solvers may not respond as well when they're on the road," Dr. Lynch explains. "They often feel endangered. When someone endangers us, we interpret it as a threat and we get angry." We express anger in a variety of ways. We yell. Flash our lights. Cut them off. And we put the lives of our passengers, other drivers, and ourselves in jeopardy.

To stay safe on the roads, Dr. Lynch recommends the following strategies.

Take 10. "Most of us lead really hectic lives and we don't leave enough time to get from place to place," she says.

Or link how you feel with a specific behavior in the other person. For example, you might say, "I felt hurt when you said the casserole was too salty and the broccoli too soggy" rather than "You were rude and insensitive."

Be a broken record. Say your mother-in-law fails to respond to or belittles your I-message. Give it again. Over and over, if need be. Repeat yourself until the other person runs out of steam or excuses.

You may even choose to spell out the conse-

Leaving 10 minutes earlier for work, school, or home keeps you from racing against the clock. Toss a book in your bag in case you arrive early. Listen to your favorite music on the way.

Avoid eye contact. We may think that a pointed look is a safe response to the obnoxious driver who cut us off, but it actually escalates the confrontation. The other driver feels challenged by our direct gaze, and we usually end up angrier, too, because then we see his rude gestures.

Keep your hands on the wheel. Shaking your fist at your fellow commuters is out, but so is a friendly wave. "People can misunderstand gestures," explains Dr. Lynch, "and interpret a friendly wave as a hostile gesture."

Think differently. When a driver makes an obscene gesture, tell yourself that they're just letting you know you're "number one." Or that the finger represents the number of friends they have. Pick any interpretation you want, as long as it makes you laugh and keeps you calm.

Make room. If someone nearly runs you off the road, don't tailgate them out of revenge; stay out of their way instead. "Tell yourself, 'That guy made a mistake. I better watch what he's doing and be extra careful,'" Dr. Lynch says.

Seek help. If you're getting angry on the road three or more times a day, you may have a problem, even if you're mild-mannered in every other aspect of your life. Consider an anger management program, many of which offer specific seminars on road rage.

quences that will result if your reasonable request (make sure it's reasonable) isn't met. Some examples: "On the phone, you said it would cost $75 to fix the fan belt in my car. But the bill says $120. If you don't honor your price, I'll call the Better Business Bureau." Or, to a rebellious teenager, "Your curfew is 11 o'clock. The next time you break it, I'll take away your driving privileges for a week."

Make your body as assertive as your mouth. "Our posture makes a tremendous difference in how we feel," says Dr. Padesky. So when you confront the target of your anger, look them directly in the eye, keep your body open and relaxed (no arm crossing, shuffling of feet, or twisting of hair), and speak in a strong, clear voice.

To sample the power of body language, try this exercise, suggests Dr. Padesky. Slump in a chair, look at the ground, and say softly, "No, I don't want that." Now, sit straight and tall and say in a clear, strong voice, "No, I don't want that" while looking directly at a lamp or some other object.

Feel the difference?

Start small. Before you take on your spouse or boss, practice assertive behavior in low-risk relationships. "If you have anger issues with your partner, he may not be the person you want to confront first, particularly if you tend to get into tumultuous arguments," says Dr. Padesky. Instead, start with low-risk encounters and relationships—store clerks, bank tellers, bag boys at the grocery store. When assertive behavior becomes more natural, and you're feeling more confident, *then* you can graduate to a more high-stakes relationship.

Enlist others' support. Before you start asserting yourself all over the place, let family and friends know that your behavior is going to change. "You might call your family together and say, 'I have a hard time saying no and expressing my anger. But I'm going to change that. So I wanted you to know that when I get angry or say no, you shouldn't take it personally. I'm changing my behavior for me,'" says Dr. Padesky. "This message can help make people your allies."

Practice, practice, practice. In the car or shower, or in front of a mirror, stage a mental dress rehearsal of how exactly you'll confront an anger-provoking person or situation.

You might also come up with two or three lines that will buy you time in an anger-provoking situation, such as "Let me think about this for a few minutes and get back to you," or the time-honored "Excuse me, I need to visit the ladies' room." Then use the time to figure out how you want to respond.

Stick to your guns, girl. If you've been picking your mate's underwear off the bathroom floor for the past 15 years, his jaw may drop when you tell him that it makes you angry and that, from now on, you want him to put them in the hamper.

"People will try to make you go back to the meek little mouse that you were," says Dr. Thomas. "They may say things like 'What's gotten into *you*?' or 'You're being a real bitch about this!'"

Not exactly ego-stroking responses. But *don't back down*, says Dr. Thomas. Tell them that your request isn't unreasonable. Then tell your partner to pick up his underwear, or your colleague to prepare her own monthly reports, for as long as it takes for them to get it.

Snuffing the Dragon-Lady Flames

For basic anger management techniques that can help keep Dragon Ladies from scorching the landscape with our wrath—and raise the odds that our needs will be heard and met—try these tips.

Inner-Space Explorers
Who was Frederick (Fritz) S. Perls?

German psychiatrist Fritz Perls founded Gestalt therapy in the 1940s with his wife, Laura. Perls believed that people instinctively seek out health, wholeness, and ways to reach their full potential. His method of therapy holds the patient responsible for herself, for her own happiness, and for creating meaningful experiences in her life. Gestalt therapy is not designed to change the patient's feelings, solve her problems, or help her release pent-up emotions. Instead, it gives her the tools to solve problems on her own. The patient becomes more aware of what she is doing, how she is doing it, and how she can change herself—all while learning to accept and value herself.

Unlike Freudian psychotherapy, Gestalt therapy focuses on the patient's present experiences. The patient links present feelings or behaviors with past experiences or issues, which may be reexperienced, sometimes through role-playing. The process of what is happening in therapy is far more important, Perls believed, than the topic that's discussed or how the patient or therapist interprets feelings.

In Gestalt therapy, the therapist does not direct the ses-

Don't react—yet. You remember the old adage, "Don't just stand there, do something!" Dr. Lerner advises Dragon Ladies to reverse it: "Don't just do something, stand there." It's a unique way to remember not to react immediately. "Not reacting gives you time to calm down and think about what the real issue is and the best way to approach the problem," she says. "Standing there" might mean taking a bathroom break in a meeting when you feel yourself about to blow, or telling your partner, "I need some time to sort out my thoughts. Let's set up another time to talk about this."

Devise an anger mantra. Choose a word

sion. The patient does. The therapist may ask questions such as "What are you thinking? What are you feeling? If your boss were here right now, what would you say to her?" These questions are merely to help the patient focus on the here and now. It is really up to the patient to decide what she wants to work on in the session.

Gestalt therapy also emphasizes interpersonal contact through group therapy and through the patient's relationship with the therapist. Unlike in Freud's model, the Gestalt therapist shares her own feelings and experiences with the patient to encourage an open, honest exchange and to set an example for the patient to follow.

This innovative method of therapy gained popularity in the 1960s and can be very helpful for addressing problems in which anger is a component. Today there are at least 62 Gestalt therapy institutes throughout the world.

While there are no national standardized certification criteria for Gestalt therapists, there are various institutes that have their own requirements, and some programs train clinicians for 3 years prior to awarding certification. For information on finding a Gestalt therapist near you, visit www.gestalt.org, but be sure to ask about your clinician's credentials and training.

logic is the enemy of anger, says Dr. Lerner. Thinking rationally helps you focus on solving the problem, rather than giving vent to your intense emotions.

To help you think logically about an anger-provoking situation, force yourself to answer the following questions: "What is it about this situation that's making me angry? What is the real issue here? What do I want to accomplish? What, specifically, do I want to change?"

Take a Zen-minute break. Ten minutes of deep breathing can calm down the physiological arousal anger can cause, says Dr. Thomas. "It isn't good for your body when you stew and seethe for hours."

Try this simple breathing technique. Inhale slowly and deeply while counting 1-2-3-4. Exhale to the same count. "Let your body go limp and hollow," says Dr. Thomas. Allow each breath to fill the hollowness with relaxation.

"If it will help, try seeing your breath as a soft, relaxing color that gently floods your being, washing away the tension and stress," says Dr. Thomas.

Put yourself in their place. "Typically, we get angry at people over things we have probably done ourselves," says Dr. Padesky. (Perhaps scooting into that parking space when it was clearly the other driver's spot?) Before you lose it, ask yourself if you've ever done to someone else what this person is doing to you. If the answer is yes, you may decide that your "adversary" isn't deliberately being unfair or insensitive.

Get physical. Taking a 10- or 15-minute walk can help you shed the physical tension that

or phrase to repeat to yourself when your anger reaches critical mass. "A word or phrase such as 'calm' or 'think' or 'cool it' will eventually be your cue to settle down," says Dr. Padesky. Slowly repeat the calming word or phrase in rhythm with your breathing.

Strike the word *you* from your vocabulary. Dragon Ladies tend to use the word *you* a lot. Such as in "You're a whining little @!##@!!," or "You're an insensitive lout of a husband." Instead, follow the same "I-language" rules described for Nice Ladies on page 66.

Make like Spock. Not the baby doctor, but the pointy-eared stoic on *Star Trek*. Cold, hard

9-to-5 Anger Management

If your office is a hotbed of backstabbing coworkers, cut-throat politics, or tyrannical supervisors, it's probably also a breeding ground for anger. But don't get mad, get smart. These strategies can help reduce workplace anger, says Ronald Potter-Efron, Ph.D., director of the anger management clinic of First Things First Counseling and Consulting Center in Eau Claire, Wisconsin, and author of *Working Anger: Preventing and Resolving Conflict on the Job.*

➤ **Take responsibility for your anger.** Nobody has the power to make you angry unless you hand them that power. To short-circuit an impending meltdown, tell yourself, "I make me mad," "It's about me, not them," and, "I *can* help it."

➤ **Don't take the bait.** A colleague who says, "You're doing it wrong again. When are you going to learn?" or "I just heard Mary got the promotion *you* wanted" is trying to "hook" your anger. Don't bite.

➤ **Learn the art of listening.** Don't interrupt. Give Mary or Joe the chance to say their piece before you start yours. Also, use active listening methods, such as restating ("So you're saying that you're upset because . . ."). Another method: reflecting, in which you restate what you think is at the heart of the dispute. You may be wrong. Correcting misunderstandings can defuse many an office battle.

➤ **Be direct and show respect.** Don't merely hint at what you want or need. State it directly, starting with "I want," "I need," or "I feel." Don't use the words *always* or *never*, which tend to put others on the defensive.

➤ **Steer clear of group gripes.** To avoid getting swept up in others' battles, politely decline any invitation to "take sides." And when a group of your colleagues gets together over lunch or in someone's office to fume about work, make tracks.

anger can create, says Dr. Thomas. At work, take a quick trip around the block, or up and down a flight of stairs. At home? Clean a closet or go at the rug with the Hoover.

Bickering: Don't Take the Bait

In the Woody Allen movie *Radio Days*, a husband and wife argue over which ocean is bigger, the Atlantic or the Pacific. That's the essence of bickering. Unlike full-blown arguing, bickering consists of little snipes over seemingly trivial issues. In the end, it usually makes no difference who's right and who's wrong. Still, persistent bickering can be corrosive to a relationship.

"Hostile language is as toxic as chemical waste," says Suzette Haden Elgin, Ph.D., an applied psycholinguist in Huntsville, Arkansas, and author of the Gentle Art of Verbal Self-Defense series. "It's as toxic for the people dishing it out as it is for the people receiving it."

So for the sake of everybody's health, it's best to either avoid bickering or short-circuit it before it escalates into a big fight. Here's how.

Remember, it takes two to bicker. "A large percentage of our bickering consists of verbal attack patterns and taking the bait," Dr. Elgin says. "If you refuse to take the bait, the other person can't continue to bicker alone."

Recognize bicker bait. Some husbandly examples: "Why do you always hide my socks?" "If you really loved me, you wouldn't spend so much money." "If you really cared about your health, you would stay on your diet."

Agree with him. In a neutral voice, say to him, "It's really annoying to not be able to find your socks." "That'll stop him in his tracks," Dr.

Elgin says. "He can try a new attack, but the first one is over."

Refuse to feed him his next line. "If you say, 'I do stick to my diet,' that gives him an opportunity to say, 'But what about yesterday when you ate that doughnut?'" Dr. Elgin says. "Women who refuse to be a partner in bickering are going to get far less of it."

Neutralize hurtful comments. "Hostile language almost always has lots of personal language," says Dr. Elgin. "Instead, respond with a bland platitude, such as 'Money is a problem in every marriage'—it doesn't have any I's or you's in it," Dr. Elgin says. When you can't think of a platitude, use this all-purpose emergency sentence: "You can't tell which way the train went by looking at the tracks."

"You can find meaning in it, and it is, in fact, true," Dr. Elgin says. "People will say, 'I never thought about it that way,' or 'Wow, that's deep.' If someone's interested in the platitude and wants to discuss it, fine. It's a conversation. If not, they'll wander off." Either way, you've accomplished your goal, which is not to bicker.

You can use the sentence only once with the same person, however. If you said it to your husband more than once, it wouldn't work.

Shadowlands of Feeling

Anger is a symptom, a way of cloaking and expressing feelings too awful to experience directly—hurt, bitterness, grief, and most of all, fear.

The speaker?

Comedienne Joan Rivers, who obviously knows the way most of us cope with our painful feelings.

And it isn't only anger that protects us. Anxiety, guilt, frustration, and jealousy also cover for us when we feel vulnerable. But unlike the protection afforded by a warm winter coat, this type of emotional cloak can be damaging. Eventually, it will be ripped away by the ghosts of hurt, sadness, helplessness, loneliness, and fear, leaving us more emotionally freezing than before.

"When you substitute one feeling for another, you don't deal with what initially evoked the emotion, so you can't take action to prevent further pain," says Anita L. Vangelisti, Ph.D., associate professor in the College of Communication at the University of Texas in Austin.

Many of us wear our emotional cloaks on the inside, where no one can see them. It's how we're conditioned. "Society expects women to turn against themselves instead of others," says

Dana Crowley Jack, Ph.D., professor at Western Washington University in Bellingham and author of *Behind the Mask: Destruction and Creativity in Women's Aggression*. So we go on, smiling and laughing with a backstabbing friend when inside we're furious. Or blaming divorce on ourselves, certain that if we were only thinner or younger, he would have stayed.

Sometimes we hide that underlying emotion even from ourselves. "We cope by ignoring our vulnerable emotions, denying them, and moving on," says June Tangney, Ph.D., professor of psychology at George Mason University in Fairfax, Virginia, and coeditor of *Self-Conscious Emotions: The Psychology of Shame, Guilt, Embarrassment, and Pride*. We're afraid to give voice to what we're feeling, lest we really will feel it.

It's a reaction we may have learned in childhood. Did Mom dismiss your pain when you were teased on the playground? Then you learned to ignore your own hurt.

Or maybe you're frightened. "When pain isn't covered by anger, it's much scarier because it exposes our vulnerability," says Ayala Malach Pines, Ph.D., professor of psychology at the school of management at Ben-Gurion University in Beer-Sheva, Israel, and author of *Romantic Jealousy: Causes, Symptoms, Cures.*

But denying an emotion doesn't make it go away. We're like emotional recycling bins; our fear, hurt, helplessness, loneliness, and sadness mix and churn inside of us, emerging later in a new form as anger, anxiety, guilt, frustration, or jealousy. Burying our emotions so deeply may also lead to depression, anxiety, eating disorders, and panic attacks, according to Dr. Jack.

Learning to recognize the type of cloak we're wearing is essential to exploring the true emotion itself. And in the end, throwing off the confines of that covering will leave us emotionally and physically healthier.

Hell Hath No Fury . . .

Consider the scenario: You're overdue on an important project at work, the kids are sick, the license plates expire tomorrow, and the dog just pooped on the rug. Oh, and your husband is at a conference in Bermuda. You can't possibly tackle everything. So what do you do? You throw your briefcase against the wall, start screaming at the kids, chuck the pooping puppy into the backyard, and leave a voice mail message giving the husband grief about the license plates.

Your rage changes nothing, but at least you've taken action (and what is anger if not action?), so there's a greater sense of control.

REAL-LIFE SCENARIO

She Seems So Happy All the Time That Her Friends Don't Believe It

Jennifer, 48, is an "up" person. She literally bubbles over with happiness, even when she's scrubbing her bathroom. No matter what her boss asks her to do, she readily accepts it with a smile. Even when bad things happen, her grin barely falters. When she was in a car accident, she chattered on about how she had needed a new car anyway. When she didn't get a long-awaited promotion, she shrugged her shoulders and said, "Oh well, I still like my job," then went back to work, her smile still plastered to her face.

But her friends are worried. No one can be happy all the time. They think she's hiding her true feelings under that smile, and that if she doesn't express them, she's going to explode. Will she?

Jennifer may just naturally be an optimistic, upbeat, and resilient person. On the other hand, she may be denying difficult facts in her life and covering them up with a false rosy outlook.

If Jennifer's smile appears plastered onto her face, and if others agree that her happiness seems phony, it probably is. Human beings have an amazing ability to distinguish a false smile from a genuine one. Will she explode? She might.

Jennifer may also be in denial. She may suppress negative feelings by constantly grinning, which isn't healthy. She needs to acknowledge her emotions to release some pressure and begin to address what's causing her distress. Talking about her feelings can get her started on problem solving.

In addition to talking to others, Jennifer needs to be honest with herself and take corrective action. If she denies her disappointment about the lost promotion, she's preventing herself from gathering information on how to solve the problem. She may only need to take a computer course to get promoted, or it may be time for her to move to another company. To get these answers, she must first admit that she's unsatisfied.

Expert consulted
Susan Heitler, Ph.D.
Clinical psychologist
Denver

BOOSTING YOUR MOOD

The difference between mood and emotion is one of connection. Emotions are connected to an event or situation. You get a raise, so you feel happy. Moods just happen, as when you wake up in a bad mood for no reason. Moods also tend to last longer than emotions. And while it may seem to take no effort at all to get *into* a bad mood, coming *out* of the slump can be as challenging as solving a Rubik's cube. To help, try the following tips.

Strolling. When you're feeling low, you probably don't have the energy to get yourself moving, but that's when you need exercise the most. A Michigan State University study showed that all types of exercise, from aerobics to yoga, can improve mood, but that Eastern exercises, such as yoga and tai chi, are slightly more effective. One reason for this is that the exercises themselves teach physical methods of becoming more conscious of our bodies and minds.

Listening. Music goes straight to our emotional system. In a Stanford University study involving 20 participants, those who listened to familiar music that they selected while performing stress-reducing exercises saw their moods improve. The most effective tunes are upbeat, energetic, and rhythmic. So put on some Rolling Stones and go to it.

Moving. A change of scenery works wonders. Put yourself in a situation that matches the mood you want. For instance, if you're feeling isolated and lonely, call and chat with an upbeat friend. Are you feeling grumpy about nothing? Go to the zoo and eat cotton candy. It's a guaranteed uplifter.

Helping. It's much more of a mood booster to do something for others than it is to have something done for you. Bake a loaf of banana bread and take it to an elderly neighbor. Offer to babysit for a friend with young children. Volunteer for an extra assignment so your coworker can get home in time for her dinner date.

back on tried-and-true anger and begin barking commands at her. Your anger gives you a sense of control over the situation, says Dr. Tangney.

Another reason you're angry is that you're hurt that she hasn't improved. "We often cope with hurt by lashing out at the people who hurt us," says Dr. Vangelisti. Take the time your mother patted you on the rear just before a clothes-shopping trip and said, "Looks like you'll be shopping in the plus-size section today." Did you tell her how devastated her comment made you feel? Nope. You just hit right back: "Like mother, like daughter, I guess!" No dealing with the pain for you.

You're so hurt and angry, in fact, that you stop talking to Mom for months on end. The funny thing is, though, that underneath your rage, you really need to talk to your mom. You need her in a way you never outgrow, no matter what your age. You pick up the phone to call nearly every day—and hang it up again. You're afraid. Fearful she'll reject your overture and hurt you even more, you stay away and stay angry.

That same fear is why we lash out when someone brings us bad news. It's the old shooting-the-messenger-for-the-message thing. Your best friend tells you she saw your husband kissing another woman in the park. "You're wrong. It wasn't him. You're either blind or lying," you say furiously (really wanting to scratch her eyes out). The reality? You're terrified of losing your hus-

Fast-forward to the office. You have an employee who's heading downhill fast. You've tried counseling, sent her to training, even reduced her workload, but nothing works. So you fall

band, so instead of understanding that your friend is just trying to help, you get angry and defensive.

Watch out for anger, though, because it can also signal depression. The more depressed we are, the more irritable we get, says Susan Heitler, Ph.D., a clinical psychologist in Denver and author of the audiotape *Depression: A Disorder of Power*. When we're depressed, we view not only ourselves but others negatively, finding fault with everything they do. It's as if the filter that normally keeps things in perspective has disappeared. Conversely, we may shift the blame for our depressed feelings onto those around us, making ourselves the "victim" and others the "perpetrators."

Take the overworked woman with the pooping dog. Helpless to gain control, she targets her family as the primary reason for the chaos. Her resentment turns her into a snippy witch, forcing her husband, kids, and dog to dance around her, wondering when she'll strike.

Frustrated or Lonely?

Sometimes the emotion isn't masking the feeling but is an extension of the feeling. That's the case with frustration, which can stem from loneliness—not the fleeting sense of loneliness you get when you know no one at a party, but a chronic disconnection from all people.

WOMEN ASK WHY

Why does my mother drive me crazy?

According to ancient tradition, women and their mothers are bound to each other in a kind of circular dance. When we were little, our mothers provided us with companionship, comfort, and protection. We viewed them as magical and immortal. As we got older, however, they began to irritate us. Why? It may be because our culture artificially continues childhood beyond the natural coming of age, which is 13 in many tribal cultures. As teenagers, we're torn between the instinctual call to become independent and the societal dictate labeling us still a child. Then there's our own ambivalence. We don't want to be treated like a baby, and we feel ready to make our own decisions, yet sometimes we just want to crawl into Mom's arms and feel safe. Responsibilities that used to be all hers— feeding us, clothing us, nurturing us—begin to fall more and more on our shoulders, which may make us resentful.

That irritation serves a purpose. It's nature's way of ensuring that we eventually leave the nest.

Once we're adults, Mom drives us crazy for both similar and different reasons. Our mothers may continue to baby us too much. Whether we're 20 or 60, our mothers still think of us as children, so they may treat us that way. That's hard for today's independent woman to accept. We want to be treated with the respect of an equal. This mother-daughter dynamic creates frustration and resentment.

In addition, we may not like the idea that we're becoming like her. Or, on a deeper level, she reminds us that someday, *we're* going to age and become forgetful. The best thing for us to do is to remember the principles of the Serenity Prayer: We cannot change Mom, but we can do ourselves a big favor and accept her the way she is. Getting wound up because she still treats us like her little girl is only harming ourselves.

Expert consulted
Patricia McWhorter, Ph.D.
Psychologist
Palm Harbor, Florida

WOMEN ASK WHY

Why can't I confront my friends about the hurtful things they've said?

Confronting a friend when she has hurt your feelings can be difficult for several reasons. First, being hurt means that you've been hit in a soft spot, so you're vulnerable. If you go back to that person and inform her of your hurt, you make yourself vulnerable once again. She may react by saying, "I never said that," or "You're being way too sensitive—it was a joke!" These responses just add to the hurt.

Second, confronting your friend may make her feel bad. If you're the type who doesn't like to rock the boat, or if you're insecure about your friendships, you may prefer to ignore your feelings rather than risk the consequences of hurting your friend.

Third, confronting your friend may lead you to learn something about yourself that you don't want to know. She may have made the hurtful comment because you hurt her first. Or the comment, while hurtful, may actually be true, forcing you to face something you'd rather ignore.

Expert consulted
Anita L. Vangelisti, Ph.D.
Associate professor
College of Communication
University of Texas
Austin

The frustration emerges when we recognize what types of relationships we want, but also realize we're not getting them. It's like finally being invited to a party, but finding that no one wants to talk to you once you're there. By the end of the party, you're feeling more alone than you were before it began, which adds to your frustration.

Frustration may also take over when we feel helpless. You've experienced that every time a traffic jam threatens to make you late for an appointment. You yell at other drivers, honk your horn, and bang on the steering wheel. Does it get the traffic moving any faster? Of course not. And studies show it can actually make you feel worse.

Anxiety Keeps Us Safe

"Anxiety is a response to a recognition of danger," says Dr. Jack. "It can make us perceive that we don't have many solutions, like we're trapped in a box. And when we feel trapped, we become anxious."

Physical responses to fear lie at the root of anxiety. When we're afraid, our bodies react: Our heart rate and blood pressure rise, we have trouble concentrating, we feel as if we can't breathe, and we become hyperalert. If those reactions don't fully settle after the fear ceases, chronic anxiety may result.

But it's the sense of helplessness, or lack of control over a situation, that drives it.

That same danger applies in social situations. If we don't have many friends, we fear rejection. That fear leads us to avoid putting ourselves in situations where we *could* be rejected. This is called social anxiety. In its extreme form, this fear may result in your being a virtual prisoner in your home.

Guilt: Never Leave Home without It

We're mothers, daughters, and wives. Cooks, accountants, chauffeurs, and dog walkers. We may feel as if we're drowning in a tidal wave of "shoulda, oughta, must, and what-would-the-neighbors-think" voices, but instead of stopping to acknowledge and deal with the sense of helplessness our multiple roles cause, we feel guilty because we can't do it all.

Especially with our children. In one groundbreaking study about working mothers and guilt, one mother said, "I have always felt a twinge of guilt when we had a babysitter. I should be home with the children instead of going to the movies." Another felt guilty because she lay in bed for an hour in the morning planning her day while her kids made breakfast and got themselves ready for school.

Getting angry doesn't help. Then we feel guilty over our rage.

Guilt can also step in as a shield for hurt, particularly for those of us who are the peacekeepers in our relationships, says Dr. Vangelisti. "If we accept responsibility for a hurtful episode and think, 'He wouldn't have hurt my feelings if *I* hadn't been so irritable,' we don't have to risk upsetting anyone, and we avoid facing our own vulnerability to emotional pain," she says.

There is also an element of shame inherent in guilt. As one mother said in the guilt study, "When I call and say I am not coming home to the children but am going over to a friend's, I feel like a bad person." The guilt reminds us once again (as if we needed any more reminders) of the discrepancy between who we are and who we think we should be.

INNER-SPACE EXPLORERS
Who was Carl Rogers?

American psychologist Carl Rogers is best known for his innovative approach to psychotherapy, called nondirective therapy, which gives the reins to the client. He believed that the patient should determine the course of the therapy, the rate of progress, and the end of the therapy.

To break free from the negative connotations associated with the word *patient*, he referred to his patients as clients. Instead of following the traditional approach in which the therapist directed the client, he felt the therapist's role was to support the client as she directed her own therapy. Later, Rogers began calling it client-centered therapy. Today, nondirective, client-centered, and Rogerian therapy are one and the same.

Rogers compared client-centered therapy to teaching a child to ride a bike. He said that just as a parent has to let go of the bike so the child can pedal and balance for herself, the therapist must allow the client to use her own insights to resolve difficulties.

The therapist fosters this independence through reflection—that is, restating what the client said to show that the therapist is listening and understands. Reflection also helps the client see herself more clearly and hear if she has said one thing while meaning something else. Rogers also said an effective therapist shows the client honesty, sincerity, empathy, acceptance, and respect.

This fresh approach to therapy, developed in the 1940s, influenced later individual and group methods of psychotherapy.

The Green-Eyed Monster

You won't be jealous if you're confident in yourself, because jealousy masks your own insecurity. "Insecure women are quicker to perceive a threat to their relationships than secure women," says Dr. Pines.

Women Ask Why

Why do I feel guilty when I have to work late and my family has sandwiches for dinner?

Many of us have an image of the "good mother" as one who has a full-course meal on the table every night. After all, *our* mothers did it. But most of us had mothers that didn't work outside the home, so there was never any danger of their working late. The disconnection between the image of what we think we should be and what we actually are is where the guilt comes in.

It may also be related to the anger we feel at having all the responsibility for dinner placed on us. Where's hubby in this picture? Or even the teenager? Of course, the anger only compounds the guilt because it doesn't fit the good wife and mother image, either.

Bottom line: You shouldn't feel guilty for the sandwiches or for feeling slightly annoyed. The definition of a good wife and mother is not as narrow as a hot meal. There are many other creative ways you can show affection to your family. Take your kids to the park on Saturday. Arrange a date with your husband. The quality time will probably mean more to them than a roast and some potatoes.

Expert consulted
Dana Crowley Jack, Ph.D.
Professor
Western Washington University
Bellingham

Unrobing

When we're blind to our deep emotions, we don't get to the root of our problems and they don't get fixed, says Dr. Tangney. You're never going to get along with your mom if all you do is yell at her, instead of telling her how her comments about your weight make you feel. Express the hurt, show her the power her words have, and the insults may stop.

It's also emotionally exhausting to hide your true feelings constantly. "Ultimately, a woman who hides her feelings will no longer know what she really feels," says Patricia McWhorter, Ph.D., a psychologist in Palm Harbor, Florida, and author of *Cry of Our Native Soul: Our Instinct for Creation-Centered Spirituality*. "This creates a pressure cooker effect, where feelings fester and build until they result in an explosive outburst." For instance, if you continue the silent treatment with your mother, when you *do* run into her, the force of your emotions may overwhelm you, resulting in a horrible scene.

There are also the physiological effects of hiding our true feelings. Prolonged loneliness, for example, can lead to high blood pressure, heart disease, leukemia, and cirrhosis (brought on by alcohol abuse). Guilt can be felt as anxiety, agitation, and butterflies in our stomach, or even fever, chills, and slowed thinking.

And, of course, if we don't face our feelings, we're more vulnerable to depression, which is

Jealousy may also hide loneliness. If your marriage is on autopilot, with no real connection and an emotional chasm the size of the Grand Canyon, it's easier to see yourself as replaceable. That's scary, and so our jealousy may also be masking our deep-seated fear of abandonment and isolation.

a significant risk factor for heart disease and overall mortality in women.

To disrobe and face these feelings, we must first admit they exist. Ask yourself these questions.

- Do I feel vulnerable in this situation? If so, why?
- If a friend, sister, or daughter found herself in this same situation, which emotions do I think she would feel?
- If I could change this situation in any way, how would I change it?

Write the answers down. In fact, you should break out the paper and pencil whenever you find yourself avoiding something because it upsets you. "Writing (or journaling) is a great way to get in touch with your feelings," says Dr. McWhorter. You not only tap into your suppressed emotions, but you also have a safe outlet in which to express them.

Set a specific schedule (for example, write 1 day a week for 4 weeks) and choose a place to write that is free of distractions. When you write, try to explore your deepest feelings—sadness, hurt, fear—and don't show anyone what you've written, so you can be completely honest. For more on the healing power of journaling, see "The Art of the Journal" on page 106.

And don't forget about that other communication tool: your voice. "To really search out what you feel, you have to talk to other people," says Dr. Jack. Join a support group or unload on a friend or anyone you trust who will lend a nonjudgmental ear. By talking, you may begin

> ## HOW TO COPE WITH FEAR AND ANXIETY
>
> We are socialized from an early age to conceal our fears. After all, we don't want to appear weak, cowardly, or incompetent. So we learn to control our fears by avoiding situations that elicit these emotions. This approach, however, is not the answer. Instead, here are some ways to face your fears and confront your anxiety.
>
> **Be informed.** "The best antidote for anxiety is information," says Susan Heitler, Ph.D., clinical psychologist in Denver and author of the audiotape *Anxiety: Friend or Foe?* Identify where your anxiety is coming from, gather information about the fear, then map out a solution based on your findings, she suggests. For example, if you are going back to school and have anxiety about taking language courses, talk to people in the department. Ask for a lighter course load, or for tips on how to grasp languages better. Learn that there are solutions.
>
> **Keep moving.** "Anxiety is like a yellow traffic light," says Dr. Heitler. When you start to feel anxious, slow down and gather information, but keep moving forward, she says. "It's okay to be anxious. You can be afraid and still do what you need and want to do," she says.
>
> **Turn the voice off.** That inner, insulting voice that tells us we're fat or ugly or stupid. "This negative self-talk is destructive and causes anxiety," says Dana Crowley Jack, Ph.D., professor at Western Washington University in Bellingham and author of *Behind the Mask: Destruction and Creativity in Women's Aggression.* To reduce anxiety, learn to ignore that mean voice. Surround yourself with friends, or begin an intense activity to take your mind off yourself.

to release emotions you never realized were there.

You should also read about emotions, says Dr. Jack. Gathering knowledge about the nature of your emotions can help you delve into what you're feeling. "Women can find their feelings explained in books in ways that make them feel more understood and less isolated," she says.

The Need for Courage

As the White House's top advisor on mental health, Tipper Gore spent years advocating better treatment and more understanding for people struggling with depression and similar illnesses. But the then–vice president's wife never revealed her own battles until 1999, when she spoke publicly about her bout with depression, which occurred after her young son nearly died in a car accident.

Gore's announcement required tremendous political bravery: 30 years before, a vice presidential candidate had lost his spot on the Democratic ticket for acknowledging the same thing.

It probably took just as much courage for Gore to admit her depression to herself. Confronting our grief, anger, and other difficult emotions is hard work, and it often seems far easier simply to power through them or to escape them with food, alcohol, or drugs.

Part of the problem is the expectations we hold for ourselves. Whether we admit it or not, we all carry around a mental picture of the ideal woman. She may be a stay-at-home mom meeting her kids at the door with freshly baked cookies every afternoon. Or she's a phenomenal professional success, respected for her business savvy and quick rise up the corporate ladder. Or she's both, a master juggler of home and office. Intellectually, we may know that it's impossible to live up to these idealized visions, but it doesn't stop us from trying. Unable to meet our impossibly high expectations, we sink into depression, begin drinking, or shop as if we'd won the lottery to bury the pain.

"When we avoid our feelings, we force our bodies into overdrive trying to stuff those emotions down," says Stephany Joy-Newman, Ed.D., adjunct professor in the counselor education department and counselor in the Western Illinois University counseling center in Macomb. "We overeat, we drink, we take drugs, we burn out our immune system." Then our misguided coping strategies become problems of their own.

Living in the Gray Zone

"I'm so depressed," we moan after a rough day at work, a bad date, or even an unfruitful shopping trip for a swimsuit. But many of us have no idea what that really means.

"We use the word *depression* to mean so many things that it strips the word of its power," says Valerie Davis Raskin, M.D., clinical associate professor of psychiatry at the University of Chicago and author of *When Words Are Not Enough: The Women's Prescription for Depression and Anxiety*.

"Depression is a very painful disease, and people who don't have it don't understand it," says Nada Stotland, M.D., chair of the psychiatry department at Illinois Masonic Medical Center in Chicago. "The 'depression' you get for 5 minutes is not the same as having your whole mind taken over by uncontrollable gloom and fear. Yet we try to help people with depression in the same way we'd cheer up someone who was sad for 5 minutes: We take them out for lunch, we buy them flowers, we send them a card. It doesn't make the depression go away."

Living with clinical depression is like living inside a dark cloud. Even getting out of bed in the morning is a struggle. In fact, often all a depressed woman wants to do is curl up in a ball and hide from the world.

No one really knows why women are more likely to experience depression than men, but one in four American women will succumb to it at some time in her life. One possible culprit is hormones: The gender gap in depression and anxiety disorders begins in adolescence. And the hormonal roller coasters of pregnancy, childbirth, and meno-

ADDICTIVE PERSONALITY: IS THERE REALLY SUCH A THING?

Controversial and ever evolving, the phrase *addictive personality* relates to the choices we make around alcohol or other substances or activities that might be troublesome for us. Initially, addiction experts thought we could be born with this personality, much the same way we're born shy or optimistic. "The idea was that you grew up headed for addiction because of your tendencies, your nature, and the way you interacted with the world," explains Margaret H. Kearney, Ph.D., R.N.C., associate professor at Boston College's School of Nursing and an expert on women and addictions. "You had this personality before you ever had any contact with alcohol or drugs. You were just like a time bomb, waiting to go off when you encountered these substances."

Today, many experts are skeptical of that original concept. "I don't think there really is such a thing as an addictive personality," says Nada Stotland, M.D., chair of the psychiatry department at Illinois Masonic Medical Center in Chicago. "Some people tend to depend on certain behaviors more than others, but I don't believe that people are born with a psychological weakness for some specific abuse."

Some use "addictive personality" to describe women who are more vulnerable to drug or alcohol addiction, thanks to a childhood of abuse or other nightmarish experiences. "These are people who have been through traumas, who have strong unmet needs, and who don't have the emotional or life skills to meet them," says Dr. Kearney.

Most commonly, though, "addictive personality" is used to refer to the way a woman's drug or alcohol use changes how she acts. "Once you have an addiction, it begins to shape your personality and behavior," Dr. Stotland says. You become manipulative, selfish, unpredictable. You may start stealing from your family or treating them with disrespect. Your husband may say he doesn't know who you are anymore.

"When you become dependent, your priorities shift from the big picture of keeping your house and job to getting the next fix," Dr. Kearney says. "It's the drugs talking."

WOMAN TO WOMAN

Cigarettes Are No Longer Her Best Friend

For 40 years, cigarettes were Roxie Sullivan's best friend. That made quitting "the hardest thing I've had to do in my life," says the Riva, Maryland, office manager, who's survived breast cancer and a stroke. But quit she did, and today the 61-year-old has a new life and a new attitude toward living it. Here is her story.

I started smoking when I was 13 years old. At the time, smoking was depicted in the movies and on television as something very glamorous. But smoking is truly an addiction. I couldn't start the car without a cigarette. Whether I was watching TV or listening to music, cigarettes were always there, keeping me company. If I felt miserable because of a relationship, the challenges of raising kids, or dealing with a bad boss, cigarettes numbed the pain.

I first started thinking about quitting in the 1970s, when the dangers of cigarettes became known. But I was smoking 2½ packs a day and wasn't ready to quit.

Then, 8 years ago, God touched me.

As I stood outside, smoking in the cold and the sleet because my office was smoke-free, I realized something was seriously wrong with my life. I was battling breast cancer at the time and had been to radiation therapy that morning. That afternoon, I had chemotherapy. I was doing everything possible to live, yet here I was smoking a cigarette.

I've been through some pretty tough stuff, but without a doubt, quitting smoking was the hardest thing I've ever had to do in my life. I wore a nicotine patch. I did jigsaw puzzles so I had something to do with my hands. I went to Nicotine Anonymous three times a week.

My life is totally different now. After I quit smoking, I couldn't go back to my old crowd of friends. If I did, I knew I'd just start smoking again. I'm more spiritual now. I'm involved with my church, volunteering in the office, going to Bible study, and serving on the board of directors of the women's group. I've also started an investment club, and no, we don't invest in companies with tobacco connections.

pause trigger depression in some women. Genetics also plays a role. If your parents or siblings have experienced depression, you're two to four times more likely to become depressed yourself.

Biology doesn't tell the whole story, though. Simply coping with life in the 21st century also plays a role. When doctors interviewed Afghan women in 1998 who had escaped the oppressive Taliban regime, for instance, they found that 97 percent had major depression. Forbidden to work, go to school, or even walk outdoors without a male chaperone, these women went into an emotional tailspin.

While our human rights as women are protected in the United States, we're still faced with sometimes overwhelming pressures. We often work full-time in a world configured for men. We do the bulk of child care and house-work. And more and more often, we're also caring for our aging parents. The result? We're tired, stressed, and tapped out emotionally, which increases our risk for depression.

We increase this risk further with our own inability to act, says Dr. Stotland. "We're ruminating instead of getting angry," she says. It's a vicious circle: The more we dwell on the problem, the worse we feel and the less likely we are to act. So we become down in the dumps, she says, which is a far more socially acceptable emotion than anger.

Not that anyone would know we're depressed.

"Women are remarkably good at functioning well on the outside," Dr. Stotland says. "People see you wearing nice clothes, going to work, getting your kids to school. They don't know you're ducking into the bathroom to cry every day." So don't be surprised if, when you first share how you're feeling, people don't fully believe you. "You may need to tell them, 'I know I look okay, but I am sick,'" Dr. Stotland adds.

Sometimes, we're the ones in denial. "I was working hard, like anyone who has this illness, on all cylinders and then (trying) to pretend everything was fine," Tipper Gore said in a 1999 *USA Today* interview. Call it the Superwoman syndrome: If we give in to our illness, we're admitting that we can't do it all.

We also may not recognize our depression because it comes and goes. "Depression creeps up on you," Dr. Raskin says. "People don't just wake up clinically depressed."

Doctors and therapists typically diagnose depression based on the answers to the following questions. If you've experienced five or more of these symptoms, you should talk to your doctor about getting the help you need.

- Am I sleeping too much or too little? Do I have trouble falling asleep or staying asleep?
- Have I gained or lost weight without trying? "When I see a woman with a weight problem, the first thing I look for is

DO YOUR MOODS GO SOUTH WHEN THE BIRDS DO?

Forget chestnuts roasting on an open fire, Jack Frost's nose-nipping, and any other ideas about a winter wonderland. When the days get colder and shorter, some of us would rather hibernate.

Burrowing under the covers represents a natural reaction to the changing seasons, says Charmane Eastman, Ph.D., director of the Biological Rhythms Research Lab and psychology professor at Rush–Presbyterian–St. Luke's Medical Center in Chicago. "Animals have seasonal rhythms, and humans are animals."

For about 6 percent of us, though, winter's darker days result in a condition known as seasonal affective disorder, or SAD. Without enough sunlight, we become depressed, lethargic, or sleepy. We crave breads, pasta, and other carbohydrates, especially at night.

Unlike clinical depression, which can last for years, SAD symptoms (which are similar to depression) lift when spring returns. With the sun high in the sky, we feel energetic, motivated, and hopeful again, at least until next fall. "There are countless anecdotes about women who fall in love every spring, have fabulous relationships during the summer, and then break up with their boyfriends during the winter," Dr. Eastman says.

Although antidepressants can be used to treat SAD, the most common recommendation is a light box. As much as 20 times brighter than the lights in homes or offices, the high-powered light box mimics the sun. It works to reset your body clock to summertime hours. Time and intensity prescriptions vary, so talk to your doctor.

Can't afford a light box? Dr. Eastman suggests that you can help yourself cope with SAD with the following strategies.

- Get out of the house. Even a cloudy day provides far more light than the brightest indoor lights.
- Be an early bird. Light therapy tends to be most effective in the mornings, so go outside as early as you can.
- Follow a regular sleep schedule. In one study, SAD patients who went to sleep and woke up at roughly the same times each day felt better.

ANTIDEPRESSANTS AND TRANQUILIZERS

"Tranquilizers are like putting blankets on a fire. Anti-depressants put the fire out," says Valerie Davis Raskin, M.D., clinical associate professor of psychiatry at the University of Chicago and author of *When Words Are Not Enough: The Women's Prescription for Depression and Anxiety*. "They correct, at a much deeper level, the chemical imbalance that may be causing the problem rather than mask it."

That's not to say tranquilizers can't be helpful when prescribed appropriately. If you're just starting to take an anti-depressant, your doctor may suggest tranquilizers as needed until the antidepressant kicks in. "Antidepressants really don't do much for the first few weeks," Dr. Raskin says. "Tranquilizers may help a woman sleep better and feel less anxious. But they won't touch the depression."

Tranquilizers also can be habit-forming. If you use them regularly for an extended period of time, you can become dependent, unable to sleep or relax without them for physical and psychological reasons. As a result, Dr. Raskin often won't prescribe them to women with a history of personal or family substance abuse.

Addiction isn't a problem with antidepressants, which take a far more targeted approach to treating mental health problems. Popular medications such as fluoxetine (Prozac), bupropion (Wellbutrin), and their pharmaceutical cousins hone in on specific brain chemicals that affect our emotions.

Some, such as paroxetine (Paxil), sertraline (Zoloft), and, of course, Prozac, help us feel better by keeping the feel-good neurotransmitter serotonin circulating in our brains. These drugs are often referred to as selective serotonin-reuptake inhibitors, or SSRIs.

Tricyclic antidepressants—amitriptyline (Elavil), imipramine (Tofranil), and doxepin (Sinequan)—work on feel-good brain chemicals such as norepinephrine and serotonin.

Others, such as Wellbutrin, influence the neurotransmitter dopamine. Despite their precision, antidepressants still have some side effects. Depending on which drug your doctor prescribes, you may experience a lower sex drive, weight gain, or a change in your sleeping habits.

depression," Dr. Joy-Newman says. "We stuff down our feelings and anesthetize our feelings with food and compulsive overeating."

- Am I enjoying the things I love to do?
- Do I feel sad, empty, or blue?
- Do I have difficulty concentrating or making decisions? Even the simple choice of what cereal to buy for your kids' breakfast may leave you overwhelmed.
- Do I feel noticeably anxious, restless, or agitated?
- Do I feel exhausted all the time? Fatigue is one of the most underrecognized symptoms of depression, particularly in older women, who may shrug it off as a sign of aging, Dr. Raskin says. Compare how you feel today with how you felt a few months ago; a dramatic change in energy level is cause for concern.
- Do I think I'm a good person? Loss of self-esteem is a sign of depression.
- Do I think about hurting myself?

Reasons for Hope

Diagnosing depression is winning half the battle. "Depression is just so treatable," says Dr. Raskin. Two of your options are counseling and medication.

Counseling. You'll want to read Getting Help on page 94 for specific tips on therapy and finding a practitioner, but nearly any type of counseling helps. "Depression is one of the most responsive problems when it comes to therapy," says Dianne Chambless, Ph.D., the William Leon Wylie Professor of Psychology at the University of North Carolina at Chapel Hill.

Sometimes, all you need is the chance to talk about what you're feeling, especially if your life has recently changed in some significant way, such as a cross-country move or a parent's death. But depression is often a recurrent illness, and you may need therapy "tune-ups" throughout your life.

Medication. More than a decade after doctors began prescribing fluoxetine (the now-famous Prozac), antidepressant medications have become increasingly precise, pinpointing specific brain chemistry gone awry and adjusting it accordingly. "Within 2 to 4 weeks after starting on antidepressants, the depression lifts," Dr. Raskin says. "Women will say they woke up and 'the black cloud was gone.' They feel more energy. They feel pleasure in activities again. They can concentrate on tasks. It's almost as if someone hit the on/off button."

You may need to try several different medications to find the one that works for you. And while some women may need to be on medication for months or even years, you may need only a short-term course in conjunction with therapy.

At the same time, according to the experts,

WOMAN TO WOMAN
She Uses Exercise to Battle Depression

For Shirley Fontaine, 58, of Annandale, Virginia, fighting depression has been a full-time job since she was a teenager. Initially thought to have schizophrenia, she was finally diagnosed with bipolar disorder when she was 32. Through the years, Shirley has found a number of helpful ways to cope with her disease. She takes medication. She talks to therapists. But the simplest, least expensive, and maybe most immediately rewarding method has been exercise. Here is her story.

I've used exercise to cope with depression off and on for years. I swam. I went to the gym. I used my treadmill. I mall-walked at a nearby shopping center. I've read a lot about how exercise can help you, and it certainly has no side effects, unlike some of the antidepressants I've tried.

The problem is, when you're feeling really down, you don't want to exercise, and coping with the depression has definitely gotten harder as I've grown older. So I've tried to make exercising as easy as possible.

Every morning, my husband and I go to our neighborhood supermarket and walk the aisles. It's huge. From the fruit and bread sections to the flowers, it takes about 20 minutes. And we never do our grocery shopping while we walk. We take a second stroll through the store to buy our food. When we first started doing this, people were suspicious. Who were these people flying through the store without buying anything? But now they know us and say hi.

It helps so much to walk. When I'm feeling depressed, I start to wonder what there is to live for and think that nothing's ever going to get better. After I walk, I have such a positive attitude. I look forward to the rest of the day. I can't wait to see my daughter's twins. The lift I get from exercise definitely makes a difference.

---

there are things you can do on your own to feel better.

Exercise. In one 4-month study, researchers found that depressed men and women who

walked or jogged three times a week for 45 minutes improved as much as a control group taking antidepressants.

Talk nicely to yourself. Replace self-criticism with sympathetic, forgiving thoughts by talking to yourself as you would talk to a friend, says Dr. Stotland. You wouldn't tell a friend that one bad presentation proved she was doomed to fail at public speaking forever or that she'd just ruined her career. So why tell yourself that?

Look to friends and family for inspiration. "Notice and understand how others deal with unexpected setbacks," Dr. Stotland advises. Do they accept situations and move on? Do they look for the silver lining? Test their approaches and see how they make you feel.

Act. If you're agonizing over a decision, list pros and cons for the different choices. Scribble in a journal. Make a meal. "Anything that translates rumination into activity, whether it's physical or mental, is helpful," Dr. Joy-Newman says.

Alcohol, Drugs, and Other Addictions

Picture two women. One wears expensive suits, carries a laptop in her leather briefcase, and has a Palm Pilot crammed with to-do lists and contacts. The other woman works nights at a convenience store to support her two kids, dresses in thrift store finds, and takes the bus to work. Which one is the alcoholic?

They both are.

Traditionally considered a man's disease, alcoholism is increasingly becoming a problem for many women as we turn to drinking to help us cope with the growing stress in our lives. In 1998, 3.17 million women were estimated to be dependent on alcohol, and almost one-half million had sought alcohol treatment.

Alcoholism is particularly devastating for women. If we're pregnant, we're putting our unborn children at risk for developmental problems. If we already have kids, we risk losing our children as getting drunk becomes our top priority. Alcohol may also increase our risk of breast cancer. Other alcohol-related health problems such as high blood pressure, heart and liver disease, and ulcers emerge faster in alcoholic women than they do in alcoholic men. One reason is that our bodies can't process wine, beer, or liquor as fast and efficiently as men's. This difference goes beyond mere body size. "Physiologically, women can become drunk on about half of what it takes for men," says Carol Prescott, Ph.D., assistant professor of psychiatry at the Medical College of Virginia in Richmond.

We also turn to drugs, both illegal and prescription, as a way to numb the pain. Nationally, drug abuse affects a small number of women; about 12 percent of the female population use illegal drugs, and one-fifth of those users develop abuse problems. The abuse, however, causes many serious problems for them and their families. Of these users, about 1.5 million women have reported emotional or psychological problems related to drug use.

"Women get into drug and alcohol use as a way of self-medicating," says Margaret H. Kearney, Ph.D., R.N.C., associate professor at Boston College's School of Nursing and an expert on women and addictions. That's particularly true for women from families with a history of substance abuse. They are genetically vulnerable to addictions, says Dr. Prescott.

Not only that, adds Dr. Kearney, but they

INNER-SPACE EXPLORERS
Who was Karen Horney?

German-born American psychoanalyst Karen Horney offered a more feminist view of psychology than Sigmund Freud. Born in 1885, Horney underwent psychoanalytic training with Karl Abraham, a friend and close associate of Freud. She disagreed, however, with Freud's theory that repressed sexual energy from childhood was the root of mental disorders. Horney was one of several psychoanalysts who suggested instead that our environment, culture, and social relationships shape our personalities and play a role in the formation of mental disorders. In particular, she said neurosis is caused by parental indifference, or the feeling that we didn't receive warmth and affection as a child.

Horney also criticized Freud's theory that women are psychologically inferior to men because they don't have a penis. "She said that women envy men's power in society, not the fact that they have a penis," says Ellyn Kaschak, Ph.D., professor of psychology at San Jose State University in California. Horney countered Freud's penis envy theory with one of her own: womb envy. She said that some men feel inferior to women because they're unable to bear children. These feelings of inferiority drive them to succeed so their name will live on.

Horney also believed self-analysis could be an important tool, and she went on to write one of the first self-help books. Her ideas influenced psychiatrist Frederick S. Perls, who founded Gestalt therapy in the 1940s. And Horney was a forerunner of the modern feminist therapy called difference feminism, which looks at the differences between men and women.

grew up watching their parents misuse drugs and alcohol to cope with stress.

The relationships we choose can be just as harmful as the ones we're born with. Women often begin using alcohol or illegal drugs because they are socializing with husbands or boyfriends who have substance-abuse problems, says Dr. Prescott.

Then, as the thin thread of connection frays, we use drugs and alcohol to drown the hurt, according to Dr. Stotland. And it works because of our brain chemistry. When we drink or use drugs, we're stimulating our brain's reward centers, which gives us pleasure. Simultaneously, we're also lowering the levels of stress-related chemicals in our brain.

But using drugs and alcohol doesn't help us resolve any of the emotional issues that led us to turn to them in the first place, such as loneliness, frustration, and stress.

"In the early months after stopping drug or alcohol use, women have a lot of emotional pain," Dr. Kearney says. "Often, this is when they uncover the early roots of that pain. Women really need an astute therapist then, because otherwise it will be so scary to feel the pain that they will just go back to using drugs."

Am I in Trouble?

When restaurants offer entire menus of martinis, and even health experts suggest that a daily glass of red wine is good for us, where does the line between social drinking and problem drinking lie? "It's subjective, and you may not draw the line where your family does," says Dr. Stotland. "Sometimes a habit only becomes an addiction when it causes a problem."

But if you can answer yes to three or more of the following questions, you may have a substance-abuse problem. More serious problems,

WOMEN ASK WHY

Why do some women get depressed after childbirth?

Having a baby is like a psychiatric treadmill test. The sheer physical and emotional stress of the experience uncovers any problems that already existed. Consider: A new mother is chronically sleep-deprived from caring for the baby at all hours. There's usually less money and more need for it. There may be identity issues as she and her husband adapt to their new roles as parents. And if she's a first-time mother, she may feel inadequate.

Most new mothers feel the baby blues to some extent, when all-over-the-place hormones can make them crabby, anxious, and teary for no real reason during the first few weeks after birth. In comparison, postpartum depression, which affects about 10 percent of women, is significantly more severe and longer lasting. While the baby blues often improve with rest or some hands-on help, postpartum depression lasts all day long, day after day. There are some situations that put a woman at higher risk for postpartum depression.

- A first baby
- A history of depression in either herself or her family
- An unanticipated cesarean section. The mother isn't mentally or physically prepared for the surgery, and the postsurgical exhaustion makes the typical new-parent stress more difficult to handle.

such as drunken driving, an arrest for an alcohol-related offense, never-ending fights with your husband over your drinking, or an inability to keep up with such basics of your life as paying bills or going to work, also indicate that you're abusing alcohol or drugs. Either scenario—substance dependency or abuse—means you need help.

- A colicky baby. When you're tired and stressed, it helps to have your gorgeous baby gazing peacefully at you. Compare that with a baby who cries constantly, needs to be held all the time, and doesn't provide any positive feedback.

- A history of sensitivity to changes in female hormones, such as PMS or emotional reactions to oral contraceptives

If you're worried that you've got more than the baby blues, talk to your doctor, spiritual leader, or therapist. Here are some signs that you may be heading into postpartum depression territory.

- All-day, relentless depression lasting more than 2 weeks (the baby blues last from hours to days)

- Insomnia (with the baby blues, you still sleep easily)

- Suicidal thoughts

- Feelings of worthlessness (with the baby blues, your self-esteem is intact)

You can contact Postpartum Support International at 927 North Kellogg Avenue, Santa Barbara, CA 93111, or visit its Web site at www.postpartum.net. Postpartum Support International maintains a network of doctors, fellow mothers, and support groups for new moms.

Expert consulted
Valerie Davis Raskin, M.D.
Clinical associate professor of psychiatry
University of Chicago
Coauthor of This Isn't What I Expected:
Overcoming Postpartum Depression

- Do I choose drinking or using drugs over socializing with friends or family?
- Do I need to drink more and more or use greater amounts of drugs to get the same buzz?
- Do I find myself drinking or using drugs more or for longer periods of time than I expected?

- Do I spend a lot of time buying drugs or alcohol, drinking or taking drugs, or recovering from hangovers and side effects from the drugs?
- Have I tried to quit, with no success?
- When I stopped drinking or using drugs, did the withdrawal effects make it difficult for me to work or interact with my friends or family?
- Do I continue to drink or use drugs even though it makes my health problems worse?

Other Addictions

We're used to calling any guilty pleasure an addiction. Chocolate, shopping, love. But, says Dr. Stotland, "every habit someone doesn't like isn't an addiction." It's when those habits begin taking over our lives that we need to worry.

Compared with misusing alcohol and drugs, shopping-'til-you-drop and overeating seem like mild problems indeed. But just because a habit can't be formally diagnosed as an addiction doesn't mean it can't destroy your life. Ask any woman who's declared bankruptcy because of overwhelming credit card debt, risked serious health problems because of compulsive overeating, or caught a sexually transmitted disease by jumping from one man's bed to another.

"It's really the same thing as alcohol," says Lucy Papillon, Ph.D., a clinical and media psychologist, founder and director of the Center of Light in Beverly Hills, California, and author of

When Hope Can Kill: Reclaiming Your Soul in a Romantic Relationship. "People use habits to numb themselves. They won't open themselves to love because it feels too risky, but they can eat or shop." Or diet to excess, spend hours surfing the Internet, smoke, gamble, or sleep around.

"The common ground among all of these behaviors is the emptiness women feel," says Dr. Papillon. "Women think they can fill that hole with food, promiscuity, possessions. What they're really longing for is a connection to themselves that they lost earlier in their lives."

That separation from self often begins at an early age, when we mistakenly begin giving up pieces of ourselves to gain approval from those we love and admire. Little by little, we lose touch with our own needs, turning the responsibility for our self-esteem and happiness over to other people, expecting our addictive habits to fill the empty space that is left when we abandon ourselves.

As one woman told Dr. Papillon, "I will binge to the point of unconsciousness until my soul is no longer starving."

Have I Crossed the Line?

Do you just love to shop or do you have a problem? To determine whether your habit is truly compulsive, ask yourself the following questions. If you answer yes to any of them, you should talk to a therapist or your doctor.

EMOTIONAL PAIN RELIEVERS

Dealing with the loss of a loved one is never easy, but some experts say it can be especially difficult for women. "Women often have an especially hard time working through grief because they are so focused on supporting others that they put their own needs and feelings aside," says James Campbell, Ph.D., professor of philosophy at Rochester Institute of Technology in New York. But grieving is good—and necessary.

"The most important thing you can do to cope with grief is to embrace it, not resist it," says Dr. Campbell. "By allowing grief to go on, it resolves itself."

Grieving is painful. Experts offer these strategies to help you work through your grief constructively.

- Surround yourself with people to support you, but be aware that in many cases, family members are not the best people to do this. Your family may be so close to you that it pains them too much to see you suffer, says Dr. Campbell. Consequently, they unconsciously send you messages that they want you to stop, when what you need to do is continue grieving. A friend who is slightly removed from the loss may be a greater support.

- Communicate with the deceased, in your own way, to help resolve some of your feelings. If you've lost your husband or another loved one, write him an honest letter telling him how you feel without him—even if that means writing an angry letter expressing your sense of betrayal that he left you. Or go to his burial site and talk to him or bring him something that he used to enjoy. "One woman I counseled used to visit her son's grave and pour cans of Coca-Cola onto the ground while she talked to him. It was his favorite beverage, and it made her feel close to him to give it to him," says Dr. Campbell.

- Be prepared to go back into the grieving state from time to time, especially on holidays or anniversaries. Just don't run away from the memory of the deceased, says Dr. Campbell. You will miss him especially during these times, so make him part of the holiday by talking about him with others, sharing favorite stories, or looking at photos. You may want to light a candle for the deceased and keep it present as a way of having him there.

- Do kind deeds for others, such as working in a soup kitchen. It will help distract you in a positive way, says Dr. Campbell. "By doing something kind for other people, you will feel that you are helping ease someone else's pain, which can also help ease your own."
- Affirm life. Go for walks, go to movies, enjoy your favorite foods and hobbies. Continue to eat right and exercise, care for yourself, and be attentive to yourself, says Christina M. Puchalski, M.D., assistant professor of medicine at the Center to Improve Care of the Dying at George Washington University Medical Center in Washington, D.C., and director of education at the National Institute for Healthcare Research in Rockville, Maryland.
- Practice your faith. "Men and women who have a spiritual belief tend to cope better with grief," says Dr. Puchalski.
- Do something to memorialize your loved one in a way that is meaningful to you. Plant a tree as a remembrance, write a poem, paint a picture, or keep a journal of your feelings and memories of the deceased, says Dr. Puchalski.
- Meditate or practice yoga. These relaxation methods have extremely calming effects and can help you feel emotionally and spiritually in touch with the person you've lost.

Grieving takes a very long time. Don't rush back to work or to all of your regular daily activities before you are ready, says Dr. Campbell. If you don't seem to be moving through the grief, however, you should see a counselor. If you aren't sure, you might consider asking a trusted friend if it seems to them that you are having an especially difficult time coping.

- Do I feel worthless, valueless, or unlovable when I pursue my habit?
- Does my habit control my life?
- Do I organize my life around the habit? Do I think about it almost all day, eagerly awaiting the next time I can do it?
- Do I pursue this habit out of desperation instead of enjoyment?
- Would I rather engage in my habit than be with friends or family?
- Is my habit interfering with my responsibilities to my family, friends, or job?
- Do I continue to pursue my habit in spite of the financial, physical, legal, or emotional consequences?
- Is this habit continuing to grow in importance to me?

If you suspect your habit has gone from a harmless pick-me-up to an uncontrollable compulsion, see a therapist.

"Women think, 'I'll never be able to come out of that deep hole of pain once I go in there,'" Dr. Papillon says. "But nobody who is willing to go through therapy and the healing process ever gets stuck in that hole."

Getting Help

The treatment path you'll follow will depend on your particular addiction and personality and how far the addiction has progressed. There are numerous resources to help.

Women's treatment programs. Clients in women-only programs tend to stay in treatment and do better afterward than women in mixed-gender

INNER-SPACE EXPLORERS

Who was Aaron T. Beck?

In the late 1970s, American psychiatrist Aaron T. Beck developed the method of psychotherapy known as cognitive therapy. This system of therapy concentrates on here-and-now problems by helping the patient change the way she thinks and interprets experiences. It departs from Freud's primary focus on working through childhood issues that are repressed in the unconscious.

Beck first used cognitive therapy to treat a few cases of depression and anxiety. Today, it is one of the most popular types of therapy, used to treat everything from depression, phobias, and eating disorders to post-traumatic stress disorder, obsessive-compulsive disorder, and chronic medical conditions such as high blood pressure.

One advantage of cognitive therapy is that it gets fast results, says Ellyn Kaschak, Ph.D., professor of psychology at San Jose State University in California. Just a few weeks of therapy can help the patient significantly.

programs. Woman-centered addiction treatment programs cover a host of significant issues for women, from low self-esteem to a history of sexual or physical abuse, that aren't part of the conventional treatment repertoire. They also address the challenges of raising children and providing child care, and offer parenting classes to meet our short-term and long-term needs as mothers. Most important, they help their clients learn to take care of themselves in honest and healthy ways, filling the space formerly reserved for alcohol and drugs with friendship, spirituality, and other self-nurturing activities.

12-step approaches. Overeaters Anonymous. Gamblers Anonymous. Debtors Anonymous. Whatever your challenge, there's a 12-step group that can offer support and understanding as you begin dealing with your addiction. Founded in 1935, Alcoholics Anonymous is the grandfather of them all, providing the now-famous 12 steps to sobriety. Surrounded by fellow addicts, members are encouraged to admit that they're powerless over their addiction as a first step toward overcoming their problem. Other steps involve making amends to friends and family harmed by your drinking and asking a higher power for support. For an appropriate 12-step group near you, check your local newspaper. But don't stop there, especially if you're dealing with a compulsive habit such as overeating or gambling. "If a 12-step group is the only thing someone does to confront their addiction, it's going to take them much longer to pull through," says Dr. Papillon, who also recommends therapy because many people stop attending their 12-step groups when their pain gets stirred up and starts overwhelming them.

Some treatment programs, such as California's Betty Ford Center in Palm Springs, use a 12-step approach as a framework for alcohol and addiction treatment. "People begin to deal with their shame and see they're not alone with their problem," says Jane Gaunt, a counselor at Betty Ford. "Using the power of the group, they begin to make the behavior and life changes necessary for sobriety."

Rational Recovery. This approach emphasizes the importance of the individual in overcoming addiction. Based on Voice Recognition Therapy, it says that people are addicted to a substance or activity because it's incredibly pleasurable. The voice in your head (called the beast in this approach) imploring you to have another drink or take another pill comes from the most primitive part of your brain. Through this approach, you learn to hear the voice but not listen to it, says Jack Trimpey, L.C.S.W., a former alcoholic, cofounder of Rational Recovery, and author of *Rational Recovery: The New Cure for Substance Addiction*. It's an old-fashioned approach, he says, but one that works for anyone who wants to take control of their addiction rather than letting it control them. For more information on Rational Recovery, write to P.O. Box 800, Lotus, CA 95651, visit www.rational.org/recovery, or call (800) 303-CURE.

Therapy. While one-on-one talk therapy isn't generally recommended for alcoholism or drug addiction, it can be helpful for compulsive behaviors such as shopping or eating. A therapist can help uncover the emotional issues that are behind your addictive behaviors. Once you know the roots of your addiction, you can begin solving the problem at its source. A good therapist also can address the behavior itself, suggesting alternative ways to react to your compulsive feelings.

Getting Help

In the movie *Sybil*, we were awed as a powerful psychiatrist expertly integrated 17 of a troubled young woman's personalities. On *Ally McBeal*, we laughed as a wacky therapist prescribed pop songs as pick-me-ups. And on the HBO series *The Sopranos*, we nodded in understanding as we watched a skilled counselor help a Mob boss slowly explore his complicated feelings about a manipulative mother.

But, as we always tell our kids, TV is not real life.

"Going to therapy does not mean spending your kids' entire college tuition money or scheduling an hour with your therapist every week for the rest of your life," says Julia Frank, M.D., associate professor of psychiatry and behavioral sciences at George Washington University in Washington, D.C., and coauthor of *Persuasion and Healing: A Comparative Study of Psychotherapy*.

Instead, we could be in and out of a therapist's office within a few months, with new attitudes toward ourselves and our lives. And while more complicated emotional issues may require extended therapy, just because Woody Allen has

spent most of his life on a psychotherapist's couch doesn't mean we will.

If you don't have the slightest idea where to begin, don't worry. Here's a short primer on therapy, including questions to ask yourself, common approaches to mental health treatment, ways to find a therapist you can trust, and even touch therapies to try. Let your healing begin.

Do I Really Need Counseling?

Whether or not you need professional help from a therapist depends on you. What have you done to shake off your feelings of anxiety or depression? Have you turned to friends for support? Changed your lifestyle to boost your flagging energy or spirits? Begun journaling to discover your hidden emotions? "If these things aren't working, you may need a therapist," says Dr. Frank.

Often what we really need is a sympathetic listener, someone who is capable of understanding our struggle. That kind of person can be hard to come by in our increasingly mobile society. "Many women go to a therapist because there is no one else for them to turn to," Dr. Frank says. Even when a woman has many acquaintances, none may know her past experiences, or be aware of her most important feelings or beliefs. A recent move, conflict with the people closest to her, or the end of an important relationship can propel a woman into a state of painful emotional isolation.

But, afraid of what friends, family, and colleagues might think, nearly two-thirds of us don't get help for treatable mental health problems such as depression or anxiety. And that's playing with fire. Left untreated, a mental illness such as depression may last for 9 months or more, while research shows that most patients feel significantly better after just eight therapy sessions. Nine months is a long time to feel desperate when help is a phone call away.

Choosing a Therapist

When we're desperate for help, the last thing we may care about is the set of letters after a therapist's name. Yet qualifications, experience, and approach matter as much with mental illness as they do with physical illness.

"With therapists, just as with medical doctors, there's a wide range of quality," says Marion Jacobs, Ph.D., adjunct professor emerita of psychology at the University of California, Los Angeles. "Think of all the physicians out there, from those who are medically brilliant but have no personal touch to those who are all-around wonderful. You want someone you will be com-

---

WHAT HAPPENED TO PRIMAL THERAPY?

In the early 1970s, primal therapy was all the rage. Celebrities and college students alike did "primal screams" to release their emotional pain or exam-induced stress.

Developed by California psychologist Arthur Janov in the 1960s, primal therapy argued that all of our psychological and physical problems stem from early traumas, or primal pains, which we've repressed. Only by allowing ourselves to regress to childhood and relive those fearful moments—and letting out a primal scream—can we free ourselves from neurotic behaviors such as anxiety, intimacy issues, and depression.

Despite its initial popularity (more than a million copies of Janov's *The Primal Scream* were sold), primal therapy has largely faded away. It's an intense, time-consuming approach requiring that patients stay at Janov's Primal Center for 3 weeks, part of which is spent in isolation. Yet there's no scientific evidence that primal therapy works, says Dianne Chambless, Ph.D., the William Leon Wylie Professor of Psychology at the University of North Carolina at Chapel Hill.

"In general, these emotionally intense therapies provoke impressive early results, but the results are not sustained," says Julia Frank, M.D., associate professor of psychiatry and behavioral sciences at George Washington University in Washington, D.C., and coauthor of *Persuasion and Healing: A Comparative Study of Psychotherapy*. "It's hard to institutionalize and perpetuate a therapy that depends on the charisma of the therapist, as primal therapy did."

---

fortable and compatible with. Don't be afraid to ask questions."

"This takes a lot of energy," admits Nada Stotland, M.D., chair of the psychiatry department at Illinois Masonic Medical Center in Chicago, "but we're talking about your life."

And, just as with medication, the first therapist you try may not be the best one for you. You should meet with several different mental health professionals, or at least talk with them on the phone, before deciding which one to see. Be prepared to pay out-of-pocket for any introductory sessions with a therapist; your insurance company probably won't cover "auditions."

To help you find a therapist you trust, here's a quick list of critical questions to ask. Don't forget to ask friends, family, and your family doctor for recommendations; you may also get referrals from national mental health organizations or professional associations.

- Is she licensed by your state? This at least ensures you're seeing a therapist who's had the basic educational and hands-on supervised training. All states require that therapists be licensed.
- What degrees does she hold? Psychiatrists are M.D.'s, which qualifies them to prescribe medications. Psychologists are Ph.D.'s, Ed.D.'s, or Psy.D.'s; they've done both psychological research and training with patients. Licensed clinical social workers (L.C.S.W.'s) have a master's degree in social work plus at least 2 years working directly with clients. You may find yourself seeing a psychiatrist for medication as well as any one of the other degreed professionals for actual therapy.
- How long has she been a therapist? What is her specialty? Has she worked in a crisis center or emergency room where she's had to confront and treat a host of unexpected mental health issues? Generally, the more varied her experience, the better. Overall, you should be sure that the therapist you

REAL-LIFE SCENARIO
Her Therapist Does All the Talking

Janet, 55, has been in therapy for 3 months for depression and anxiety attacks. She's stuck in a bad marriage and feels helpless to change the situation. She came into therapy hoping to learn some coping skills so she could move forward in her life. But it seems as if her therapist spends much of their hour preaching to Janet and giving her advice, rather than listening to what Janet has to say. Janet tries to interject, but assertiveness has never been one of her strengths, which is one reason she's in therapy. What should she do?

Janet's found herself in a common situation. The way people choose a therapist—either by word of mouth or through their insurance company—often has very little to do with how they're going to get along with the therapist. The same goes for therapists, who believe they can help virtually anybody. Very few professionals will say to a patient after their first meeting, "I don't think there's a chemistry here that's going to work for you."

With a situation such as Janet's, there are two schools of thought. The first says she should stay with her therapist and work it out; that's how emotional growth happens. The second says that bad matches happen, and Janet will get the best therapy when she's well-matched with her therapist. If she hasn't dumped therapists habitually in the past, she may do better with a new person.

But Janet needs to talk to her therapist first and tell her

choose has expertise in dealing with your specific concern: depression, substance abuse, eating disorder, anxiety disorder, or sexual or other physical abuse.

- How would she treat your problem? If you're seeking short-term help for depression in 12 sessions or less, you don't want a psychoanalytic therapist who plans to spend 3 years dissecting your childhood.

she can't get a word in edgewise. If Janet just walks away without making a serious effort to straighten things out or without a clear sense that the therapy relationship is unfixable, she may end up feeling guilty and responsible. Confronting the issue will help Janet clarify whether it's her problem, the therapist's, or their chemistry. It will also keep her from feeling that she's the one who failed.

After all, her therapist simply may be trying to fill in the blanks Janet is leaving open. It's a clumsy way of trying to help, but it's well-intentioned. It sounds as if Janet is very silent and lost and doesn't know how to put her thoughts together. But "filling in the blanks" may not be what she needs.

If her therapist acknowledges the problem and recognizes that it's related to Janet's reluctance to assert herself, then the therapist may be able to adjust her treatment style so the two can work together. And, although it may not seem this way to Janet, it's a good thing when a problem she's having in her life begins to manifest itself in treatment. This represents a great opportunity for Janet to overcome her anxieties about speaking up.

Expert consulted
Julia Frank, M.D.
Associate professor of psychiatry and behavioral sciences
George Washington University
Washington, D.C.
Coauthor of Persuasion and Healing: A Comparative Study of Psychotherapy

➧ Can you trust her? You'll be telling her fears and hopes you may not have shared with even your husband or best friend, so you need to feel safe with this person. "Don't settle for just any response," Dr. Stotland says. "Wait until it resonates with you that someone hears what you're saying." It is especially reassuring to have a referral from someone you know personally who has had a positive experience with a particular therapist.

What Are My Options?

Gestalt. Freudian analysis. Cognitive-behavioral therapy. When all we want is someone to talk to, the array of therapy choices may be confusing and overwhelming. But it's not as complicated as it looks. "Most therapies will get you better, sooner or later, depending on the therapist," says Dorothea Z. Lack, Ph.D., clinical assistant professor of psychiatry at the University of California, San Francisco.

While some therapists specialize in particular forms of therapy, most use what's called an eclectic approach. That means they borrow elements from different psychological schools of thought to provide a treatment that's tailored to us and our difficulties.

Still, they may have their own personal preferences. To help you make an informed choice, here's a short primer on the most common approaches. Try not to get hung up on the theoretical designations. "You're not really signing on for a particular kind of therapy as much as you are choosing a certain type of relationship with a therapist," says Dr. Frank.

Psychoanalysis. This classic therapy, which is based on the teachings of Sigmund Freud, delves into our childhood memories to uncover the unconscious thoughts and memories that hinder our adult happiness. It's an "evocative" therapy rather than a "directive" one; expect to do most of the talking and lots of free-associating, jumping from thought to thought, with limited

COPING WITH THE COST OF THERAPY

Mental health may be priceless, but it's not always afford-able. When fees start at an average of $80 an hour for so-cial workers and climb higher for Ph.D.-level psychologists and M.D.-level psychiatrists, therapy soon soars out of finan-cial reach for those with limited or no health insurance. Luckily, there are resources to help you cope with the cost.

Nonprofit family and children's services. Often affili-ated with religious denominations or with as the Milwaukee-based Alliance for Children and Families, these agencies provide nonreligious counseling to people of all faiths. They accept insurance, but they also offer a sliding fee scale. De-pending on your income and household size, you could pay as little as a few dollars for each session.

Pastoral counselors. Generally less costly than social workers, pastoral counselors are religious leaders with mental health training that allows them to provide therapy as well as spiritual guidance. If you belong to a church or synagogue, you may be able to talk with your pastor or rabbi for free. The cost is generally less than what professional therapists charge.

Community mental health centers. While many states focus their resources on only the most serious mental ill-nesses, some states fund walk-in therapy clinics.

Your therapist. She may be willing to establish a payment plan for you.

You'll work with your therapist to discover how your emotions and be-haviors are influenced by the self-defeating thoughts that leap to mind when something goes wrong ("I knew I'd mess this up—I can't do anything right," after you flubbed the presentation) or even unexpect-edly right ("She's only saying that to be nice," after a friend compliments you).

You'll learn to challenge the truth of those damaging (and often equally inaccurate) self-perceptions actively, exchanging them for healthier self-talk and actions. You won't become a Pollyanna; "CBT isn't about taking off gray-colored glasses and putting on rose-colored ones," says Diane Spangler, Ph.D., assistant professor of psychology at Brigham Young University. You might, however, find yourself feel-ing unexpectedly empowered, espe-cially if you've been struggling with depression or anxiety, both of which respond especially well to CBT.

Thanks to its action-oriented emphasis on solving your emo-tional problems by permanently changing your thoughts and behaviors, CBT is associated with lower relapse rates than other therapies. "People walk out the door with the skills and abilities to live their lives in a different way," says Dr. Spangler. To find a CBT specialist, visit the Association for Advancement of Be-havior Therapy Web site at www.aabt.org.

Gestalt. In contrast to psychoanalysts, who concentrate on our childhood, and cognitive-behaviorists, who teach us how to change our negative thinking patterns in specific ways,

interference from your therapist. This approach takes longer than other therapies, and may in-volve sessions several times a week, making it most appropriate for women willing to make an intense time commitment to exploring their psy-chological history. For this type of therapy, look for a psychiatrist who's been trained by a psycho-analytic institute.

Cognitive-behavioral. If you're a believer in self-help, and you're looking for an active, shorter-term therapy with proven success, cog-nitive-behavioral therapy (CBT) may be for you.

Gestalt therapists encourage us to talk about what we're feeling at this very moment, both physically and mentally. As we become more aware of our emotions and sensations, we gain insight into our behaviors, choices, and even physical problems. To achieve this, the therapist may ask us to recall particular moments in our lives, encouraging us to re-enact, not simply discuss, them during the session. "Intensifying the experience like this clarifies your perception of it," says Dori H. Middleman, M.D., staff psychiatrist at the Pennsylvania Gestalt Center for Psychotherapy and Training in Malvern. "You're able to find your own wisdom there." You work very independently, as a Gestalt therapist believes in guiding a client through her own discovery process, not just telling her what to do. Finally, the importance Gestalt places on physical sensations makes it a great complementary talk therapy for women using bodywork or massage (covered later in this chapter).

Couples. What couples therapy is not: the solution to domestic abuse. "The abusing partner must be seeking help and must accept responsibility for his acts," says Dr. Frank. What couples therapy is: a way to get beyond the irresolvable issues in a relationship, whether the impasse revolves around his interfering mother, your workaholism, or your hurtful patterns of relating. You'll focus on communication skills, understanding your spouse's viewpoint, and negotiating solutions

WOMEN ASK WHY

Why does every medication warning label say not to mix it with MAO inhibitors? What are they?

MAO inhibitors are early antidepressant drugs. When we're depressed, our brains often don't have enough of certain chemicals that regulate our moods. MAO inhibitors boost our spirits by keeping the critical neurotransmitters serotonin, dopamine, and norepinephrine moving through our brains by preventing an enzyme known as monoamine oxidase (or MAO) from breaking them down.

The problem is, we have dopamine, serotonin, norepinephrine, and monoamine oxidase all over our bodies—not just in our brains. These early antidepressants are not specific for any particular part of the body; they essentially take a shotgun approach, firing 100 bullets at the problem. One bullet will treat the disease and the other 99 will cause problems.

Potential side effects include dizziness, constipation, headaches, sleep problems, and weight gain. Also, MAO inhibitors may cause strokes when they interact with over-the-counter drugs and certain foods, such as aged cheeses, red wine, and fava beans. That's because these foods contain an amino acid called tyramine. Normally, your body breaks down tyramine, but the MAO inhibitor keeps this from happening. Thus, the substance builds up in your body, causing higher blood pressure, which may lead to a stroke. That's why very strict dietary monitoring is necessary when taking MAO inhibitors, which are often a last resort for women who've tried multiple antidepressant medications.

The newer antidepressants, such as fluoxetine (Prozac), are much more precise. They act more like a single bullet, treating depression where it originates.

Expert consulted
Valerie Davis Raskin, M.D.
Clinical associate professor of psychiatry
University of Chicago
Author of When Words Are Not Enough:
    The Women's Prescription for
    Depression and Anxiety

that you can both accept, with the ultimate goal of enhancing your intimacy and relatedness.

Family. This approach works best for families whose lives have been disrupted by illness or other trauma, Dr. Frank says. Basically, when a parent or child becomes physically or psychologically ill, they're no longer able to fulfill their family roles. This can have consequences for everyone: A previously angelic son may start misbehaving because his anorexic sister is getting all the attention, or a daughter may become depressed as she watches her mother undergo chemotherapy for breast cancer. Family therapy teaches you how to share the burden, helping each member of the family get what they need and give what they can. Depending on the issues and the therapist, family therapy may involve just the immediate family or the extended clan.

Group. Group therapy is faster, cheaper, and just as effective, if not more so, as individual counseling, says Bonnie Buchele, Ph.D., president of the American Group Psychotherapy Association. But it's not for the faint of heart. In individual therapy, you can portray situations the way you want them to appear, and there's only one person to impress (or fool). In a group of 5 to 10 people, there's nowhere to hide.

You'll be expected to be honest and direct with other group members, which often represents a dramatic change from real life. "Your best friend rarely tells you if you're bothering her. She'll just try to work around it," explains Bonnie Jacobson, Ph.D., adjunct professor of psychology at New York University, director of the New York Insti-

---

JOIN THE GROUP!

From support groups to self-help organizations, personal growth groups such as Alcoholics Anonymous can show us we're not alone, provide inspiration, and help us develop awareness of ourselves and our relationships with others.

What these groups don't provide is therapy. Therapists draw clear distinctions between personal growth groups and group therapy, which is led by a trained professional focused on helping clients make major changes in their lives and relationships. Instead, personal growth groups such as those below are run by members or facilitators who aim to provide softer benefits: personal growth, new perspectives on old problems, a nonjudgmental place for revealing feelings. Here are some of the most common.

Self-help groups. Organizations such as Alcoholics Anonymous (and its many offshoots) and Recovery, Inc. provide programs for members to overcome their problems without professional help. While AA expects members to surrender to a higher power as a first step toward sobriety, Recovery, Inc. emphasizes taking personal responsibility and developing problem-solving skills. "It's sort of a poor man's cognitive therapy," says Julia Frank, M.D., associate professor

---

tute for Psychological Change, a clinical psychologist specializing in group and relationship therapy, and author of *If Only You Would Listen*. That won't happen in group therapy, where you'll simultaneously clarify your feelings and develop interpersonal skills.

But you'll also find that you're not the only one feeling depressed, angry, anxious, or ashamed. "Group therapy takes people's problems out of the closet," Dr. Jacobson says. Groups generally meet weekly, and, as with individual counseling, there are different ways of running group therapy. Expect to pay about one-third to one-half of what an individual hour with a Ph.D.-level psychologist costs.

of psychiatry and behavioral sciences at George Washington University in Washington, D.C., and coauthor of *Persuasion and Healing: A Comparative Study of Psychotherapy*. Recovery, Inc. members meet weekly for highly structured sessions in which they discuss situations they've recently encountered, and most important, how they solved them. Between meetings, they practice their newfound skills by putting them into action. Dr. Frank says that Recovery, Inc.'s approach can be particularly helpful for women who need its empowering message of self-help. It is not the best resource for substance abusers, she says.

Support groups. Revolving around anything from breast cancer to Alzheimer's disease caregivers, these groups offer empathy and an opportunity for group problem-solving. "If a woman's recently divorced, a support group can help her build a new life," says Matti K. Gershenfeld, Ed.D., president of the Couples Learning Center in Jenkintown, Pennsylvania. It can also provide a safe haven for emotions that are too raw to share with friends and family. Just be wary of a group in which every meeting turns into a bitch session, Dr. Gershenfeld cautions. "It's not supportive when all you hear is the reasons why something won't work."

Touch Therapies

Anyone who's been hugged by a child after a tough day knows the power of touch.

From the tightness in our chests to the tension in our necks, all our physical and mental worries seem to melt away as they throw their pudgy arms around us.

That's kind of how touch therapies such as massage and acupressure work. They're effective because our emotions so often manifest themselves in physical ways. A stress-filled day at work leaves our shoulders tight and contracted. Our mother's upcoming visit ties our stomachs in knots. We may not even realize how tightly strung we are until the tension is gone. "People adapt to tension," says Adela Basayne, a licensed massage therapist and a past president of the American Massage Therapy Association. "Even if we're not aware of it, it's still a fatigue factor because other muscles have to compensate. You'll feel tired, but you won't realize it's because you've been holding your shoulders up."

Touch therapy massages away those emotional-turned-physical strains, leaving us relaxed and less anxious. It even helps us sleep more soundly. "By taking away the aches and pains, bodywork helps us weather the storm of life's daily challenges a little easier," says Lynn Meffert, co-owner and director of To Your Health in Charleston, South Carolina, and eastern regional director for the American Oriental Bodywork Therapy Association.

Massage therapies can also enhance talk therapy. By encouraging us to be more aware of what's happening in our bodies, "touch provides rapid access to our emotional experiences or past traumas," says Basayne, who is also a trained Gestalt therapist. Touch therapy may be especially helpful if we're having trouble opening up to our talk therapist. By kneading away the tension, massage and other bodywork leave us more comfortable in our own skin and thus more trusting of others. The result? We're more willing to tackle painful topics with our therapist.

But we don't have to wait until we're emotionally drained or barely able to move to try touch therapy. "We want people to relieve their stress before their body breaks down into disease," says Meffert. Depending on your location

INNER-SPACE EXPLORERS

Who was Albert Ellis?

Discouraged by the poor results of psychoanalysis, American psychologist Albert Ellis went on to develop rational-emotive therapy. This highly effective form of therapy was the first to fall under the umbrella of cognitive-behavioral therapy.

Ellis used a Greek philosophical principle as the basis for rational-emotive therapy: "People do not get upset by things, but by the view they take of them." Ellis said that no thing or situation automatically upsets us. Rather, our irrational beliefs, such as "I have to be the best at everything I do" or "Everyone must like me," shape how we react to things and are the real cause of our sadness, anger, or frustration.

Rational-emotive therapists help people recognize their irrational beliefs and replace them with rational ones. They use a tough-love approach of directly telling their patients what they're doing wrong and how they should change. Therapists will even argue with their clients, attacking any beliefs they find foolish or illogical.

To guide the therapy process, Ellis established the now internationally acclaimed A-B-C model of human emotions. In this model, "A" refers to an event a person reacts to, "B" represents her beliefs about that event, and "C" is her emotional response. Ellis said that to change your emotional reaction (C) to an event (A), you must adopt more realistic personal beliefs about that event (B). This model, from the 1950s, has proven to be one of the most useful psychotherapy tools in the 20th century.

(deep-tissue massage, sports massage, and trigger point therapy) benefit our spirits and health by relieving tension, improving circulation, and boosting our immune systems through kneading and stroking of the muscles. "We have this idea in our country that massage is a luxury that only the wealthy can indulge in," Basayne says. That's not true. "With women so often the designated caretakers, there's something quite wonderful about letting someone care for us for an hour." Look for a state-licensed massage therapist who's a member of the American Massage Therapy Association (AMTA) or certified by the National Certification Board for Therapeutic Massage and Bodywork. For more information, contact the AMTA at 820 Davis Street, Evanston, IL 60201, or visit its Web site at www.amtamassage.org.

Acupressure. If you're intrigued by the ancient Chinese art of acupuncture, but you faint at the sight of needles, acupressure may be the answer for you. It's based on the same philosophy as acupuncture—that certain points in the body correspond to physical ailments—but instead of needles, hand pressure is applied. You can find a qualified practitioner through the American Oriental Bodywork Therapy Association (AOBTA) at 1010 Haddonfield-Berlin Road, Suite 408, Voorhees, NJ 08043, or visit its Web site at www.aobta.org. You can also get information from the National Certification Commission for Acupuncture and Oriental Medicine (NCCAOM) on its Web site at

and the practitioner's expertise, expect to pay $45 to $75 for a 1-hour bodywork session. Some practitioners offer their services on a sliding fee scale, or will provide 30-minute sessions. Like talk therapies, touch therapies differ in the approaches they take.

Swedish massage. Soothing and relaxing, Swedish massage and its touch therapy cousins

I don't know doc . . . sometimes I think you're not listening to me . . .

www.nccaom.org. Both of these organizations require considerable education and experience.

Shiatsu. Shiatsu, a Japanese form of acupressure, is the complete opposite of Swedish massage. It is based upon principles of traditional Chinese medicine for assessing and evaluating the energy system of the human body. Treatment strategies are designed for chronic and acute conditions of physical and emotional distress, such as irritable bowel syndrome, fibromyalgia, insomnia, and depression. You stay fully clothed during a shiatsu session, which involves active stretching and breathing exercises. "This is not a passive, feel-good massage," says Meffert, a certified shiatsu practitioner. Instead, shiatsu practitioners lean on, press, and move your limbs and muscles quite intensely, releasing energy that is "stuck" in your body and providing physical and emotional relief. It is designed to create a condition of harmony and balance in the human energy field. Afterward, women say, they feel lighter, more balanced, and, depending on their bodies' energy patterns, either more relaxed

or more energetic, making shiatsu helpful for symptoms of anxiety or depression. Look for AOBTA or NCCAOM certification as described above.

Reflexology. Call this a foot massage, and Valerie Voner may tickle your toes in revenge. Voner, a certified reflexologist and director of the New England Institute of Reflexology in Onset, Massachusetts, says reflexology differs from massage in multiple ways. First, it focuses not on muscles but on pressure points and nerve endings, much as acupressure does. Second, reflexology involves only the hands and feet. But it has full-body results. "When we apply light pressure to the feet or hands, it affects the central nervous system," Voner explains. "The body immediately begins to release its stress." To choose a reflexologist with credentials from the American Reflexology Certification Board, contact it at P.O. Box 620607, Littleton, CO 80162, or log on to its Web site at www.arcb.net. The board provides free information for referrals and national certification testing.

Rolfing. Imagine a touch therapy that transforms your life by improving your posture, and you've got Rolfing. Unlike Swedish massage, which simply rubs the tension away, Rolfing seeks to realign your entire skeletal and muscular system by concentrating on the connective tissues that knit your muscles and bones together. More intense than a deep-tissue massage, Rolfing, known generically as structural integration, can be physically uncomfortable at times. But by manipulating and teaching your muscles, limbs, and joints to move in more efficient ways, Rolfing can dramatically change how your body works.

Most people notice the difference halfway through the 10-session therapy, says Linda Grace, a certified Rolfer in Philadelphia. "There's a profound psychological impact on people. They realize they can move in ways they never thought of," she says. By the end of the treatment, they feel like a new person, physically and emotionally. "You respond better to stress. You can reach over your head more easily. You see better because your neck swivels better." Research shows that people even say they think better after they've been Rolfed. Look for a Rolfer certified by the Rolf Institute, founded by Ida P. Rolf, Ph.D.; only its graduates are allowed to call themselves Rolfers. You can contact the institute at 205 Canyon Boulevard, Boulder, CO 80302, or visit its Web site at www.rolf.org.

Helping Yourself

or some of us, the idea of visiting a shrink's office and pouring out our innermost thoughts, worries, fears, and hidden stories to a complete stranger has all the appeal of a hike through a minefield.

We'd rather confide in our best friend, our mother, our pastor, the dog. Anyone who is willing to listen, except for a therapist. This could be for financial or cultural reasons or because of fears associated with a past experience, inconvenience, or believing that only "crazy people" need counseling.

That's okay, as long as your issues are not so debilitating that you can't function or are having thoughts about hurting yourself or someone else. That's when you need professional help. But if you're grappling with a career change, problems in a relationship, or struggling with wondering why happiness always seems to elude you, you may be able to address those issues yourself.

There's one requirement you'll have to meet first, though: You can't be afraid to dig deep within yourself and explore the inner depths of your soul.

Digging Beneath the Surface

The key to emotional health is knowing what makes us tick. We have to stay in close touch with our emotions and examine our feelings if we're going to find solutions to our daily problems. To do this, we need to set aside quiet time for ourselves—time away from the office, our kids, our partners, and our friends. This allows us to think clearly and bring order to our lives. It's a four-step process.

1. Grab a pen and notepad and find a quiet place where you won't be disturbed. Write in three-word sentences what you're feeling at the moment. "I feel lonely. I feel sad. I feel angry." Focusing on your feelings will help you identify the situations in your life that are giving you trouble. "Our emotions are like keys that unlock the door to important thoughts," says Susan Heitler, Ph.D., a clinical psychologist in Denver and author of *The Power of Two: Secrets to a Strong and Loving Marriage* and of the audiotape *Depression: A Disorder of Power.*

2. Jot down the situation causing the feeling. Why are you lonely? Is it because you have few

THE ART OF THE JOURNAL

Writing in a journal is better than confiding in a best friend. We can divulge our best-kept secrets, knowing that those pages won't talk. It also slows us down, forces us to relax, and helps us zero in on who we are and what we desire.

"Putting your thoughts on paper helps you make sense of your life, sort out problems, and come up with solutions," says Linda Cameron, Ph.D., a senior lecturer in psychology and a journaling researcher at the University of Auckland in New Zealand.

It's also an incredible outlet to express our creativity. "Journaling is an art form," says Susan Heitler, Ph.D., a clinical psychologist in Denver and author of the audiotape *Depression: A Disorder of Power*. "It's like writing poetry, painting, or playing a musical instrument, which all contribute to our emotional health."

There are other bonuses as well. Studies show that writing about our stress boosts our immunity, reduces visits to the doctor, and even relieves asthma and rheumatoid arthritis symptoms.

So what are you waiting for? Whip out that journal and start writing. Here are some hints to help you get started.

Buy a notebook. This may seem obvious, but journals come in a wide array of beautiful colors, designs, textures, and sizes. You can even have your name engraved on one that's bound in leather. Pick one that you think is attractive, is convenient to carry, and fits your personality. That way, you'll be more likely to write in it.

Be creative. Instead of just jotting down what you did today in chronological order, write your thoughts and feelings about what happened to you. Sort out your problems and come up with solutions by writing poems or short stories. If you're an artist, draw the events in your life and how you feel about them. Make your journal fun and interesting.

Take five. You don't have to write for hours to keep a journal. Carve 5 minutes (or less) out of your day to write a sentence or two. If you have more time, write for 20 minutes, or 2 hours. Just be flexible. Journaling is something you should look forward to, without any added pressure.

friends or family members in your life? Because you're working too hard to have a social life? Listen to your inner voices, "the voices of your values and principles, your wishes, your dreams, and your preferences," says Dr. Heitler. "And really be honest."

3. Write what you'd like to change about the situation. Maybe you would like a more active social life, or closer relationships with the people already in your life.

4. Create solutions to the situation causing your feelings. For instance, join a church, start a women's book club, invite the few friends you do know over for dinner. You can reduce your work hours, get home earlier, and spend more quality time with your family and friends. "The sky's the limit when it comes to problem solving," says Dr. Heitler.

The Mind-Body Connection

Another way to identify your emotions is to listen to your body. Very often, our feelings manifest themselves in physical problems. Lower-back pain may indicate that we're carrying too heavy a load. Pain in our reproductive area may symbolize our sadness at our inability to conceive. Muscle tension and frequent headaches may be signs that we're internalizing our pressure-filled lives.

Of course, any physical pain may

also be a sign of disease or other problems, so check with your doctor. If she rules out any serious health concerns, then you can begin to trace those body aches from their physical locations to their emotional origins.

Question yourself. Close your eyes and take deep, relaxing breaths. Think about the part of your body that's hurting and ask yourself, "What does this feel like?" Your headache may feel as if someone is jabbing you, or your stomach may feel as if it's tied in knots. Then ask, "At what other times in my life have I felt like this?" and "What is different about my current circumstances compared with the past?" Given the differences, "What new options do I have for handling my present situation?" Write down your answers, and a pattern will emerge.

Snap a picture. Visualize your physical pain as an image. For instance, your stomach is a bunch of ropes tied in knots. Then ask yourself, "How can I turn those knots into a smooth silken cord?" Now picture that cord. Is it in the dark, or in bright sunshine? Look for the reason you see your solution in a particular setting. If it's in sunshine, it might mean that you've been very much on edge lately and now you need some bright moments in your life, says Dr. Heitler.

Living the Spiritual Life

As women, we are composed of body, mind, and spirit. Each part

WOMEN ASK WHY

Is it true that physical activity can actually prevent stress and depression from happening in the first place?

Exercise can blast away fat, shave years off your figure, boost your energy, and fight disease, but to say that it can prevent stress and depression altogether is a bit of a stretch. Research shows that regular aerobic activity can relieve symptoms of depression and significantly reduce stress to the point where it's barely noticeable. When we're stressed out, our bodies release large amounts of the hormones cortisol and adrenaline, which tense our muscles and speed our heart rate, blood pressure, and breathing. Exercise keeps these hormone levels down and protects us from irritability, panic attacks, throbbing headaches, stomachaches, ulcers, and heart disease.

Research also shows that regular aerobic exercise produces mood-enhancing chemicals called endorphins that keep us cheerful, bolster self-esteem, and restore feelings of hopefulness in depressed women. So moving our bodies definitely helps. There's even evidence showing that exercise can reduce the amount of antidepressant medication you take, depending on the severity of your depression.

But with depression, exercise alone isn't enough. Prescription medications are usually taken to raise low levels of serotonin, dopamine, and norepinephrine, those precious brain chemicals that regulate our moods. Weekly therapy sessions may also be necessary.

To control stress and depression symptoms, exercise aerobically 3 or 4 days a week for at least 20 to 30 minutes. Jogging, vigorous walking, cycling, stair climbing, and step aerobics are great choices.

Expert consulted
Ellen McGrath, Ph.D.
Chair
American Psychological Association task force
  on women and depression
Washington, D.C.

RELAX WITH HERBAL TEAS

While they don't compare to basking in the sun on a pink-sand beach, teas made with herbs called nervines, can help send your tension and anxiety packing, according to Jennifer Brett, N.D., a naturopathic doctor at the Wilton Naturopathic Center in Stratford, Connecticut. Here are some of the best-tasting blends. Drink up to four 1-cup servings of these teas throughout the day as needed to reduce anxiety, tension, and stress.

Chamomile tea. A member of the daisy family, chamomile is used to treat insomnia, tummy troubles, and jittery nerves. Buy it in tea bags or make your own infusion. Put 2 to 3 ounces of dried chamomile flowers in a jar and cover with freshly boiled water. Let it steep overnight. Strain and drink. (Because of the strength of this infusion, drink only one-quarter cup, or add hot water to make a tea.) If you're allergic to ragweed, asters, or chrysanthemums, use caution with chamomile.

Kava kava. Native to the tropical forests of South Sea islands, kava relaxes your body while keeping your mind alert. Buy the prepared tea, or make your own from kava root, which is available at some health food stores. Place 2 tablespoons of fresh (or 1 tablespoon of dried) kava root and 1 cup of spring or filtered water in a pot. Cover and boil for 20 minutes. Let it remain in the covered pot for another 10 minutes. Strain and drink. Don't take kava with alcohol or barbiturates, and use caution if you have to drive or operate machinery.

Skullcap. Also known as mad-dog weed and helmet flower, skullcap relieves anxiety, stress, exhaustion, and depression. You can buy the tea in health food stores, or make it yourself. Pour 1 cup of boiling water over 2 teaspoons of dried (or 1½ tablespoons of fresh) skullcap leaves. Let it steep for 15 minutes in a covered pot. Strain and drink.

Passionflower. This herb eases stress, tension headaches, anxiety, insomnia, and PMS. Additionally, it increases levels of serotonin, a brain chemical that regulates mood. Buy it in tea bags or use the dried leaves to make your own. Pour 1 cup of boiling water over 1½ teaspoons of the dried herb. Steep for 15 minutes. Strain and drink.

interacts with the others to help us achieve overall physical and spiritual health.

Just as we nourish our bodies to survive and stimulate our minds to stay sharp, we have to nurture our spirits to be truly complete. If we don't, we'll feel a void, says Elizabeth J. Canham, founder and director of Stillpoint Ministries in Black Mountain, North Carolina, and author of *Heart Whispers: Benedictine Wisdom for Today.*

Numerous studies show that people who practice their faith are healthier than those who do not and are less likely to die prematurely from any cause. A spiritual life can also speed recovery from physical and mental illness, surgery, and addiction.

"We're less likely to be anxious, depressed, and pessimistic when we lead a spiritual life," says Canham.

Spirituality isn't just about religion. It's about getting connected with a higher power, whether that is God or some other life force. By bringing your concerns and joys to this higher power, knowing that you have spiritual support as you walk this journey, you're able to come to a deeper appreciation of your emotions, your feelings, and yourself. These emotions and feelings are gifts to help us stay in tune with ourselves and our higher power.

You're also activating your inner voice, your intuition. Doing this helps you become more attuned to your own feelings. Once you're in touch with your spiritual side, your inner healing power is unleashed.

You can't, however, suddenly become spiritual simply to prolong your life or help you recover from an illness. Your desire for spirituality has to come from the heart. But if you are sincerely searching for it, or would like to develop your own faith, here are some ways to make it a part of your daily life.

Become one with nature. Stop and smell the roses—literally. Go for a walk and really notice the beauty around you. Watch the clouds move. Listen to the birds chirp. Nature helps us relax and restores our spirit. "It's similar to taking a nap, or getting a massage," says Lucy Papillon, Ph.D., a clinical and media psychologist, founder and director of the Center of Light in Beverly Hills, California, and author of *When Hope Can Kill: Reclaiming Your Soul in a Romantic Relationship*. "You've moved out of one space and into another."

Schedule prayer time. Prayer is a conversation with your own higher power. And it involves both talking and listening, says Ann Bauwens, director of program development at Christian Healing Ministries in Jacksonville, Florida. Prayer can provide a connection to the Divine in your life, and help you develop a relationship with this higher power.

Not sure how to pray? "You can begin by sharing your thoughts and feelings in conversation. It can be either verbally or in writing," suggests Carol Schoenecker, R.N., a certified healing touch practitioner and spiritual director

---

THE MERITS AND DANGERS OF KAVA KAVA

Stressed? Anxious? Can't sleep? Pop a kava capsule. It's considered one of nature's best chill pills.

Kava is a native perennial shrub of the South Pacific islands that dates back thousands of years. It's known for its powerful abilities to calm jangled nerves, relax tense muscles, and provide a sense of well-being. And it's fast acting, so you'll feel calmer and even a little euphoric in as little as 30 to 60 minutes. It can also prevent stress if you take it prior to a situation you know will be nerve-racking.

The secret behind kava is a group of chemicals called kavalactones that have a mild tranquilizing effect similar to that of Valium, but without its side effects, says Jennifer Brett, N.D., a naturopathic doctor at the Wilton Naturopathic Center in Stratford, Connecticut. Animal studies show that these ingredients act on the limbic system, the part of the brain that is the center of emotions. Dr. Brett says kava is not addictive and will remain effective for insomnia over time. It doesn't leave you feeling spaced out or groggy the next morning, as many prescription drugs do.

Kava is considered very safe if you follow the dosage instructions on the label. At very high doses or with prolonged use, it may cause stomach upset or a dry, scaly skin rash, says Dr. Brett. On rare occasions, it can cause intoxication or drowsiness, so use caution if you have to drive or operate any machinery. An overdose may impair vision, cause liver damage, or lead to spinal cord injury. Don't take kava with alcohol or barbiturates. And don't use the herb if you're pregnant, trying to conceive, or breastfeeding.

---

at the Mind Body Spirit Clinic at Fairview University Medical Center in Minneapolis. "Prayer is empowering because you realize that you are not alone," she says.

Read from a good book. Pick a passage from the Bible, inspirational writing, or even a poem that speaks to your emotions or current situation. "I've found that reflecting on scripture

ADAPTOGENIC HERBS AND STRESS

These particular herbs, also called tonics, can improve how we react to stress and protect us from the negative effects it can have on our physical and emotional health.

The beauty of adaptogens is that they adapt to our bodies' needs. If our adrenal glands pump out too much adrenaline in response to stress, the herbs help reduce the supply. If the glands aren't releasing enough hormones, the herbs help them produce more. So the adaptogen goes where it's needed, bringing our body back into a more balanced state, says Jennifer Brett, N.D., a naturopathic doctor at the Wilton Naturopathic Center in Stratford, Connecticut.

These herbs can act as stimulants by increasing alertness, reaction time, respiratory output, and motor coordination. Or they can have a milder tonic effect, lowering blood pressure, regulating blood sugar, and maintaining the immune system.

Ginseng is one of the best adaptogens around to restore vitality and boost energy. It's been used for thousands of years as a tonic to elevate mood and reduce fatigue.

There are different varieties of the herb, including Siberian ginseng, Asian ginseng, and American ginseng. They all have similar properties, although Asian ginseng is more of a stimulant than the Siberian variety. So if you're acutely stressed or recovering from a long illness, Asian ginseng is the way to go, says Dr. Brett. She recommends up to three 500-milligram capsules daily. She cautions, however, that overuse could cause sleeplessness and jitters.

Oats are also a supreme tonic for the nervous system. They help you make slow, sustained progress against stress-related disorders such as shingles, herpes flare-ups, and chronic depression. Your daily bowl of quick oats won't cut it, however. Only whole oats, the kind you cook for 30 to 40 minutes, provide this benefit.

Other adaptogens include astragalus, schisandra, codonopsis, and gotu kola, all of which are safe to take on a regular basis and are available in capsule form from your health food store. Follow the package instructions for recommended dosages.

early in the morning before I start my day is very calming. It puts me in a better frame of mind," says Canham.

Join a spiritual community. Connect with friends who meet once or twice a month to discuss spiritual topics. Meet with a spiritual director or mentor. You can become part of a scripture-study group in your neighborhood, or work in a ministry at your church or synagogue. Yoga classes or prayer and meditation workshops are other good ways to get in touch with your inner spirit, says Schoenecker.

A Calming Ritual

Meditation, a form of contemplation that is thousands of years old, is rooted in the traditions of the world's greatest religions. Today, nearly all religious groups practice it in one form or another. At its core, meditation involves being quiet and still, clearing your mind, and focusing on a word or phrase, or on the rhythm of your breathing. All of these things seem about as possible as winning the lottery in our hurry-up lives.

But it's worth a try; meditation provides the time and space to tend to your emotional needs and nurture yourself. For that reason, it's a great stress buster. Research shows that daily meditation can reduce anxiety, panic attacks, depression, anger, and other emotional health problems, says Joan Borysenko, Ph.D., president of Mind/Body Health Sciences in Boulder, Colorado, and author of *A Woman's Journey to God: Finding the Feminine Path.*

Moreover, meditation can ease tension headaches and symptoms of PMS when practiced on a regular basis.

"Meditation reduces your heart rate, your breathing, and your blood pressure. And the more you do it, the longer you'll remain in that state throughout the day," says Dr. Borysenko. Here are some tips to help you get started.

Get comfy. Sit on the floor with your back against a wall, or in a chair with your feet on the ground and your hands resting on your knees or thighs.

Breathe. Breathe in slowly and deeply for five counts, then exhale slowly for five counts.

Take a mental vacation. Close your eyes and visualize yourself in a tranquil place where you feel safe and calm. A quiet beach is an ideal place to start. Picture yourself resting on the sand. Feel the warmth of the sun on your skin, hear the water rushing against the shore, listen for the sounds of seagulls, or picture the ships passing by. You can use the same technique for any serene place that brings you peace.

Do it again. While you don't need to spend long hours meditating—20 minutes is enough—you should do it twice a day, in the morning and evening. A peaceful meditative journey upon awakening can set the tone for your entire day.

St. John's Wort

True depression is not just the blues. It's a deficiency in the brain's mood-altering chemicals that maintain our emotional equilibrium. These "feel-good" neurotransmitters include serotonin, dopamine, and norepinephrine.

That's why medication is often a first-line treatment for depression. And while recent years have seen an explosion in new drugs to treat depression, including fluoxetine (Prozac), paroxetine (Paxil), and bupropion (Wellbutrin), there are also natural supplements that may be just as effective. One of the most popular is St. John's wort.

What is it? An herb used for mild-to-moderate depression. One of the most widely studied herbs for depression, it is prescribed regularly in Germany.

How does it work? Researchers speculate that St. John's wort inhibits an enzyme that breaks down serotonin molecules and other brain chemicals, enabling the serotonin to circulate longer in the brain. It may also increase the uptake of serotonin in the brain.

What are its benefits? In studies, St. John's wort has been shown to be just as effective at treating mild-to-moderate depression as prescription drugs such as Prozac.

Does it have any drawbacks? In rare cases, some people experience insomnia, loose bowels, and sun sensitivity. St. John's wort isn't strong enough to treat severe depression or other disorders characterized by hallucinations and suicidal thoughts. Do not use St. John's wort if you are already taking a selective serotonin-reuptake inhibitor, otherwise known as an SSRI (such as Prozac, Paxil, or Zoloft), or if you are taking digitalis for an irregular heartbeat. St. John's wort may cause photosensitivity; avoid overexposure to direct sunlight.

Eating for Emotional Health

Remember the "body" in the mind-body-spirit trio? Just as we nourish our souls with spirituality and our minds with meditation, we must nourish our body with healthy foods.

INNER-SPACE EXPLORERS
Who was Ida Rolf?

New York native Ida Rolf founded the holistic philosophy and hands-on therapy known as Rolfing. Rolf, a biochemist, first presented the system, which she called structural integration, to osteopaths and chiropractors in the 1950s. It wasn't until a decade later, however, that Rolfing really became popular.

Rolf began with the idea that a person's physiological function and anatomical structure are related. From there, she developed a system to change a person's structure by manipulating their myofascia, the thin web of elastic tissue that covers organs and blood vessels and attaches muscles to bones and other muscles. A person's myofascia is greatly influenced by gravity and can become distorted from injury, emotional trauma, or poor posture. Rolfing is designed to "fix" the distorted myofascia and bring the body's structure back into balance within gravity.

While Rolfing resembles massage therapy, it does much more than release muscular tension; it improves a person's overall well-being. The therapy makes you feel light and fluid; improves your posture; eases pain, stiffness, and chronic stress; and even promotes emotional release.

Rolf's work not only led to her system of Rolfing, but also has influenced most of the "deep tissue" therapies and many other types of soft-tissue manipulation that have been developed in this country.

During times of stress, your brain runs through its supply of serotonin, dopamine, and norepinephrine (neurotransmitters that stabilize your moods and promote emotional well-being) the way a marathoner guzzles liquids. When levels of these chemicals drop, we can get depressed, anxious, irritable, and stressed, says Joan Mathews Larson, Ph.D., founder and executive director of the Health Recovery Center in Minneapolis and author of *7 Weeks to Emotional Healing.* But modifying your diet with specific foods and supplements may help.

Chow down on fish. Just another example of how Mom was always right: Fish *is* brain food. Cold-water, fatty fish, such as salmon, mackerel, trout, and canned white tuna, is loaded with omega-3 fatty acids, which may help fend off depression. Some research suggests that adequate amounts of omega-3 fatty acids, particularly DHA, may reduce the development of depression in some people. Other research has shown that worldwide, the more fish people eat, the lower the incidence of major depression. Although research evidence is preliminary, it is promising. So try to eat 2 to 3 playing-card-size servings of fatty fish a week for the omega-3s your brain needs.

Chomp on carbos. Eating foods high in carbohydrates such as pasta, whole wheat bread, brown rice, and whole grain cereals triggers the release of insulin, which allows the amino acid tryptophan to enter your brain freely, causing serotonin levels to rise. So make sure every meal contains some carbohydrate-rich foods. Good snacks include low-fat oatmeal cookies, bananas, popcorn, and whole wheat crackers.

Turn to comfort foods. After studying women who craved sweets and fats, Adam Drewnowski, Ph.D., director of the nutritional sciences program at the University of Washington in Seattle, concluded that comfort foods serve only one basic function: stress relief. Certain foods stimulate the brain's opiate receptors, areas that trigger pleasant feelings. When Dr. Drewnowski gave the women an opiate-blocking drug, he found that their cravings melted like a candy bar on a hot sidewalk.

There are four main comfort food categories, says psychologist Doreen Virtue, Ph.D., author of *Constant Craving*. Women who crave ice cream, for instance, are very different from women who crave popcorn. See if you recognize yourself in the following categories.

❧ The chocoholic. Problem: You need more love. Chocolate contains chemicals that make you feel as though you're in love. To lift your spirits, take a whiff of fresh coffee; pleasant scents stimulate nerves in the body that trigger wakefulness.

❧ The ice cream fiend. Problem: You're depressed. Dairy foods contain chemicals that pull you out of the dumps. Try low-fat yogurts, skim milk smoothies, and cubes of cheese.

❧ The chip head. Problem: You're stressed, possibly because of a high-pressure job. Eating popcorn, pretzels, chips, and other salty, crunchy snacks is calming because you're gnawing out of anger, anxiety, and frustration. Gnaw on carrots, celery, broccoli, or cauliflower dipped in low-calorie, fat-free salad dressing.

❧ The sweet tooth. Problem: You're bored, so you gobble candy and other sugary snacks to make you feel more alive. Find a neighborhood fruit stand that sells fresh apples, peaches, and watermelon. The sugars in candy and in fruit are similar in that they are both nutritive sweeteners, and they provide similar amounts of energy. "At first, women think that fruit won't satisfy them, but that's because they've been eating poor-quality, store-bought fruit," Dr. Virtue says. "If they spend the extra money to get high-quality fruit, they won't consider it a compromise."

Pop some Bs. If you're feeling down, tense, and anxious, you may be deficient in the B-complex vitamins. These vitamins, which include thiamin, riboflavin, niacin, pantothenic acid, and vitamins B_6 and B_{12}, help us relax and lift our mood by raising levels of several of those all-important neurotransmitters. "Without them, we'd be nervous, irritable, and moody," says Dr. Larson. Vitamins B_2 (riboflavin) and B_6 (pyridoxine) in particular have been linked to higher spirits.

Boost your intake of vitamin B_6 by eating several servings daily of low-fat, protein-rich foods such as chicken, nuts, legumes, and fish. Other good sources include bananas, avocados, and dark green leafy vegetables. Eat whole grain breads and cereals, and brown or enriched rice. Look for a multivitamin supplement containing at least 2 milligrams of B_6. The safe upper limit is 100 milligrams, unless your doctor advises you to take more. Large doses of B_6 supplements can cause nerve damage, including numbness and tingling in your hands and feet.

Slurp some citrus. Vitamin C also increases levels of serotonin, dopamine, and norepinephrine, says Dr. Larson. What's more, vitamin C relieves stress by suppressing surges of adrenaline, the hormone our body pumps out when we face danger or a stressful situation. Too much adrenaline coursing through our veins leaves us feeling nervous and irritable. To get these benefits, however, you'd have to supplement with at least 2,000 milligrams of vitamin C a day in divided doses, says Dr. Larson. Excess vitamin C may cause diarrhea in some people; if that happens, cut back on your supplementation and try to get as much vitamin C as possible from food. Foods high in vitamin C include broccoli, brussels sprouts, strawberries, oranges, cantaloupe, kiwifruit, papaya, sweet potatoes, watermelon, and red bell peppers. You're likely to get over 500 milligrams of vitamin C simply by eating five to nine half-cup servings of fruit and vegetables a day.

INNER-SPACE EXPLORERS

Who was Matina Horner?

Psychologist Matina Horner, who served a 17-year post as president of Radcliffe College in Cambridge, Massachusetts, is well-known for her research on how gender differences influence people's drive for success. Horner conducted a classic study in 1968 from which she concluded that some women shy away from striving for success because they are socialized to believe competition and achievement are masculine traits. These women fear that success will make others view them as less feminine. For that reason, they underachieve, especially when competing with men, and may avoid socializing with successful women, Horner said.

This female fear of success, known as the Horner Effect, may not be as prominent in today's society as it was some 20 years ago, but as psychologist Barbara Kerr notes in her book *Smart Girls: A New Psychology of Girls, Women, and Giftedness*, "The Horner Effect may still live on in girls' and women's tendencies to negotiate or avoid conflict or competition when friendship or intimacy is at stake."

Pass on the refined sugar. If you are depressed, sugary treats may enhance your mood in the short term, but in the end, the depression inevitably returns. Why sugar has this effect on some people isn't clear. Some experts speculate that sugar produces a temporary release of feel-good chemicals called endorphins, which is followed by a crash as the endorphins plummet to lower-than-normal levels. What's more, your blood sugar levels also take a nosedive shortly after you eat sweets, which can make you irritable, says Dr. Larson. If you're hungry and you crave something sweet, mixing fruit with a bit of protein, such as pineapple with cottage cheese or frozen blueberries with fat-free yogurt, is your best bet, she says. You'll still satisfy your sweet tooth, but the protein will help balance the rise in blood sugar caused by the fruit's natural glucose.

Nix the caffeine. Coffee, tea, and soda serve as quick pick-me-ups that can boost your energy and increase alertness. But in the long run, the caffeine can make you jittery, anxious, and more tense. So if you're under a lot of stress, go for decaffeinated coffee or soda, herbal tea, water, or juice, says Dr. Larson.

PART THREE

The Truth Shall Set You Free

Turning Lead into Gold

For years, we've absorbed the message that emotions such as anger, fear, hurt, and envy are bad. That to feel them somehow makes us lesser women, "not nice," or "selfish." But, as we've already learned, hiding these emotions can be truly damaging not only to ourselves but to those around us.

The challenge, then, is to find a way to turn the negative energy of these emotions into positives. To do with our feelings what the ancient Romans were never quite able to do with their lead ingots: transform them into gold.

While they may be uncomfortable, anger and fear can energize us. Along with envy and hurt, they are powerful teachers. They are clues that we need to change something in our lives. Listening to them can give us the strength we need to transform ourselves into stronger, healthier women.

Anger into Action

So you're learning to cope with your anger by writing in your anger journal, talking about your feelings, and better understanding your anger style. You know now that you're a Nice Lady with bits of Dragon Lady mixed in, and it's been weeks since you expressed your rage at your husband by banging pots and pans instead of talking to him. Last month, when the hotel clerk couldn't find your reservation, you didn't even make her break down in tears. Now it's time to take the next step: Transform the energy and knowledge that anger brings into something worthwhile.

"A lot of us fight our anger," says Deborah Cox, Ph.D., psychologist, anger researcher, and assistant professor in the department of guidance and counseling at Southwest Missouri State University in Springfield. "But inwardly, we know that the 'Bitch' knows something. She understands her own power in a way that many of us are afraid to."

Are you angry at your boss for ignoring your skills and skipping you for a much-deserved promotion? Take a management-training course or learn a new computer skill, then apply for another job elsewhere in your company or outside it. Raging at your husband's inability to start dinner when he gets home before you? Corral him into spending a Sunday preparing casseroles and other dishes for the freezer that he can just pop into the oven.

This works with societal anger, too. Say you're furious at sneaker companies using overseas child labor to produce those $20 shoes. Channel your ire into letters or e-mail messages to legislators and top management at the offending company.

After all, the 3-million-member-strong Mothers Against Drunk Driving, which has toughened drunk-driving laws and penalties throughout the country, was formed on the back of one woman's rage.

Or maybe turn into an anger exhibitionist. Join a local theater group or take an acting class. You'll be forced to get in touch with all your emotions—even the ones you don't like. Try the irate Martha in Edward Albee's *Who's Afraid of Virginia Woolf?* or the unruly Katharina from Shakespeare's *The Taming of the Shrew.*

You can also bring the emotion of your anger into the visual world through art.

"Art can transform even the darkest emotions into something valuable, even beautiful," says Vivien D. Wolsk, Ph.D., executive director of the Gestalt Center for Psychotherapy and Training in New York City. "Painting, drawing, sculpting, and any other form of art can be used as a way to display those inner demons legitimately."

Forget about painting pink flowers and golden sunsets. When you're

PMS: MYTHS AND REALITIES

"Do you have PMS or something?"

All it takes is one outburst, and we're accused of being irrational women at the mercy of our hormones. Then we start questioning ourselves: Do I have a right to be mad, or am I letting my hormones control me?

With so many other things going on in our bodies and our lives, it can be hard to tell whether our emotions are a result of our cycles or not. Symptoms can occur up to 2 weeks before your period and there can be as many as 150 of them, says Shari L. Maxwell, M.D., F.A.C.O.G., division head physician of obstetrics and gynecology at Henry Ford Health System in Detroit. Here, she shatters some other myths about PMS.

Myth: There's no telling if my symptoms are a result of PMS.

Reality: By keeping a symptom diary for at least 2 months, you'll be able to keep track of mood swings and other symptoms. If they go away at the beginning of your cycle and come back during the 2 weeks before your next period, then they're a result of PMS.

Myth: PMS is a psychiatric disorder.

Reality: Only up to 5 percent of women have the severe form of PMS, called premenstrual dysphoric disorder.

Myth: I'm too emotional to make smart decisions during PMS.

Reality: Along with the more uncomfortable symptoms, women often experience intellectual clarity during premenstrual weeks, along with feeling happier.

Myth: Exercising can't help my emotional symptoms.

Reality: Exercise releases endorphins in your brain and stabilizes your mood, which means you're less likely to go from laughing to crying after your 30-minute walk.

Myth: My doctor won't believe my complaints.

Reality: Chances are, your female doctor will be able to relate to your symptoms just fine.

angry, embrace the dark colors and images of your mood. Follow Sylvia Plath's lead and create a poem so powerful that people will *have* to pay attention to your rage. Or take a lesson from mystery writer Sue Grafton and let your anger inspire you to write a short story or a novel. Grafton launched her successful career with the mystery *'A' Is for Alibi* while in the midst of a bitter divorce. The premise of the plot? The heroine's husband is murdered.

Anger into Forgiveness

Imagine a long steel chain wrapped around your ankle, dragging behind you everywhere you go, weighing you down, holding you back.

Now imagine the freedom you'd feel removing that chain—link by rusty link. That's what happens when you forgive. All of the energy you spent on anger, bitterness, and resentment suddenly reappears, providing an opportunity for emotional and physical healing to begin. And none too soon: Keeping these negative emotions bottled up inside you for months or years puts you at a higher risk for developing high blood pressure, heart disease, stroke, depression, or even cancer, says Norma Dearing, director of prayer ministry at the Christian Healing Ministries in Jacksonville, Florida.

"When you forgive, you're not letting the person who wronged you off the hook, you're really letting yourself off the hook," says the Reverend Linda Shaheerah Beatty, an ordained minister at Transforming Love Community Church in Detroit. "Forgiveness is letting go;

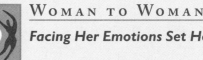

WOMAN TO WOMAN
Facing Her Emotions Set Her Free

Susan, a public relations consultant and freelance writer in central New Jersey, spent more than 4 decades disengaged from her emotions, leaving a wall between her and the rest of the world. Her father committed suicide when she was 9 years old, and her mother was physically and emotionally absent from her life. Not knowing how to love, she became rigid, hiding her pain with food and other excesses. While she was outwardly successful in her life and career, she felt disconnected from others, as if she didn't "belong," until she learned to experience her feelings. As a result, she transformed her life, leaving her happier and healthier, both physically and emotionally. Here's her story.

I didn't know how to deal with the pain of my father's death and the loneliness and rage I felt afterward, so I became closed off from my feelings at a young age. They were simply too painful. My mother didn't want the responsibility of my sister and me, so she took an evening job. She was never home after school and she slept in every morning. My grandparents moved in, but did very little parenting.

I was alone most of the time, with no one to tuck me into bed, comb my hair, or give me hugs. After my grandparents went to bed, I stuffed down my feelings with cookies and doughnuts. At home, I was a difficult, bratty little girl, but when I visited relatives who paid attention to me, they thought I was delightful.

I tried to gain my mother's attention by getting good grades and doing all the chores around the house after my grandparents moved out, but nothing worked. She was as incapable of giving love as I was of asking for it. As I grew

it's discovering what hurt us and healing those hurts."

Here is a step-by-step guide to who, what, where, when, and how to forgive.

Whom should you forgive? No matter how many people have hurt you, it's important to forgive everyone, even if they've never apolo-

older, I functioned well, but a deep emptiness permeated my life.

Later, I married a good man who, like my mother, didn't know how to fulfill my emotional needs. I reacted the same way I always had. I didn't know what those needs were and I didn't know how to ask for anything, so I buried my feelings with food and rigidity. After I made dinner, my husband and sons ate and disappeared into the den, leaving the cleanup to me. I ate everything in sight while doing the dishes.

The truth about my shut-off emotions dawned on me when I told a friend about my father and said, "He was very young when I died."

This led me to the therapy that gave me a new life. In therapy, I relived the pain from my past and learned that, by not letting my feelings out, I had been crippled by them.

Therapy also helped me understand that my mother had experienced great suffering of her own, which closed off her emotions.

My husband came to some counseling with me, but I knew that to move on, I had to put the past behind me, so we divorced.

Eventually, I became the person I am today, a woman who knows how to experience both the pain and the joy of life. When I'm hurt, I know how to say, "I need a hug." My relationship with my sons has become much warmer. On the rare occasions when I'm upset, I try to understand my pain instead of stuffing it down with chocolate. I'm a far happier woman now (and, incidentally, a thinner one) because I learned to recognize and live through the hurt and anger instead of trying to bury it under food and other excesses.

gized, says Reverend Beatty. "Most of the time, when people hurt us, they are acting out pain that they've endured in their lives. We just end up getting the brunt of it because we're in the line of fire."

What should you forgive? Betrayal, gossip, infidelity, broken promises, and even verbal and physical abuse. These offenses—and the people who committed them—may seem impossible to forgive at first, especially if you've lived with the pain for years. Just try to be patient and ask for divine help in the forgiving process. It may take longer for you to forgive an unfaithful husband than a gossiping friend. But that's okay. Once you start dealing with your past hurts and decide to release yourself from the anger, the guilt, and the shame, you'll begin to heal, says Dearing.

Where do you forgive? Face-to-face is probably best, says Reverend Beatty. "You can look into that person's eyes and soul. The true essence of you is going to speak even louder than your words. And if that doesn't work, you can always write a letter. They can read it over and over again, and they won't be able to add anything to your words," she says. A phone call can work well, too—but before deciding, consider the situation and the person you're forgiving.

When do you forgive? The best time to speak to someone is when you're not angry. It's always best to deal with your anger first, then approach the other person once you've calmed down. A good way to alleviate anger is to talk to a close friend about the situation. Getting it off your chest not only reduces tension but may also give you new insight, says Reverend Beatty.

How do you forgive? When confronting someone you want to forgive, explain how their actions or words made you feel. Use phrases such as "I felt hurt when you . . ." or "I felt betrayed when you . . ." The "I" phrases take the

REAL-LIFE SCENARIO

She's Afraid to Go Outdoors

Marcia, 56, has always led an active, full life. Two years ago, she saw the last of her children off to college and increased her hours at work. But last month, she finally had to quit. The problem: She feels as if she can't breathe every time she leaves the house. It's as if she's becoming a prisoner in her own house. What should she do?

Marcia probably had a panic attack while she was outside. Panic attacks come on when we're very stressed and include the symptoms she's had: shortness of breath, apprehension, fear, terror, heart palpitations, and nausea. They are so intense and powerful that some people think that if they go back outside, they'll have another one.

The cause of Marcia's attack could be the change in her life, whether it's not having the kids at home or facing a strain in her marriage as a result.

But feeling anxiety doesn't mean Marcia is bound to her house forever. A relaxation technique called systematic desensitization can help her venture out once again. Either with a cognitive-behavioral therapist or on her own, she can learn the art of deep relaxation by closing her eyes, breathing deeply and slowly, and relaxing all her muscles, particularly her facial muscles, until she feels them sag. She could pair this with a silent chant in her mind such as "I feel calm" or "I am a competent person."

Once she's relaxed, she should imagine going outside in a hierarchy of steps, starting with the lowest intensity, such as going into the garage. Then she can think about getting into her car, opening the garage door, starting the engine, pulling out of the garage, driving down the street, and eventually getting out of the car and walking outside.

It will probably take several sessions to be able to imagine all the steps without feeling anxious.

Expert consulted
Carolyn Saarni, Ph.D.
Professor of counseling
Sonoma State University
Rohnert Park, California

blame off the other person and focus on your feelings, says Reverend Beatty. You can also write daily forgiveness affirmations on paper that say something like "I forgive so-and-so for . . ." or "I forgive myself for . . ."

A Helpful Hint

If you like to pray, make a list of all the people you haven't forgiven and the hurtful things they've done to you, suggests Dearing. Give each person her own separate, but small, sheet of paper. You could also verbally state what everyone has done as you pile the sheets of paper in your hands. Put your hands together, and hold them up to God. Turn them over and release the papers and all of that pain and hurt to God, asking Him to take away the anger, resentment, and bitterness that you have in your heart. Then burn or throw away the papers.

Fear into Accomplishment

We wouldn't go to amusement parks and ride "The Whip" if we didn't like to be scared. Like anger, fear propels us into action by increasing our heart rate and blood pressure, tensing our muscles, sharpening our senses, and slowing our digestion.

But that doesn't mean we always enjoy the loops on the roller coaster of life.

Too often fear, or its cousin, anxiety, brings us screeching to a halt. Think about the time you became paralyzed at just the thought of giving a speech, going to a job interview, or even calling a potential new friend.

Although we're born with a built-in response to potentially life-threatening situations, the type of fear most of us confront these days is learned, says Lucy Papillon, Ph.D., a clinical and media psychologist and director of the Center of Light in Beverly Hills, California. Think about how fearless kids are, venturing into the unknown with boundless curiosity and wonder. It's only when they *touch* the stove that they learn it's hot. Or when they fall down on the ice that they realize that ice-skating can be painful.

We learn to avoid certain situations in the same way. We have one bad experience, and the next time we're thrown into a situation where we don't know what to expect or how we'll be received, we freeze.

The key is not only moving beyond the fear to give the speech, go to the interview for the job, or call the new neighbor, but using the fear to do an even better job than we thought possible at what scares us.

Start by releasing the fear: Tell a friend exactly why you're afraid. Simply saying it out loud often makes anxiety disappear like a cat at a dog show. Listen to your friend as she bulks up your ego, reassuring you that how you appear to others—the audience, the employer, the new neighbor—matters little in the overall scheme of the great woman you already are. (This is what friends are for; don't worry, your turn will come.)

Then, list all the reasons you're so nervous. Are you afraid the interviewer is going to ask you a question about the company that you can't answer? Spend time beforehand researching it. Call for annual reports, check out its Web site, and talk to others in the same business. Have your friend walk you through a mock interview.

Are you worried about that speech? Videotape yourself presenting it before a mirror. You'll not only be surprised at how polished you appear, you'll be able to find any small flaws and fix them before the real event.

Always ask yourself: What's the worst thing that can happen if I do this? When Marcia Reynolds, author of the audiotape *Being in the Zone: The Secrets of Personal Excellence*, wanted to quit her regular job and start her own business, she was petrified at the thought of failure. But when she analyzed her feelings, she realized that the worst thing that could happen was she'd find another job and have another boss. She plunged ahead and today is a successful personal coach in Phoenix.

Finally, revel in the adrenaline rush that fear brings. It means you're alive and anything is possible.

Hurt into Self-Awareness

Like fear, hurt also paralyzes us. We avoid friends when they forget our birthdays. We give our husbands the silent treatment when they neglect to notice a new hairstyle. We ignore coworkers who steal our ideas.

Drawing into ourselves, like a turtle hiding in its shell, only damages us more. "Our world gets smaller," Dr. Papillon says. "Instead of knowing that we live in a big mansion, we begin to exist in one room, metaphorically speaking. That is, we shut down huge aspects of ourselves, thinking we are protecting ourselves."

But as with fear and anger, we can use hurt to move forward in our lives, to learn more about ourselves, and to make the changes necessary to avoid pain in the future.

If we have a healthy respect for ourselves and strong self-esteem, we don't allow the hurt to penetrate us, says Dr. Papillon. That's difficult for many women, who are used to drawing their

INNER-SPACE EXPLORERS
Who was Eric Berne?

After failing to be accepted into the psycho-analytic fraternity in 1956, American psychiatrist Eric Berne created a new approach to psychotherapy known as trans-actional analysis. He designed this therapy to help people communicate better and improve how they give and take compliments and criticism.

He theorized that our personalities are made up of three "ego states": parent, adult, and child. Each one has an entire system of thoughts, feelings, and behaviors that determines how we interact with others. Berne also believed we need "strokes," or recognition, to survive and thrive.

But he is best known for his book *Games People Play*, which enjoyed great popularity in the 1960s. In this book, Berne described the patterns of socially dysfunctional be-havior or games we use to get recognition. It's as if we un-consciously and repeatedly live out the script of a play that was written from our childhood expectations and decisions. Berne gave the games distinct names such as "Why Don't You, Yes But," "Now I've Got You, You SOB," and "I'm Only Trying to Help You." The problem with these games, he said, is that they reinforce negative feelings and self-concepts while masking our true thoughts, wants, and needs. Trans-actional analysis, in turn, helps us recognize the games we play so we can begin interacting without them.

Berne's transactional analysis is now used by some 7,000 therapists throughout the world, and the International Transactional Analysis Association he established in 1964 continues to offer certification and training to over 3,000 members.

her he loved her, told her, "You make me sick. Get out of my face." He made her feel empty, as if she were nothing, but she stayed silent. She stayed through 2 years of his lies and her tears, occasionally thinking she deserved better, but burying those thoughts under the cotton wool of self-doubt. Until one day, as she listened to a patient de-scribe *her* abusive relationship, Dr. Papillon saw the similarities to her own life.

Thus began intense introspection, in which Dr. Papillon, who inte-grates spirituality and psychology into her practice, began to under-stand that she accepted whatever men told her about herself—nega-tive as well as positive—because she craved their attention. With that self-knowledge, she was able to stand up for herself and leave the abusive boyfriend. She accepted that she was smart, attractive, and suc-cessful, and that the only opinion that mattered was her own. Since then, she has put the steps she took to move from pain to power into her book, *When Hope Can Kill: Re-claiming Your Soul in a Romantic Relationship*.

"The mark of any good relation-ship is that you come away from it feeling better about yourself," says Elizabeth Herron, coauthor of *What Women and Men Really Want: Creating Deeper Understanding and Love in Our Relationships* and director of the Gender Relations Institute in Santa Barbara, California. "If someone makes you feel diminished and you have lower self-

sense of self from others. So in many cases, al-lowing ourselves to be hurt is a signal that we need to strengthen our own self-esteem.

That's what happened to her.

She once dated a man who, hours after telling

esteem when you're with them, they're not a good friend."

So trust your instincts when you meet someone new. Do your stomach and chest tighten when you're around them? Do you somehow feel uncomfortable, even though you can't put your finger on why? Does their teasing take on a hint of cruelty? Answer yes to any of these questions and you should be walking away from that relationship.

If you're already enmeshed with this person, consider your hurt and pain as a red flag that something's wrong. Also examine your own reactions to the hurt. Do you close that person out? Jump from relationship to relationship? Slam doors because you can't express your pain? Consider these actions signals that something's got to change.

Then next time, instead of giving your husband the silent treatment, tell him that you feel unimportant in his life when he doesn't tell you he'll be home late. If you avoid statements like "Look what you've done to me," he'll probably be less defensive. And this way, you're redirecting your hurt into assertiveness.

If someone belittles you, take control with your own voice by saying, "I'm not stupid (or fat or slow or whatever other ugly thing they're calling you)."

One way to find the courage to stand up for yourself is to conjure up an image of someone you know loves you. What would your mother, daughter, or great-grandmother say about the way this person is treating you? It might be easier to hear your mother tell you to break off a relationship than it is to tell yourself, says Dr. Papillon.

ALL IN THE GENES?

Why do I sweat when I'm nervous?

When we're nervous, we feel threatened, whether we think we might say something stupid in a job interview or we might trip on the steps to a stage where we're giving a speech. That type of stress puts our sympathetic nervous system into action, triggering the fight-or-flight mechanism. Several changes that we have no control over happen then: Our hearts beat faster, our body heat rises, and we start sweating. The sweat helps us cool off and keep a normal body temperature.

Expert consulted
Lila A. Wallis, M.D., M.A.C.P.
Clinical professor of medicine
Weill Medical College of Cornell University
New York City
Author of The Whole Woman: Take Charge
of Your Health in Every Phase of Your Life

Most important, says Dr. Papillon, "tell yourself, '*I'm* going to be here for me. And I'm the one that must stay on my own side, no matter what.'"

Envy into Understanding

If jealousy is a green-eyed monster, then envy is a crystal-clear mirror, because looking at what we envy gives us clues about what we need to be happy.

You're on the treadmill at the gym dripping in sweat when a taller, slimmer woman saunters past in skintight bike shorts. Suddenly, you feel like a stuffed turkey in your oversize sweatsuit, and the 5 pounds you've lost over the past month seems like the tip of the Everest-size mound of weight you still have to lose. Why, you wonder, do I have to work so hard so stay in

ALL IN THE GENES?

What makes the hair rise on our arms and necks when we're frightened?

We've all seen Halloween images of black cats with their hair raised to look frightening. Well, that's probably why we feel the hair rise on our arms and necks, too. Back in the days when hair covered our entire bodies, it helped us look larger and more intimidating to an attacker.

Adrenaline is the real culprit. When we're frightened and adrenaline is released into the bloodstream to give us energy to fight or flee, it tightens the muscles that hold our hair follicles. Even though today our hair is softer and shorter and doesn't look very intimidating when it's raised, we still have that natural reflex.

Expert consulted
Lila A. Wallis, M.D., M.A.C.P.
Clinical professor of medicine
Weill Medical College of Cornell University
New York City
Author of The Whole Woman: Take Charge
of Your Health in Every Phase of Your Life

garden or paint your walls to give yourself at least some of what you're craving right now.

Then expand your vision. Think about how you would like life to be in 1, 5, or 10 years. Be very specific: What city would you like to live in? What kind of house will you have? What type of friends or job?

Write it all down and tuck a copy in your purse, pin one to your bulletin board, and put one on the refrigerator door. To make your statement even more visual, create a collage of pictures of everything you want to accomplish in the next year and display it prominently in your office or home. It will serve as an instant motivator to keep brown-bagging it so you can afford that vacation or to go to your class that night because you need the degree for a better job.

Then, instead of drowning in envy, you're riding its waves toward a better life.

Jealousy into Love

You know that nobody's perfect, especially your husband's ex-wife. But it infuriates you that they're still friends. It bothers you even to see them talking together. You can just picture them running away, hopping on a jet, and writing you a "Dear Joan" letter from a nude beach in Jamaica.

That's jealousy, a complex mix of anger, sadness, and fear that can cause irrational, uncontrollable behavior, such as spying on his whereabouts or calling him a half-dozen times a day at work and demanding to know his every move.

shape while *she* barely breaks a sweat and looks like that?

You can't change your body shape or height overnight. But you can mimic that woman's posture, hold yourself as tall as she does, and buy some slimming new spandex workout outfits.

Pay attention to what's unique about you, too. She might be tall and slender, but you have beautiful, curvy legs.

Sometimes we covet things because we *can* have them, we just don't know it. Envying a friend her new house but know there's no way you could take on a mortgage that big? Break down your envy into its specific components.

Is it the big house or the nice garden you really want? The extra bathrooms, or the pristine rooms of a brand-new house? You can plant a

You may believe it's a sign of devotion. But unless you have good reason to believe your husband is fooling around, you're dead wrong. Jealousy is as corrosive as battery acid. When you turn into an inquisitor, it eats away at the core of your marriage. Monogamous men resent being mistrusted, so they withdraw and become more protective of their privacy. This sets in motion a vicious circle in which their wives become even more panicky, paradoxically increasing the likelihood that their worst fears will come true.

"Jealous women are hard to live with. In their jealousy, they drive their husbands away," says psychologist Paul Hauck, Ph.D., of Rock Island, Illinois, author of *Overcoming Jealousy and Possessiveness*. To help control your jealous tendencies, try the following strategies.

Turn the tables. If you have a habit of frequently calling your husband at work, stop and make him play the role of jealous spouse. Have him call you a half-dozen times a day to ask what you're wearing, whom you've been with, and whether you still love him. "The men love it because they've been on the receiving end for so long," says Ayala Malach Pines, Ph.D., professor of psychology at Ben-Gurion University in Beer-Sheva, Israel, and author of *Romantic Jealousy: Causes, Symptoms, Cures*. "The wives also like it because their husbands are making the effort to call. For them, jealousy is a show of love."

Try aversion therapy. "A jealous response is a learned response, and you can unlearn it," Dr. Pines says. "So whenever jealousy rears its head, take a whiff of smelling salts." Available at pharmacies, smelling salts are a combination of alcohol and ammonia sold in little glass ampules. Popped open, they release a noxious smell to revive someone who has fainted. Sniff some whenever you feel jealous; eventually, your brain will so strongly associate jealousy with the smell that it'll erase jealous thoughts before they can come into your conscious awareness. Just be careful not to inhale too deeply because it could bring on a coughing fit.

Reach Out and Touch

We're grown women, with children and credit cards, husbands and houses. We manage projects, budgets, carpools. Yet among our multiple multitasking skills, there seems to be one we haven't yet fully mastered: making and maintaining meaningful connections with the most important people in our lives.

Maybe we're shy. Toss us into an unfamiliar crowd and we feel as if we're reliving the first day of high school as "the new girl," regardless of the power suit and Palm Pilot. But even if we're the life of the party, we may still withdraw like a turtle into our shell when someone brings up anything more emotionally loaded than how much water to add to the Hamburger Helper.

"We tend to be self-protective," says Beverly Steinfeld, Ph.D., a clinical social worker and psychotherapist in Pittsburgh. "We resist trying anything that may cause us danger, rejection, or pain." And that means intimacy. It's an understandable reaction: Revealing our thoughts and emotions can feel like we're taking a psychological bungee jump.

If intimacy is so scary, why take the leap? Because it's good for us (although the same argument could *not* be made for bungee jumping). We make friends. We bond with our family. We deepen our relationship with our partner. And we end up healthier, happier women than before.

Love's Healing Power

When we were children, we knew who to find when we were hurt: Dr. Mom. She could magically cure our scraped knees with nothing more than a kiss.

She knew instinctively what researchers are just now beginning to discover: Love heals.

"People don't do as well in their lives when they're isolated and hanging from a tree limb," says Barbara Saltzstein, M.S.W., a psychotherapist in Cambridge, Massachusetts, and a lecturer on psychiatry at the Harvard Medical School, who found that women with chronic fatigue syndrome were more hopeful and healthy if they had support from friends, spouses, and especially their physicians. When we're lonely, we're more likely to die of a heart attack, to be problem drinkers, or to visit the emergency room.

In contrast, if we have strong support networks, we're more likely to experience the following benefits.

We live longer. This applies even to women with serious illnesses. One groundbreaking study found that women with breast cancer who went to a weekly support group lived twice as long as women who didn't.

We strengthen our immune systems. One study found that the more types of relationships (friends, family, colleagues, church members, neighbors, and so on) a woman had, the less likely she was to catch a cold.

We reduce our risk of heart disease. Just telling your husband that you love him may lessen his chances of heart pain, even if he has other risk factors such as high cholesterol or high blood pressure. The same is true for women.

We remain calm in stressful situations. Remember how your heart pounded the last time you had to give a speech? Next time, ask a friend to attend for moral support. Both your heart rate and blood pressure may stay lower than if you go it alone.

We recover from stress faster. We will probably still panic when we're presented with an unexpected deadline or other stressful event, but our blood pressure and heart rate may return to normal faster if we have a strong support network on which we can rely.

SETTING BOUNDARIES

In today's let-it-all-hang-out society, no question is too personal to ask—or answer. Over lunch, a coworker reveals the sexual problems of her short-lived marriage. Mom fishes around for your dress size. Neighbors ask how much money you put down on your house.

All this querying makes New York psychiatrist Ann Turkel, M.D., want to ask a question of her own: "Why do you want to know the answer to that?"

When it comes to personal boundaries, she says, "we walk around with blinders on," neither respecting other people's rights nor enforcing our own. We can't learn to trust if we don't know where to draw the line, says Dr. Turkel.

"When you've got healthy boundaries, it's safer to take a risk on intimacy," says Beverly Steinfeld, Ph.D., a clinical social worker and psychotherapist in Pittsburgh.

"Healthy psychological boundaries are like skin," says Dr. Steinfeld. "They protect us. They're flexible. They're permeable." And they're very individual. Your best friend may be perfectly comfortable sharing her family's finances, whereas you classify your home phone number as "personal." That's okay. We simply need to know where our personal lines in the sand lie and when to defend them with respectful assertiveness.

Here's how to draw your lines.

Listen to your gut. If something just doesn't feel right, such as your neighbor's question about the down payment, it probably isn't.

Keep quiet. "We seem to have been raised to think that if someone asks us a question, we have to answer it," Dr. Turkel says. We don't. Raise your eyebrow, give your interrogator a pointed look, or turn the tables and ask with a smile, "Why do you want to know?"

Follow the Golden Rule. Would you feel uneasy if your friend or colleague told you what you're about to tell them? If so, stop.

Speak up. Urgent problems require urgent action. If a neighbor appears at your door with a sick 8-year-old on the day you'd planned to work at home, tell her you're sorry, but you can't care for her child today.

WOMEN ASK WHY

Why do I always feel that "if I don't do it, it won't get done"?

Because we set ourselves up. Every time we pick up toys and clothes off the floor, we're teaching family members that they don't need to do their part because we'll do it anyway.

Our family's reluctance to help may be legitimate. If we're constantly criticizing their efforts or redoing the job when they're done because we have such high expectations, they're doomed to fail to meet our standards. Yet we like imposing these standards. It puts us in the role of boss, which can be very appealing to women who don't have any other personal or professional opportunities to exert power.

And maybe we *like* feeling that we're more responsible and more conscientious than everyone else; it may be part of our identity. But for things to change, we need to reject that martyr role. (For help doing that, see Belle of the Masquerade Ball on page 42.)

If you're feeling exploited by the unfair division of labor in your household, you need to ask yourself what *you're* getting from the status quo and then decide what you're prepared to give up: your role as martyr, perfectionist, and boss, or some help around the house.

Expert consulted
Catherine Chambliss, Ph.D.
Professor of psychology
Department chair
Ursinus College
Collegeville, Pennsylvania

We can overcome depression. In one study, more than 75 percent of chronically depressed women who were befriended by a volunteer significantly improved within a year, compared with 39 percent of a similar group who weren't befriended.

We choose healthier lifestyles. Studies show that people with strong support systems are more likely to quit smoking, lose weight, and exercise.

Roadblocks to Love and Connection

Although we may long for connections to others, our reaction to people, especially men, sometimes echoes Groucho Marx's famous line about refusing to belong to any club that would want people like him as a member.

"We think, 'If this person loves me, there must be something wrong with them,'" says Lisa Firestone, Ph.D., a clinical psychologist and education and program director for the Glendon Association in Santa Barbara, California. Their love makes us feel exposed. Uncomfortable with our own vulnerability, we close ourselves off from intimate relationships.

We may choose men who are wrong for us, opting for chemistry over compatibility. But when the good sparks fade, "the relationship becomes polarized and the couple start to hate each other for the same qualities they were initially drawn to," Dr. Firestone says.

Sometimes we do choose caring, responsible men who love us in return. They may even bring out qualities we didn't know we had. Dr. Firestone had a client who always thought of herself as a hard-boiled, tough career woman. Yet with her partner, she turned into a superaffectionate, loving woman who greeted him at the door each evening with hugs and kisses. Her partner loved that she was so sweet, and told her so. That's when she panicked and completely withdrew from him. Her self-identity threatened, she responded by withholding the affection he cherished.

Sometimes, we provoke conflict, spurring our partner to say aloud all the negative things we believe internally but refuse to confront. "It's more comfortable to fight it out with them than to deal with our own divided feelings about ourselves," Dr. Firestone says.

Discarding our emotional armor can be frightening. But you don't have to strip all at once. You can ease into intimacy the same way you would enter an icy pool: starting with your big toe and very slowly going deeper until you're totally submerged. "Intimacy requires risk," says Dr. Steinfeld. "You can't have true intimacy without revealing your vulnerabilities."

It starts by reaching out. Ask a coworker to lunch. Tell your husband you miss the walks you used to take. Invite your mother for a (short) visit. Share with your sister your dream to become a painter. You'll never have the intimacy you want without stretching out your own hand.

Portrait of a Healthy Relationship

From the blue screen to the silver screen, and everywhere in

MEN, WOMEN, AND STRESS: UNDERSTANDING THE GENDER DIFFERENCE

When it comes to stress, men and women are not created equal.

First, different events stress us out. While men worry most about losing a job or getting a pay cut, we fret about situations happening in the lives of those we love, such as our mother's arthritis, our best friend's marriage, or our children's academic problems. "People tend to get stressed out the most by whatever they're responsible for," says Catherine M. Stoney, Ph.D., professor of psychology at Ohio State University in Columbus.

Second, our physiological response to stress is different from a man's. Our blood pressure doesn't go up as high, even after accounting for the fact that women tend to have lower blood pressure than men. Our heart rate doesn't increase as much. And neither does our cholesterol level, which represents a major risk factor for heart disease. We release fewer stress hormones, such as adrenaline and noradrenaline, that prepare the body for "fight or flight." All of this helps us live longer than men.

Female hormones may play a protective role. If postmenopausal women are on hormone replacement therapy (HRT), their blood pressure goes up about the same as that of young women when confronted with a stressful situation. But those not on HRT show blood pressure levels that increase nearly as much as a man's.

Still, stress takes a toll on us. We're more frequently sick, take more sick days (even after accounting for childbirth and our children's sick days), go to the doctor more often, and get more minor infections, from colds to the flu, than men do.

Why? Since we're primarily the ones running the household (in addition to running the children around), we have elevated levels of stress, which can negatively affect our bodies' systems. As a result, our immune systems don't function the way they should, and we become more vulnerable to disease.

WOMEN ASK WHY

Why do women stay in abusive relationships?

Actually, most women don't stay. If you look at many of the well-publicized cases, the women have left in multiple ways and at multiple times, but the abuser has dragged them back by threatening to kill them. In fact, the likelihood of murder increases when a couple in an abusive relationship separate.

The problem with asking why women stay is that it reframes the abuse as their problem, implying that if they would just leave, it would all go away. But batterers don't stop abusing just because a woman has left. They leave telephone threats. They come to women's workplaces. They argue about visitation with the children.

Domestic violence is much more common than we like to believe. Batterers may be our pastors, our doctors, or the neighborhood cop. And their victims may be very strong, professionally savvy women. In fact, women who are abused tend to be superior in economic standing and training to the men who abuse them. That's one reason for the abuse: Their partner feels threatened.

Abuse also occurs on a continuum, and it's often hard to know at what point you should leave. Is it when your partner pounds the wall with his fist? When he throws something? And then there are complicating factors such as the fact that you still love him and you have children together.

And where do you go for help? Society doesn't support women breaking up the family. Churches certainly don't. Sometimes, a battered woman is economically dependent on the abuser.

The law can make a difference. Although stories about women who were killed despite protection orders get the publicity, most times, protection orders work.

Expert consulted
Joan Meier, J.D.
Director, Domestic Violence Advocacy Project
George Washington University Law School
Washington, D.C.

between, we're bombarded by images of happy couples. On the television series *Mad about You*, we watched newlyweds Paul and Jamie Buchman adjust to married life with humor and grace. In the pages of *People* magazine, we read the dish about celebrity couples from Warren Beatty and Annette Bening to Paul Newman and Joanne Woodward. Finally, there are our parents, who shaped our romantic ideas of what marriage is like in a real-world way, for better or for worse.

Despite all of these images, we often still don't know what a healthy relationship looks like, much less how to create one. It's an equal-opportunity problem, says Dr. Firestone. "Men want intimacy just as much as women do. But they don't know how to get it either."

Here's a place to start, with guidelines for qualities to seek in your relationship and yourself and actions to take when things get off track.

Honesty. When we talk about honesty and its flip side in relationships, we often think of the most extreme betrayal: extramarital affairs. But our everyday truth-fudging, from covering our overspending at the mall last week to swallowing our hurt about his forgetting our anniversary, also damages the integrity of the relationship over time. "Our actions need to match our words," says Dr. Firestone.

Affection. When couples grow apart, sex becomes infrequent and unsatisfying. "To connect, sexuality needs to be personal," Dr. Firestone says. "When people are making eye contact, they're still relating." So look your partner in the eye when you compliment him. Hug him when he comes home from work. Hold his hand at the movies.

Openness. Be receptive to new ideas in whatever form they come. If your partner wants the two of you to try sailing, go for it. This principle applies to more than just activities, though. If your partner needs to talk about his frustration with the long hours you're working, let him speak—without getting defensive yourself. In both situations, maintaining an open mind helps keep the relationship alive and growing even in challenging times.

Empathy. Few things soothe us more than pouring out our troubles to someone who loves and understands us. Be that person to your partner and ask him to be that person for you.

Individuality. As a couple, it's easy to slip into "we" language. "We like the movies." "We like museums." "We like spending Sunday afternoons at my mother's house." But if you constantly finish his sentences, you'll never find out what he really thinks. There can be such a thing as too much togetherness, says Dr. Firestone. "It's important to see each other as separate people." Otherwise, she says, "We start to see the other person only in relation to how they can meet our needs. Once we

ALL IN THE GENES?
Are women hardwired for monogamy?

When we talk about the origins of sexual behavior, it's important to keep in mind that we're talking about a society that lived a million years ago. And, if our theories are right, none of these behaviors resulted from conscious decision making. They just happened to be behaviors that, many years later, resulted in more descendants than other behaviors.

Given that framework, the answer to the question is no. As compared with men, some women, under certain circumstances, may be more monogamous, but I wouldn't say women in general are hardwired for monogamy.

Women have extramarital affairs. Women have multiple sexual partners during their lives, just as men do. Women may do this on average less than men, but this difference doesn't prove they're genetically monogamous.

In addition, there's some new research that argues that women evolved with one of two sexual styles.

The first group of women is more hardwired for monogamy because they evolved with a preference for mates with resources who could provide what was needed to raise and protect children. Today, this might mean a man wearing an expensive suit or driving a Porsche. In ancient times, it might have meant a good hunter who could feed the family.

The second group of women increased their reproductive success by being less restrictive sexually. They took multiple partners, giving their children the benefit of genetic diversity and greater potential for immunity should disease strike. These women also allowed their male partners to take other female partners, which means they were willing to give up their sexual access to these superior men temporarily in return for the chance to mate with them.

Bottom line: When it comes to sexual behavior, there's a lot of variability in both men and women.

Expert consulted
Diane Berry, Ph.D.
Professor of psychology
Southern Methodist University
Dallas

WOMAN TO WOMAN
Love Caused Her Spiritual Rebirth

From the outside, Ann looked as if she had it all. She operated her own thriving business, competed in triathlons, and had a serious boyfriend, who'd given her a diamond-studded ring from Tiffany's. Then her world came crashing down. A close relative died. She broke up with her boyfriend. She had a miscarriage. Lost in anger and self-doubt, she deepened her yoga practice. Now 37, Ann, who lives in northeastern Pennsylvania, says she's rediscovered love and spirituality as a result. Here is her story.

When I was living in the city, I was in a pretty bad relationship. My boyfriend was an all-around loser: He pretended to be nice and sweet, but he had a nasty edge. He was jealous of my friends and family. He wanted to control my time and my career. We fought a lot. But I thought everything would be okay. He'd given me a ring; I thought we'd get married some day.

Then I got pregnant with his baby. When he said he didn't want children, we broke up for good. At my first prenatal visit, I had a miscarriage.

My grandfather had died only a few weeks before. It was hard to go through a breakup, the loss of a dear family member, and then the loss of an unborn child.

With friends and family, though, I pulled myself together. I decided to take classes in yoga, which I'd been practicing on my own for years. I even went to a weeklong retreat at a yoga ashram in the Catskills.

An ashram is where people, young and old, single and in families, go to heal: They meditate, chant, practice yoga. I thought immediately that this was where I belonged, and that these were the loving people I needed to be around.

When I returned to the city, I soon realized that I didn't want to live the kind of stressed-out life I'd been leading. I went to California to learn how to teach yoga. I took a spiritual journey to India. I connected with an old friend, who was also rediscovering yoga. We fell in love and got married, and still practice yoga together daily.

It's been a slow process, but I finally feel spiritually centered. I love myself. I believe in a higher power.

do that, we lose our attraction to them."

Communication. Too many couples go out to eat at a restaurant and converse more with the waiter than they do with each other, Dr. Firestone says. Instead, share the highlights of your day and ask your partner about his.

Freshness. At the beginning of a relationship, we do all those sweet things like exchanging funny cards, making special meals, and buying small gifts. Don't let those gestures disappear as the relationship deepens. These are the kinds of things that prevent us from taking our partners for granted. Another suggestion is to go back in time to the dates you had when you first met: walks, bike rides, trips to the ice cream shop. "They don't cost much money, and there's much more opportunity to talk than at the movies," Dr. Firestone says. Don't have time? Everyday activities such as shopping for groceries and reading the newspaper together can boost your connection to the one you love if you use them as opportunities to share time and thoughts with each other.

Support. When it comes to emotional support, men and women follow different playbooks. We want a shoulder to cry on; he wants to tell us how to fix it. Yet, "instead of talking about what they need, women think their husbands just don't care," says Susan Lynch, Ph.D., director of the bachelor of social work program at the University of Arkansas at Little Rock. So ask your partner, "How do you show me you love me?" Maybe he waxes your car by hand every 2 weeks. Perhaps he lets you have the first shower in the mornings, while the water's still steaming hot. Once we realize how *they* express their love, and begin to ask for what we need in return, we won't feel so neglected.

Reciprocity. If you're doing all the reaching out and the work on a relationship, you will eventually burn out if you don't get something back. Make certain that your friends and family also care for you in return.

Navigating the Emotional Minefields

So you're in a good relationship, things are going along fairly smoothly, and then you decide you want to go back to school. Or quit your job and freelance. Or shift the balance of power in the relationship by taking over the finances. You're about to build some major speed bumps in the smooth highway of that relationship. "We wonder: Can they accept this about me?" says Dr. Steinfeld.

They can—if you approach them in an open, honest way. Here are some other suggestions to keep in mind.

Give warning. Don't spring the news that you're returning to the workforce the day before you start a

INNER-SPACE EXPLORERS
Who is Ellen Langer?

Ellen Langer, a social psychologist at Harvard University, believes that we spend much of our lives unconsciously living instead of mindfully living. In her book *The Power of Mindful Learning*, she argues that we need to be conscious of what we do, whether typing a memo or folding laundry, instead of simply doing tasks because they're routine.

Thinking about what we're doing, she says, will enable us to enjoy the experience more.

Langer compares mindfulness to play. When people are at play, she says, they are mindfully engaged, learning something new. For instance, if you did a crossword puzzle and then did it again, knowing all the answers, it wouldn't be fun. If you went to the theater and watched a performance exactly the same way you did the first time, intentionally seeing nothing new, you wouldn't enjoy yourself. The essence of having fun is noticing new things: being mindful.

When we're mindless, however, we're trapped in a single perspective. We behave like automatons, without any choices, without any uncertainty. Langer believes that we have to keep open the possibility of uncertainty, because if we think there's a best way to do something and we've learned that best way, there's no need to pay attention to what we're doing anymore. So certainty often kills mindfulness.

Plus, Langer says, the more mindful you are, the more you pay attention to what you're doing or learning, and the more you'll remember. This is not the same thing as memorizing. Memorization, she says, is the epitome of mindlessness.

In her book, she tells a story about an Air Florida plane in Washington, D.C., leaving for Florida one winter day. The pilot and copilot were going through the checklist before takeoff, a mindless routine as they called off one item after the other. Even though there was snow in Washington, however, the anti-icing device was mindlessly turned off, and the plane crashed. Her point is that the pilots had practiced to the point of not being there, so they were unable to make corrections and adjustments to their routine.

INNER-SPACE EXPLORERS

Who was Anna Freud?

Sigmund Freud's youngest daughter, Anna, was also a prominent figure in psychology. But while Sigmund focused on psychoanalyzing adults, Anna led the way in child and teen therapy. The former elementary school teacher developed child psychoanalysis in the 1920s, and later founded and directed the Hampstead Child Therapy Clinic in London, where she conducted much of her research.

Anna encouraged long-term studies of children from their early years through their teens, urged analysts to pool their findings, and was a pioneer of natural experiments, which involved studying groups of children with similar disabilities such as blindness. Anna also concluded that in order for a child therapist not to undermine the parents' authority, it is best to play the role of caring adult rather than playmate or substitute parent.

While Anna remained faithful to her father's basic ideas, she was more interested in the conscious, or ego, than the unconscious. Her best-known work, *The Ego and the Mechanisms of Defense*, describes the defense mechanisms we use both as teens and as adults and how they work. Her focus on the conscious led to a movement called ego psychology, which built upon her father's theories so they could be applied to more practical day-to-day issues.

new job. You need to prepare your partner in much the same way you'd prepare the soil before planting a garden. Begin talking about your desire to go back to work even before you start job hunting. That gives him time to adjust and both of you an opportunity to brainstorm what this will involve.

Write a letter. "You can take all the time you need to choose your words and make your points, without worrying about being interrupted or getting distracted," says Dr. Steinfeld. Your partner also receives time and privacy to react to your thoughts. You still need to talk with each other; the letter is a catalyst, not a substitute, for conversation.

Be patient. Other people aren't always as emotionally prepared as we are for the shifts we want to make in our lives. So give them time to adjust to the new game plan. As long as you're both committed to making things work, you'll find a solution together that you can both accept.

When Your Inner Genius Comes Out to Play

While going through an ugly divorce, Mary Rockwood Lane was enraged and depressed, so she did what many women do in that situation: She went into therapy. Somehow, though, the counseling didn't even begin to touch her pain.

Then, while flipping through a magazine, Lane, then a 36-year-old nurse from Gainesville, Florida, saw a picture of a "broken and distorted" woman. That's exactly how I feel, she thought. And an irresistible urge came over her to paint that woman.

With her first strokes of paint on canvas, Lane began to heal. She'd never considered herself an artist before, but at that moment, the anguish from her divorce eclipsed her fear of inadequacy as a painter.

As Lane learned, creativity resides deep inside all of us, like a bottomless cache of fresh, pure water, waiting to be unearthed. Letting it out will help us not only paint pictures but also shape our self-images, cope with stress, banish boredom, and heal emotional and physical ailments.

The science behind the process goes like this:

Our brains have left and right sides. The left side specializes in verbal and mathematical reasoning and logic. It allows us to read, write, do math, analyze, and schedule time. The right side specializes in visual and spatial perception. When activated, it triggers our autonomic nervous systems, which control our heart and breathing rates.

It also triggers the release of feel-good endorphins and other hormones that relieve pain, help us relax, and boost our immune systems.

"True creativity relies on the use of both sides of the brain," says Lucia Capacchione, Ph.D., an art therapist in Santa Monica, California, and author of *Visioning: Ten Steps to Designing the Life of Your Dreams*. Why? Right-brain flights of imagination need left-brain structure to make them reality.

Healing is their natural by-product.

More than likely, you've tapped into your creative genius several times today without even knowing it. Each time you whip up a casserole without a recipe, or make a stranger feel at home, you're being creative. Sure, they're part of the "lighter" levels of creativity that frequently go

Her Friends Think Her Hobby Is Too Weird

Mary Ellen, 42, has always loved to make things. In the past, her hobbies have included needlepoint, sewing, hand-painting sweatshirts, and designing floral arrangements. But her newest hobby is garnering some strange looks from friends. On the Internet, she learned about making modeling clay out of dryer lint, and now she has boxes of the fuzzy stuff in her basement. She spends nights and weekends making the clay, then shaping it into animals, bowls, and mugs to sell at craft shows. Her friends think she's getting too weird: It isn't normal to play with dust in the basement. But she finds her hobby relaxing, inexpensive, and fun. Who's right?

It sounds as if Mary Ellen has discovered a new creative modality that excites her, and she's having fun with it. It clearly fascinates her, and who knows where it will lead. Unfortunately, it sounds as if her friends are uncomfortable with her choice of material and perhaps a bit jealous of how much time she spends on her creative projects. Mary Ellen has to decide whether or not these friends are valuable enough in her life to make time to spend with them. If they are, she should carve out some regular time to spend together. If not, perhaps she needs some new friends who are more supportive of her creativity. If that's the case, she could join a local arts organization, take some classes, or surf the Internet to connect with other artistic souls. Above all, she should stay true to her passions.

Expert consulted
Gail McMeekin, L.C.S.W.
Author of The 12 Secrets of Highly
Creative Women: A Portable Mentor

What Is Creativity?

Ask five different people to define creativity, and you'll get five different answers. But at the core of each is the fact that when you're being creative, you're taking two existing things and changing their relationship to each other to form something new. Picasso once took the handlebar and seat from a bike and created a bull's head. It's one of his most famous sculptures; many consider it a work of genius. But all he did was shift his perspective on the pieces from objects that allow you to sit and steer a bike to the head and horns of a bull.

You don't have to sculpt farm animals out of old sports equipment to be creative. All you need is a problem to solve, an open mind, and a shift in perspective.

The problem can come from anywhere: everyday challenges (what's for dinner?), relationships (how can I make her laugh?), or self-exploration (will I ever be able to love again?). Shifting your perspective can be as simple as concocting that new casserole or as complex as writing a book about your pain so you can move beyond it.

It's the amount of mental energy you expend and the degree to which you control the creative process (or the process controls you) that determine the level of creativity you're able to reach.

❧ Everyday creativity. This is no-frills creativity, such as using a paper clip to reattach the earpiece of your glasses, or putting on a pair of polish-soaked socks and "skating" across your

unrecognized. But acknowledging even these small, everyday bursts of creativity can help you reach that deeper level where Lane, coauthor of *Creative Healing: How to Heal Yourself by Tapping Your Hidden Creativity*, discovered her hidden artist and healed herself.

hardwood floor to clean it. At this level, you have total control over the process. It doesn't require much mental energy. You're focused on the outcome—glasses that stay on your head, a clean floor—more than on the process.

❧ Relationship creativity. "Relationships are one of the strongest ways for women to express their creativity," says C. Diane Ealy, Ph.D., a national speaker and author of *The Woman's Book of Creativity*. At this level, you still have control over the process, but it takes more mental energy than everyday creativity. For instance, to ease someone's discomfort, you have to combine an understanding of who that person is, what makes them tick, and the immediate environment around you. Take the grandmother who pops out her dentures to make her cranky grandson smile. Her product, a giggle, though intangible, is creative because of *how* she made him laugh. By shifting her view of the dentures from false teeth to a humorous tool, she eases a child's pain.

❧ Flow creativity. This is the highest level of creativity. Here, the process controls you. You

lose track of time, go hours without eating or drinking, even forget to go to the bathroom. With creativity in the driver's seat, the direction you thought a project was taking may change. And you allow that to happen. "When I let the process take over, it comes up with much better stuff than I ever could," says Dr. Ealy. When Lane gave into her creativity, her true self—gray, scared, and hurting—emerged onto the canvas. What you create at this level is very personal. It's holistic, involving every ounce of you: physically, intellectually, spiritually, and, most important, emotionally.

Combining these four elements inspires passion. "And it's in passion that we both lose and find ourselves," says Lane. We see our true selves. We begin to heal.

Creativity's Healing Power

The highest level of creativity, flow, is the most healing level. The process will either give you a much-needed mental escape from your problems, or it will help you face them. Which

WOMAN TO WOMAN

She Grew in Her Garden

Many beautiful things have grown in Patty Martin's garden, and she's one of them. After this 51-year-old personnel management specialist for the Navy had surgery to remove a cancerous tumor from her breast, she turned to gardening to deal with her fears of radiation therapy and death. She never suspected that when she planted spring bulbs, she would cultivate a new outlook on life. Here's her story.

I turned to gardening after my breast surgery because I wanted to show my family that I was normal. I had been an avid gardener nearly all my life, and if I wasn't digging dirt or pulling weeds, they would know something was wrong.

It was early October 1995. My surgery, just 2 weeks earlier, had gone well, and my prognosis was good. But I still had to face radiation therapy in another week. I had no idea what that meant or how it would change me. I was angry about what I had already gone through, and scared about what was to become of me and my family.

I didn't go into that patch of dirt with a design in my mind, or with the intent of healing myself. All I knew was I wanted to replant some pink and white tulips that I had previously had in the garden.

Somehow, I lost myself in the process of digging in dirt and nurturing plants, and my anger dissipated. I realized that, whatever happened, I would be okay. I might not be there when the bulbs came up, but my family would have something there to remember me. That didn't take away the pain, but it did lessen it, making it easier to confront.

In October, I started radiation therapy, and it wasn't as difficult as I had feared it would be.

In the spring, gorgeous pink and white blooms appeared. I was extremely excited to see them. They reminded me of what I had gone through and survived.

The tulips come up every year and are a symbol of my strength during that hard part of my life. They are proof that during that time, I didn't give up. I was productive and hopeful. I remained alive.

path it takes you on depends on what you can mentally handle at the time.

Lane once had a patient who was preparing for a bone marrow transplant to cure her leukemia. Attempting to lift her spirits before the procedure, the hospital nurses encouraged the woman to draw. Nauseated, in pain, and depressed, she reluctantly started drawing the chair next to her bed—the one she was supposed to try to climb into by herself but couldn't.

The next day, the nurses found her sitting in that same chair, still drawing. Her pencils and paper became her escape. Thoughts of her leukemia, pain, and nausea were replaced with vivid colors and landscapes.

Eventually, her art led her to a greater understanding of herself and her illness. She realized that she kept drawing pictures of lakes and other bodies of water because they represented her illness. The day she drew a beautiful island in the midst of a lake and a bridge to the island was the day she realized she would get better. It was as if crossing that bridge to the island represented her own power to move beyond her sickness. "I felt like I had power in this situation where I had felt helpless before," she told Lane. In drawing, she could create whatever she wanted, even a new reality.

The woman survived the bone marrow transplant, continued painting, and exhibited her work. Expressing herself on paper made her feel alive again.

Myths and Barriers

Sometimes, it seems as if our creative well has dried up, when really it is only clogged with the common myths about creativity.

Myth: I'm only creative at work. Once you tap into creativity, it's like hitting an oil gusher. It oozes into every part of your life. "The more you acknowledge the smaller acts of creativity, the more creative energy becomes available to you," says Dr. Ealy.

Myth: I'm not creative. You may not lose yourself in an innovative process every day, but that doesn't mean you aren't creative. Bringing out the best in an employee or helping a child learn how to get along with another child may not require as much mental energy as a poem about the challenges in your marriage, but they are just as valuable.

Myth: Creativity runs out. There's an ocean of creativity in all of us. It doesn't dry up or run out, but it does come in waves. Sometimes, it comes in small waves lasting for minutes; sometimes, in big waves lasting for years. After each wave crashes, we may need to rest. Take a mental break, get away from your work space, and give yourself time to let the next wave form.

Myth: I'm too old to be creative. Marie Curie was 45 when she shifted her scientific perspective and discovered medical uses for radiation. Georgia O'Keeffe was in her eighties when her failing eyesight forced her to switch from painting to clay sculpture. Need we say more?

Sometimes, it's not the myths that are blocking us, but our own inner voice that is raising the barriers.

Criticism. "You're not qualified." "What will others think?" "What were *you* thinking?" Criticism sabotages our desire to take risks, and we can't be creative without these leaps of faith. Focus on the passion behind your creative endeavor, what motivates you to draw or establish rapport, and you can drown out your fears.

Burnout. "Burnout is a key enemy of innovation," says Gail McMeekin, L.C.S.W., author of *The 12 Secrets of Highly Creative Women: A Portable Mentor.* When work or home completely drains you, there are two things for you to do: Take a break and change your routine. Get away for a week, or at least a weekend. Then, when you return to your daily grind, do things differently. Drive another route to work. Sit on the other side of your desk. Eat lunch with your left hand. This will exercise your brain and lead you into new paths of creativity.

Perfectionism. "Creativity and perfectionism, like oil and water, don't mix," says Dr. Ealy. Perfectionists fear losing control. They're driven by unrealistic self-expectations and are unable to move on until everything is "just right." Creativity, on the other hand, is about taking risks, making mistakes, and experiencing the unknown. You have to give yourself permission to fail.

Tapping into Your Creativity

There are as many ways to tap into your creativity as there are colors in an artist's palette. The important thing is to start with the one that feels natural to you. Chances are, once you tap into your creativity one way, you'll want to express it in other ways. Lane, for example, moved from painting to dancing, and eventually to writing. "Before I began painting, I never realized I was an artist, let alone a dancer and a writer," she says.

Art

What is it? Painting or drawing your emotions.

How do I do it?

1. Create a studio. Find a room where you can close the door, and furnish it with a table, a comfortable chair, and good lighting. Turn off the

phone, and tell your family and friends to leave you alone for at least an hour.

2. Let go of your insecurities and fear. Say to yourself, "I am an artist."

3. Think about the topic or person that is most meaningful or compelling in your life right now.

4. Draw or paint the emotions and images the subject conjures up—the first thing that comes to mind, be it purple streaks, a cartoon figure, or a huge red blotch.

5. Play like a child. Be in the moment. Let go of judgment. Experiment with different materials, shapes, and colors.

6. Look for signs of your power and strength in your art. Respond to the materials, shapes, colors, and textures that capture your attention. Note, as the woman with leukemia did, what the repeating images in your work really mean.

7. Return to your studio at the same time the next day and the day after that until it becomes a habit.

8. When you're ready, share your art with a friend. Talk about what the picture means to you. Together, you may discover deeper meaning in your work.

Dance

What is it? Expressing your emotions and experiences through body movements.

How do I do it?

1. Find a space where you can move freely. It can be as small a space as the corner of your bedroom.

2. Stretch to warm up your muscles and release any tension.

3. Choose music you love or want to move to and follow its rhythms.

4. Connect with the energy inside your body. Allow your body to move spontaneously, yet be aware of your movements. Later, the reasons for them may become clear.

5. Let your emotion merge with your movement. If you're angry, shake your arms. Stomp. Scream. Visualize your spirit and body becoming one. Make sounds—grunt, purr, yodel—if it feels right.

6. Wave scarves to depict flowing movements or to simulate water. Dance an animal, the emotion of fear, or your spouse.

7. Dance every day.

Writing

What is it? Putting your thoughts and emotions on paper, whether in the form of a poem, a short story, or stream of consciousness.

How do I do it?

1. Create a space and time to write. Escape to your bedroom after dinner or wake up a half-hour early to write.

2. Using a computer or a notebook, start writing.

3. Let your words flow out. Don't edit or censor them. Don't worry about making any sense. Just write whatever comes to mind.

4. Write a story. Having trouble starting? Try "Once upon a time . . ." and continue with the first thing that pops into your mind, whether it's Snow White or Silly Putty looking for its missing shell. Have conversations with your characters.

5. Create poetry. It doesn't have to rhyme or have form.

6. Write a letter to yourself or to someone else from your heart.

7. Draw pictures along with your words.

8. Find words in your writing that come up again and again. They are your themes.

9. Focus on your themes to bring out deep memories.

10. Make time for writing every day.

11. Create a writers' circle with friends and read your work to one another.

Dreaming

What is it? Asking yourself a question in the meditative state that occurs just before you fall asleep and waking up with the answer.

How do I do it?

1. Determine what problem you want to work on. Think about it in depth. What is your goal? What has gotten in the way? What things seem impossible? Settle on a single question that sums up your concerns. Be specific. Write it down in a dream journal or on a piece of paper and slip it under your pillow. As you go to sleep, repeat the question in your mind.

2. Allow yourself to fall asleep, remaining open to all possibilities.

3. After each dream, note any particularly vivid dream images, words, or feelings, and write them in your dream journal. You may wish to use them later for a drawing, dance, or story.

4. If you don't get an answer the first night, try again. Sometimes, rephrasing is the jump start your dreaming mind needs to provide a solution.

Finish What You Start

Creativity is a process, with a beginning, a middle, and an end. And just as it may be hard to get started, it may be difficult to finish. That's because our creations result from our innermost feelings. This makes us vulnerable. Sharing our product, whether it is a painting or a never-

INNER-SPACE EXPLORERS
Who are Masters and Johnson?

Because the men who wrote textbooks in the 1950s reported that women didn't have the capacity to reach orgasm, gynecologist William Masters knew that if he wanted to study sexual behavior, he had to recruit a woman. So in 1957, he and psychologist Virginia Johnson teamed up to study the physiological changes of the body during intercourse. They were the first to map out sexual phases and find that women are not only orgasmic, but, in many cases, multiorgasmic.

Even though sex wasn't freely talked about in the 1940s, Alfred Kinsey managed to survey thousands of Americans about their sex lives. Although critics said Kinsey was trying to undermine the family structure, he raised enough awareness to allow Masters and Johnson to do their own research in the 1960s.

They measured the sexual responses of 700 men and women while they had intercourse or masturbated. The two researchers noticed a pattern of four physiological phases: excitement, plateau, orgasm, and resolution.

They found that during excitement, or foreplay, our stomachs, breasts, throats, and necks become flushed, our muscles become tense, our hearts beat faster, our blood pressures rise, our labia and clitoris swell, our nipples get hard, and our uteruses and inner vaginas expand. During the plateau phase, sexual arousal levels off. Finally, we reach orgasm, in which we experience intense contractions in our genital muscles for 5 to 7 seconds. During the resolution phase, our bodies return to normal, sometimes leaving a thin layer of sweat covering us.

The doctors published their findings in a book called *Human Sexual Response* in 1966. Later, they studied and wrote about sexual inadequacy, homosexuality, and AIDS.

Along the way, Masters and Johnson married each other, but they divorced in the 1990s.

The techniques they used to help couples improve their sex lives, such as showing how to give and receive sensual pleasure, are still used by therapists today.

INNER-SPACE EXPLORERS

Who is Kay Redfield Jamison?

Psychologist and Johns Hopkins University professor of psychiatry Kay Redfield Jamison, Ph.D., created a furor over her theory that creativity and mood disorders are linked. She explored that idea in her book *Touched With Fire: Manic Depressive Illness and the Artistic Temperament.*

In the 1980s, Dr. Jamison started applying diagnostic criteria to the art and biographical material of dead poets, composers, and artists and revealed that many had mood disorders. She also did a study of 47 artists who were still alive, and found that 38 percent of them were treated for depression or manic depression (also called bipolar disorder), compared to 1 to 6 percent of the overall population.

Her critics say that she romanticizes depression and implies that mood disorders are necessary for creativity, and that she doesn't take into consideration the numerous people with mood disorders and depression who aren't creative. One critic even called her book propaganda. Others worry that she could make those with psychiatric diseases who aren't creative even more depressed.

But her proponents argue that by looking at the poetry of Anne Sexton or the paintings of Vincent van Gogh, she raises awareness among people who may not normally pay attention to mental disorders. Dr. Jamison says that research on the connection between creativity and mood disorders is important to our overall understanding of these diseases and to counteracting the stigmas associated with mental illness.

Dr. Jamison is known for something else. In 1995, she publicly announced that she was diagnosed with bipolar disorder when she was 16. Also in 1995, she published *An Unquiet Mind*, her own story of manic depression, including a suicide attempt at age 28 from a lithium overdose.

an idea if we are too attached to the feelings connected with it," says Dr. Ealy.

Fortunately, we have a built-in detachment system that allows us to let go once we're satisfied with our creation. For instance, suppose after an argument with your husband you write a poem that begins "Monday Night Football. How do I hate thee. Let me count the ways . . ." If you let your creative process run its natural course, you disconnect from both the poem and the anger entwined in it just before it's finished.

You know you're detaching when you become bored and want to write a new poem or move on to another creative endeavor. It's at this moment that you are ready to share your creation with someone else, such as your husband or a friend. Their criticism won't hit you as hard.

Many women never let that creative process run through to completion. They fear letting go. And so they miss out. If they can't let go and move on, they can't encounter new ideas and feelings, and they won't grow.

Lane, for example, didn't stop with painting the woman she saw in the magazine. Next, she took photos of herself in poses that expressed her pain, fear, and anger, and painted those images. "I painted how I felt, instead of thinking how I felt," she says. "For the first time, I saw my true self."

been-tried-before solution, too soon can be deadly to the creative process if we can't handle rejection.

"Even a well-intended comment can squash

Before she knew it, she had created a series of self-portraits. Each image captured a feeling that had passed. Looking back over the series, she realized that there was movement, and that she was witnessing her own transformation.

But detachment has its own drawback: loss of interest in completing the project.

For many women, it's the creative process, not the product, that is the most exciting. It's more fun to choose the colors and fabrics of your new bedroom than it is to paint the walls. So before the work is actually finished, you may shift your interest to the next project: redecorating the basement.

One of the main attributes of geniuses, says Dr. Ealy, is that they finish what they start. One way to do that is to imagine the results. "The more vividly you can imagine the results of your creative efforts before you begin them, the more likely you will be to complete what you start," she says.

Imagining your bedroom with periwinkle walls, a new comforter with yellow irises on your bed, a spider plant hanging in front of your window, and your dresser against the far wall instead of next to the bed can activate your enthusiasm and inner drive and get you to pick up the paintbrush.

You may still feel your interest waning just before completion, but you're more likely to stay with your project and finish it.

The Pleasure Principle

What's your idea of pleasure?

A languorous afternoon in bed with your partner? Dancing until the wee hours? Racing around the yard in a wild game of tag with your kids?

Whatever it is that puts a curl in your toes or a glow in your cheeks or simply takes you outside the same-old, same-old for a few minutes—it's a good bet that you don't indulge in it often enough. And it doesn't count if you take your indulgence with an unhealthy dollop of guilt on the side.

Subconsciously, many of us believe that we're not deserving of joy, says Jennifer Fahey-Gigliotti, a spa director at Canyon Ranch Health Resort in the Berkshires in Lenox, Massachusetts. In fact, some of us catch ourselves in the act of relaxing and actually get tense. "We think, 'Oh my gosh, I shouldn't be having such a good time,'" she says, when in reality, "we should be having pleasurable experiences."

When—and why—did we stop seeking out all that makes life delightful? More important, can we actually become gluttons for pleasure while still accomplishing all that our frantic work and home obligations demand?

You bet we can. (We're women!) With a little creativity, we can return to that guilt-free, cart-wheeling sense of fun, play, and enjoyment we had as children, and find new ways to pamper ourselves and replenish our energy.

Why We Deny Ourselves Pleasure

How many times have your coworkers asked what you did over the weekend, and you literally couldn't think of a single thing to share?

You know you were busy (that's why you feel so exhausted on Monday mornings). It's just that none of the things you did would actually count as "fun." After all, how interested would they be in 20 loads of laundry and a trip to the hardware store?

But it's not just time that impedes the amount of pleasure we allow into our lives.

Traumatic events in our childhood, such as losing a parent, growing up in a dysfunctional family, or being the "little mother" of the house, may hinder our ability to relax as adults.

Some of us equate letting go with losing control, which makes us uncomfortable. "Some women feel that if they hang a little loose, they'll never regain their composure," says Mindy R. Schiffman, Ph.D., a clinical psychologist in New York City. Or we may fear that if we relax, inertia will set in, and we won't ever get moving again.

Or, perish the thought, maybe we're emulating our mothers.

"A woman might have grown up with a long-suffering mom who carried all the family burdens on her shoulders," says Lisa Firestone, Ph.D., a clinical psychologist and education and program director for the Glendon Association in Santa Barbara, California. "Allowing herself to have the fun her mother didn't would break that mother-daughter connection. After all, many of us get our identity directly from our mothers."

Whatever our reasons for not enjoying the banquet that is life, we have to start bellying up to the table, because pleasure keeps us healthy, both emotionally and physically. The more we laugh and play with our kids, our partners, and our friends, the less irritable and uptight we are, says Stella Resnick, Ph.D., a psychologist in Los Angeles and author of *The Pleasure Zone: Why We Resist Good Feelings and How to Let Go and Be Happy*. Weekend getaways, cooking classes, gardening, and just hanging out with friends release tension and energize us. "Our bodies become more relaxed. We breathe easier. Our blood flows freely. And we're less susceptible to illness," she says.

Just laughing is good for us. Studies show that laughter helps increase the level of oxygen in our bodies (which maintains healthy brain function),

IS HAPPINESS REALLY A WARM PUPPY?

You try not to smile when a 10-pound ball of wagging tail and licking tongue hits you at the door—even though you just stepped out to get the mail. Even research points to happiness as one of the top three benefits of owning a dog. (Companionship and protection are the other two.)

One reason for this could be the play factor. Adult dog owners spend 44 percent of their time with their pooches playing. Those who are age 65 and older take twice as many walks as people in the same age group who don't have dogs. They're also significantly less dissatisfied with their social lives and physical and emotional health than their dogless peers.

"Pet people describe themselves with more positive adjectives than non–pet owners," says Lynette Hart, director of the Center for Animal Alternatives at the University of California, Davis.

But then, it's easy to feel good about yourself when you're around someone who shows love so easily and who doesn't care about your social status, dress size, or bank account.

All dogs ask for is a fresh bowl of water, a run in the park, and a table scrap once in a while. They don't talk, so conflicts are few. This unconditional support system can be drawn on day or night, when your family or friends may be busy with other things or unreachable, says Hart. And, of course, dogs are a good source of entertainment. (*You* try not to laugh when they chase their own tails.) That may be why in one study, about one-third of dog owners felt Fido was as important to them as the human members of their families.

Another way that dogs contribute to our happiness: By helping us feel safe and focusing our attention on something other than ourselves, they lessen our anxiety, loneliness, and depression and lower our blood pressure.

stimulates the activity of our immune system (which fights off colds and other illnesses), lowers blood pressure, and relieves muscle tension. It may also help alleviate depression, anxiety, stress, hostility, and anger, and spark creativity. What's more, doing what gives us pleasure boosts our self-esteem and helps make us more resilient to life's pressures. The bottom line is: We're just happier women.

Then there's the added bonus of intimacy. Time spent with your partner that doesn't involve the kids, errands, bills, or dishes fosters a closer bond. "There will be more hugging, kissing, smiles of appreciation, and better sex, all of which help us chill out and de-stress," says Susan Heitler, Ph.D., a clinical psychologist in Denver and author of *The Power of Two: Secrets to a Strong and Loving Marriage.*

Discovering Your Pleasure

So the last time you had fun, the engine in a Volkswagen Beetle was in the rear. These days, "fun" is finding a sale on rump roast or minimizing your pores.

Well, hang on, ladies. We're going to tell you not only how to rediscover your inner child, but how to play so hard with her that you keep smiling even in your dreams.

Make a list. Write down everything you've ever wanted to do but were too afraid, broke, time-starved, or embarrassed to try. Maybe it's riding in the front seat of a roller coaster, your

WOMEN ASK WHY

Why do women hate the Three Stooges?

Have you ever sat down with a man while he watches the Three Stooges? You come to the part where Moe, Larry, and Curly poke each other in the eyes and then fall down, and you don't laugh. You may even yawn and start flipping through a magazine. But the guy you're with rewinds the scene, thinking you missed a subtle nuance of the fall.

"No," you say, "I understood it. I just didn't think it was funny."

To many men, them's fightin' words. The Stooges are the epitome of comedy to the male species. So if you don't laugh, you're considered humorless.

Hey, we've got a funny bone. But like many pieces of our anatomy, it differs from a man's.

Think about it. You never see two women at the grocery store grabbing each other by the nose and going, "Nuk, nuk, nuk." Yet that hazing, fraternity-type humor is the way *men* greet each other. It's okay for them to say, "Hey, Bob! Nice jacket. You sleep in it all weekend?" instead of just asking how their buddy's weekend went.

We'd never do such a thing. Can you imagine going up to another woman and saying, "Hey, Mary, are you 3 months pregnant or going heavy on the gravy?" You'd lose a friend, and probably a few teeth while you're at it. It's not that we're uptight. It's that we follow an entirely different set of ground rules in the social arena.

Another reason the Stooges aren't as appealing to women is the hierarchy of humor. Moe holds all the power and beats up on Larry and Curly, the dim-witted (relatively speaking),

hands waving over your head. Galloping on horseback along a foam-flecked shoreline. Water-skiing, snowmobiling, or swimming with the fish off a tropical island. Or even just taking a yoga or

powerless Stooges. This is a perfect match for men, since their humor laughs downward. But women's humor laughs upward. We tend to laugh when the person *in power* gets it, such as a pompous boss, not the fat kid who stutters. We don't laugh at things people can't change.

Some people believe that the Three Stooges are too violent for women's tastes. But the eye-poking and pan-slamming really aren't the problem. After all, most women loved it when Thelma and Louise blew up the vulgar trucker's rig. The Three Stooges is an attention-deficit-disorder kind of entertainment. You don't have to pay attention, remember the plot, or even listen carefully. Men can crunch on chips and flip back to the football game while watching the Three Stooges and never miss a thing. Women have a slightly more sophisticated sense of the absurd than someone spitting in their soup or falling down. And we'd like a plot with our movie.

The disparity between funny bones doesn't stop there. Even the ways we share humor are different. When a woman wants to tell you something funny, she tells a story. Lines such as "Oh my God, you mean that happened to you, too?" are heard frequently in our conversations. We want to know we're not crazy. Men's sense of humor, however, is often competitive, with each man trying to top the other's jokes.

So women definitely have a sense of humor. In fact, we're riotously appreciative of the absurd. If we weren't, we wouldn't have put up with men for so many years.

Expert consulted
Regina Barreca, Ph.D.
Professor of English
University of Connecticut
Storrs
Author of They Used to Call Me Snow
    White . . . But I Drifted

meditation class to learn whether you have the ability to sit still for 20 minutes. "Whatever it is, it will require you to let down your defenses and take the plunge," says Dr. Firestone.

The point is, the list gives you a starting place. Maybe roller coasters make you nauseated. So how about hitting an amusement park? You live in Kansas, thousands of miles from any beach. But there are still horses around. Diving makes your ears hurt. So how about snorkeling? The important thing is to identify some key areas in your life that are different from the everyday and that you feel would bring you pleasure.

Revisit your childhood. What did you enjoy doing most when you were a young girl? If you loved to tap-dance, play the piano, dunk a basketball, or even visit the zoo, chances are you'll find all of these activities just as pleasurable now as an adult, says Dr. Heitler.

Scan the papers. Open any newspaper, and you'll find loads of unique and interesting things to do, from plays and lectures to art fairs and dance classes. Start a "pleasure scrapbook" of ideas and commit to trying one each month.

Visit a bookstore. Pay attention to what captures your attention. If you spend most of your time browsing through the gardening section, plan to attend a floral exhibit or start your own garden. If you're attracted to books on exercise, join a walking, jogging, or cycling club. Perusing the spirituality section? Start your own prayer group. Picking up coffee-table books on photography? Take a class at a local college or university.

Fulfill your fantasy. Assume that money is no object, your boss gave you an extra 2 weeks'

GOSSIP CAN BE GOOD FOR YOU

Shooting the breeze. Chatting with the girls. Tapping the grapevine. Gossip by any other name is still gossip. Although it's best known for ruining friendships and destroying reputations, gossip can also help us explore our values, expose maltreatment, and laugh away anger, all the while strengthening friendships.

We like to believe that when we share kind words about a friend, we're not gossiping. But anytime our conversation takes a detour from its main focus and we start talking (naughty or nice) about someone who isn't present, we're gossiping, says Anne Skleder, Ph.D., associate professor of psychology at Alvernia College in Reading, Pennsylvania.

For example, during a family dinner you and your sister-in-law chatter about the beautiful floral centerpiece. That's not gossip. But if you talk about how sweet it was of your brother's new girlfriend to bring it, that's gossip.

Often, when we gossip, we reveal our belief system, leaving ourselves wide open to criticism. So if you whisper to a coworker that you think it's shameless of the secretary to take an hour-and-a-half lunch without making up the time, you risk her thinking you're a drill sergeant. If she accepts what you say and doesn't criticize you, however, you're more likely to share even deeper thoughts next time, which builds intimacy and trust.

Although women who gossip excessively aren't widely liked—probably because they break trust—what's surprising is that those who *don't* dish aren't trusted (or liked) either. At least, that's what Dr. Skleder found when she studied women in a sorority house. In fact, the women who didn't gossip at all were nearly as disliked as those who gossiped too much.

Another gossiping tidbit: Those who gossiped the most were the most gossiped about.

Gossip's side effects can be good. Gossip can segue to conversations about our own values that we wouldn't otherwise discuss, or it can lead to discoveries about others. For instance, through gossip, Dr. Skleder and her neighbors learned that no one had seen an elderly neighbor for days. It turned out that the neighbor was ill and unable to leave her house. Thanks to gossip, the neighborhood women began helping her.

vacation, and your mom will care for the kids. What would you do? The idea here is not to censor yourself. So whether it's an Alaskan cruise, a full-body massage, or hiking the Himalayas, write it down.

Then break your fantasy down into steps. For the cruise, for instance, the first step might be to talk to a travel agent and collect some catalogs. It may take you 3 years to save for it, but in the meantime, you can read books about Alaska, surf the Internet for cruise bargains, and begin putting together your cruise wardrobe. And every time you bag your lunch, walk instead of take a taxi, or watch network television because you've nixed the cable, you'll be clear about what you're saving for. "The point is to turn your fantasy into a reality," explains Dr. Resnick.

Question. Ask yourself, "What's the last thing my friends and family would ever expect me to do?" Then do it.

The Time Factor

So now you know what fun looks like to you. It's a morning hike, followed by a gourmet picnic overlooking a scenic vista, just you and your journal. Next, you have to figure out how to shoehorn it into your schedule without simply adding another item to your overflowing to-do list; therein lies only more stress.

"Those of us who claim 'I don't have time' say that out of habit," says Dr. Resnick. We're raised to believe we're the sole caregivers in our families, despite having careers. "So we're constantly giving and never taking for ourselves," she says. By the time we've given it all, it's 10:00 P.M.

It's a vicious circle that, if not broken, keeps us irritable, anxious, short-tempered, and tense: all of the things this inner journey is designed to prevent. So forget "can't." If you have time to man the bake sale table at the school carnival, you have time for that hike. Experts believe the following strategies may help.

Delegate. If you're the one making dinner, cleaning the kitchen, folding the laundry, vacuuming the hallway, reading the bedtime stories to the kids, and ironing his shirts, you're doing too much. The solution? Divide the after-work chores with your partner. Appoint him (or your teenager) chef for dinner 2 nights a week. Take turns putting the kids to bed. Hire someone to clean your house. Presto! You've stolen time for that after-work class or walk. (Your man or kids won't help? Tell them to order takeout, ignore the dust balls, and hit the road anyway.)

Disappear. Pick one weekend a month on which you vow not to set foot in a grocery store, dry cleaner, Wal-Mart, or shopping mall. Then use those 2 delicious days to explore what gives you pleasure and to have some guilt-free fun.

Prioritize. Make a pie chart of your day, labeling the pieces according to the tasks: commuting, work, cooking, cleaning, homework,

ALL IN THE GENES?

Why are men content with three pairs of shoes total while women are unwilling to settle for just three in one color?

It's political.

In the early 18th century, men wore heels just as high as women's. In fact, from their heads down to their toes, men were just as stylish as their female counterparts, sporting pink silk suits, blue velvet vests trimmed with lace and jeweled buttons, and shoes with red high heels.

But that all changed as capitalism and democracy rose. An aristocratic sense of fashion was replaced by bourgeois practicality. Work became a priority, and clothing reflected that new attitude by becoming more uniform, sober, and reliable.

Since women were excluded both economically and politically from the capitalist and democratic environment, their attitudes toward clothing and fashion evolved from the gaudy to the conservative more slowly. So as working clothes grew more staid, fashion naturally became linked with femininity.

Shoes magnify that difference. Although these days women have also adopted the somber workforce uniform of the business suit, shoes are one of the few areas in which we can still play and be expressive with fashion. Think about it: Different pairs of shoes can make the same old business suit appear uptown, funky downtown, girly, or ultrachic.

Plus, there's the shopping factor. Shopping exists on a continuum of pleasure. Footwear tops the joy-giving list because you're never too old or too heavy for beautiful shoes.

You don't even have to wear them to have them look great. Unlike most clothes, which just lie there when you take them off, shoes retain their shape. They're like pieces of sculpture. That's why some women buy shoes they know they'll never wear. For instance, I buy vintage shoes. They may not fit, but they're beautiful. I set them on my desk or shelves like other pieces of fine art.

Expert consulted
Valerie Steele
Author of Shoes: A Lexicon of Style

relaxing and fun, making love, and sleeping. Which is the biggest slice? (If it's making love or sleeping, then you don't need to read any further.) Now you can clearly see what's out of balance.

Next, make another list of ways in which you can equal out some of those pieces. Is your commute too long? Maybe you can telecommute part-time, or maybe you need a different, closer-to-home job. Does your work take up half the pie? Commit to leaving at 5:00 P.M. for 1 week, without bringing any work home. Do you find yourself chauffeuring the kids more than you talk to your husband? Limit them to one activity each and explain that Mom is entitled to a little fun and games, too.

Schedule. Pleasure comes in small doses, too. So set aside 30 minutes to 1 hour each day for something enjoyable, and don't let anything take its place. Some wild ideas to get you started: Paint your toenails bright green (no one will see them if it's winter). Shoot some hoops out on the driveway. Eavesdrop in an Internet chat room for exotic dancers. Blast the Rolling Stones on the stereo and dance around the house.

Pleasure for Two

There's one area of pleasure that definitely takes two: sex. Unfortunately, this is another area of our lives from which exhaustion, tension, stress, and boredom may have driven out all the fun. It's time to recapture the passion of your dating days.

WOMAN TO WOMAN

She Found Her Best Friend When She Began Playing Outdoors

When the careers and hobbies of Amy Morgan, 47, of Mendham, New Jersey, and her husband separated, so did their relationship. But rock climbing helped her rediscover her best friend. Here is her story.

You know that couple you see at restaurants, the one you can tell has been together forever? They have a 2-hour dinner and never say one word to each other. I've always feared that. Much to my horror, after 18 years, my husband and I were becoming that couple.

When we first met in April 1980, we immediately hit it off. Having been through a divorce, I knew what a bad relationship was like, and this wasn't it. We became best friends and loved doing everything together. Our relationship naturally segued into marriage 6 months later.

It was fun right from the beginning. We loved exploring and trying new things together, especially if it involved making things from scratch. We even went so far as to make homemade liverwurst!

But that changed. We started focusing more on our careers, which were very different (I'm a copy editor and he's a computer programmer). Our hobbies went in different directions: He hiked and went mountain biking, I sewed. We didn't even maintain our home together anymore because we started renting. No more painting walls or gardening shoulder-to-shoulder.

It's well worth your time, too. "Couples with wonderful sex lives are less anxious and less depressed and have greater self-esteem than those whose sex lives are dull or sporadic," says Dr. Resnick.

Enjoyable sex can also make you more playful, less self-conscious, more spontaneous, and, of course, a better lover. It releases "feel-good" endorphins that bust stress, lift our spirits, and

With nothing in common, we began leading parallel lives, coexisting with one another. It seemed as though I was looking at him through an impenetrable cloud. I was losing my best friend, and it scared me.

We have always believed that marriage takes a lot of work, time, energy, and thought to keep it healthy and strong. And that it is a commitment. We never entered into it with an exit strategy. But the prospect of staying together and having completely separate lives was a living hell I couldn't bear. You can't just watch a marriage of 18 years drift apart.

So after 2 years of ever-growing distance, in the summer of 1998, we finally did something about it.

We knew we needed to do things together. So I learned rock climbing and inline skating (new interests of his) and he learned Spanish. (I knew a little but wanted to learn more.)

Those changes woke us up and made us realize we were both too stuffy and needed to get a little silly. We began goofing around more, quoting silly lines from *The Princess Bride* and getting into pillow fights.

Today, we play by exploring, learning new things. Plans are under way to build a climbing wall of our own, and we bought a tandem bike—the only way I can keep up with him on the trails. We want to know what's around the next bend. It's a childlike curiosity that keeps us feeling young. It even makes others think we are younger than our age.

And it worked. In 2000, we celebrated our 20th wedding anniversary exploring Puerto Rico.

produce feelings of well-being (we know this as the afterglow). Plus, it's just a whole lot of fun. To recapture the passion, experts suggest the following ideas.

Change the location. It's amazing how making love in different surroundings can rev up a relationship. Got a private backyard? How about under the stars on a summer night when there's a full moon. Are your kids away on a sleepover? Try the living room. Rent a cheap hotel room for a quickie, or check out the back seat of the minivan (you'll never view it as the mommy-mobile again).

Share your fantasies. And then find a way to make them come true.

Make a date. Not for dinner and a movie, but for sex. Put it on your calendar in a code word only the two of you know. Don't roll your eyes. After all, you schedule your dentist appointments and haircuts, don't you?

Use e-mail. Open a free account on an Internet site such as Yahoo.com and send each other mushy messages throughout the day.

Abstain. This might seem to be a silly way to get more lovemaking into your life, but some sex therapists suggest that couples with problems first consciously abstain from sex for a week. The catch is that each night of that week, they spend time together just touching each other. Remember necking in high school when you were already 5 minutes past your curfew? Wouldn't you like to have those I-just-can't-help-myself feelings again?

Create a love nest. If you last bought sheets when Ronald Reagan was president, you're due for a major white sale. Splurge on satin or high-quality cotton. But don't stop there. Add lots of pillows for positioning, jettison the work-related reading for a table full of erotica and candles, and put a couple of bowls of sandalwood potpourri around the room. And don't forget to banish the TV to the basement.

Kiss him. *Really* kiss him. In the kitchen. In front of the kids. In front of friends. In the

INNER-SPACE EXPLORERS

Who was Erik Erikson?

This ego psychoanalyst was born Erik Homberger in Germany in 1902, but he changed his last name to Erikson after he moved to the United States in 1933. The illegitimate child of a Danish father he never knew, the blond, blue-eyed Jew suffered an identity crisis, a term he later coined and a subject to which he devoted his research.

Once Anna Freud's patient, Erikson called himself an ego psychoanalyst because he based his thinking on Sigmund Freud's theory that personality consists of an id, an ego, and a superego. He emphasized the ego, which is the conscious aspect of our personality.

Until he developed his theory of psychosocial development, psychologists believed that intellectual and emotional development stopped at the age of 12. But Erikson noticed that identity crises happen throughout our lives and that every time we have to deal with them, we grow as a person.

He listed the crises we face in eight stages of development: trust versus mistrust at age 1; independence versus doubt at age 2; initiative versus guilt from ages 3 to 5; competence versus inferiority from age 6 through puberty; identity versus confusion in adolescence; intimacy versus isolation in early adulthood; familial love and care versus loneliness in middle age; and wisdom versus despair with life in old age. The outcomes from these identity crises ultimately shape our personalities.

Erikson's theory doesn't have much empirical support because it can't be tested in the laboratory. Other psychologists also argue that life development isn't so predictable. But that hasn't stopped other psychologists from taking Erikson's lead and developing stage theories of their own.

dreamed up. Have an adventure together. (Skydiving can do amazing things for your sex life, assuming you're still alive.) Take a cooking class together and then sample the results (preferably with the lights out and some towels spread on the bed).

Call in sick together. The kids are in school, the dog is outside, and—finally—it's just the two of you alone in the house. You take it from there.

A Pleasure Prescription

When it's time for some pleasure on your own, you might want to try these suggestions.

A spa. One of the fastest-growing segments in the beauty industry is the day spa, with facials, massages, and other forms of pampering becoming a regular part of the routines of many beauty salons.

A massage. Yield to your need to be kneaded. It feels amazing. And although you may not care while in the midst of having your feet rubbed, research suggests that massage strengthens our immunity by helping our bodies produce more disease-fighting white blood cells, lower blood pressure, reduce stress hormone levels, and improve our mood.

An exercise class. If the very thought of step aerobics makes you groan, consider that there are tons of activities you've yet to try, such as Spinning, rock climbing, fencing, freestyle dance,

middle of the evening news. We're not talking a peck on the cheek here, either.

Play together. No, not in bed. Get him involved in some of the fun activities you've

ballet, and the minitrampoline. You'll get a great cardiovascular workout in an atmosphere that allows you to be playful and uninhibited. An added bonus: Studies show that 30 minutes of aerobic activity 3 days a week may be just as effective as medication for relieving symptoms of depression. Moreover, there's evidence that regular exercise slows our bodies' responses to the stress that makes us cranky and anxious.

Aromatherapy. Sweeten the atmosphere in your home and office with fresh flowers, gorgeous green plants, potpourri, and aromatherapy sprays, candles, or oils. But don't just indulge your nose. Indulge your other senses, too. By continuously stimulating your five senses, you allow yourself to experience pleasure in entirely new ways. For example, treat your ears to lush Beethoven symphonies or the lavish waltzes of Johann Strauss. Pamper your eyes with a beautiful poster, calendar, or painting. Treat your tongue to the bite of cayenne pepper or the sweetness of ridiculously expensive, out-of-season fruit. Touch the soft nape of a child's neck, your dog's silky coat, or your friend's or partner's hand.

Feel. Breathe. Be here now.

All That We Can Be

When we're thrown a curveball, we can either go down swinging, or we can keep our feet planted, our eyes on the ball, and whack it over the fence. In the game of life, that means making the most of our turn at bat by transforming challenges and tragedies into opportunities for personal growth.

And there will be challenges. You've probably already faced several: college, first job, marriage, children. Part of you hopes that each time you slide safe into home plate will be the last time you're at bat. Sorry—the pitcher in this game never stops throwing.

Which is why this chapter was designed to help you handle some of the fastballs that come toward you in middle age. Use it as a game plan for facing your challenges and turning them into victories.

But, as with any baseball game, recognize that you are a unique player with individual needs that must be met in order to win the game. If you are like some people, this process may require time, a support network, or professional therapy before you can begin redefining your life.

Surviving the Teenage Years

The phone startles me from sleep. I look at the clock and it's 12:08 A.M. My teenage son was supposed to be home by midnight. I grab the receiver, my heart pounding. Please tell me he wasn't in an accident . . .

The transition from childhood to adulthood is often a trying time for parents. Not only are we scared for our teen's safety, we're also confused and frustrated about how to handle this kid . . . um . . . adult . . . uh . . . adolescent, who changes more often than our dress size. It's as if body snatchers took our sweet, innocent children and turned them into pimply, sullen, half-adults overflowing with raging hormones. Getting through this passage of parenting is about as easy as collecting feathers in a hurricane. But experts say that there are coping skills that can make surviving the teenage years a bit easier on both of you.

Share with your spouse. Remember the guy holding your hand in the birthing room? He's got a stake in this, too. So share your frustrations, fears, and other feelings with him. You both may want to talk to friends who have the same overgrown aliens inhabiting their homes. "It helps to know you're not alone," says Roberta Nutt, Ph.D., professor of psychology and director of the counseling psychology doctorate program at Texas Woman's University in Denton.

Stay in plain view. When it comes to communicating with a teen, it often feels as if we're talking to a brick wall. Every once in a while, however, we break through with a meaningful conversation that lasts more than 15 seconds. The problem is, there's no way of knowing just when those moments will come. The solution? Hang out. The more you're around, the more likely you'll be within spitting distance when your kid decides to come clean about the party last weekend. Plop on the couch when he's watching TV, drive her to her guitar lesson, or team up with him to make dinner. If you've had open communication with your kids since they were small, Dr. Nutt says, they will talk to you.

Become a fan. If your daughter pitches for the Wildcats or has a part in the school play, be there for her. Supporting your kids' interests shows them you care and gives you something to talk about with them. (And we all know how hard *that* is to come by.)

Don't take it personally. Realize that their rebellion is not malicious. He's not breaking curfew to be disrespectful. It's just his way of pushing the limits, something he has to do to become more independent. Along those same lines, she isn't skipping out on the family camping trip because she doesn't love you. She just needs her own space to begin defining herself.

Be honest. If the guys he hangs out with dress all in black and pierce their cheeks with dangling skull-and-crossbones jewelry, tell him you're concerned. But don't attack him. He'll hear the message much better if you present it as "I'm scared" rather than accuse him or try to control him, Dr. Nutt says. And *you're* going to feel better if you've been heard.

Relax your rules. The more controlling you are, the more likely it is that he'll rebel to gain more freedom. "If we've brought our kids up right and they're growing well, they need more independence and control over their lives," Dr. Nutt says. "It's appropriate to start treating them more like adults, to grant them more privileges and to negotiate with them in ways we wouldn't have when they were younger." So let him borrow the car even if you're petrified of an accident. Just as you let them go so they can grow, you need to let your anxieties go, too.

Empty-Nest Syndrome

Ironically, just as you learn to loosen those apron strings, they reach behind you and cut all the way through them. Suddenly, you've got that sewing room you always wanted.

It's called empty-nest syndrome for a reason. As mothers, we have an incredible bond with our children. They depended on us for survival, and we changed our identities and skills as they grew. Whether they came from our bodies or were adopted, they are, in essence, part of us. So when they leave, we may feel empty because we're actually losing a part of ourselves, both emotionally and physically, says Phyllis Koch-Sheras, Ph.D., a clinical psychologist in Charlottesville, Virginia. Fill that void by beginning a new chapter in your life, shifting the focus from your children to yourself.

Pursue new interests. Remember the eternal moan of parenthood? "I don't have time!" Well, you have time now. "Use this as an opportunity to start some new things or to go deeper into interests that maybe you didn't have time for before," Dr. Nutt advises. Travel, take golf lessons, plant a flower garden, or follow that dream (you know, the one about the garret in Paris). For more ideas, see The Pleasure Principle on page 144.

Befriend your child. When the kids move out of the house, it doesn't mean they're moving out of our lives. Instead, it can mark the beginning of a new kind of relationship, one that's based not on meeting their needs, but on mutual respect and understanding. Start relating to your child as an adult by taking an interest in her life almost as you would a close friend's, and by having faith in her competence and judgment. Of course, you won't want to reveal everything about your personal life, as you might to your friends, but you want to be available for your child when she needs your support. It may feel strange and awkward at first, but someday, this new bond you've formed may turn out to be one of your most meaningful connections.

Fall in love all over again. It's been nearly 2 decades since you and your partner have had any major quality time. Now is the time to reignite your relationship and recapture the novelty and excitement of your early years together.

Splitting with Your Spouse

Sometimes, however, the children leave behind more than an empty room. Their absence may make the emptiness in your marriage stand out like an elephant in a china shop. Maybe you've known all along that your marriage was slipping, but now that your kids aren't around to distract you, you can't deny it anymore. And now you're faced with the decision to work on the marriage or end it. Perhaps it's no surprise, then, that although the divorce rate in couples over

WOMEN ASK WHY

Why can't my husband understand my point of view no matter how much I explain it?

Your husband might not be listening because he can't handle the situation.

In our laboratory, we found that when a wife and husband get in a heated discussion over money, their kids, or something as simple as doing the dishes, both their heart rates rocket up to about 90 to 100 beats per minute—but he feels much more overwhelmed than she does.

The reason might be that women are socialized to deal with emotions and men aren't. It's as if girls get an education that boys miss out on. Girls are expected to be inclusive in games and sensitive to others' feelings. If someone gets hurt in a game, they stop playing to comfort her.

Boys, on the other hand, are criticized for showing emotion. They're called babies if they cry when they're hurt, so they feel less comfortable talking about their feelings.

By the time men get to marriage, they have a lot of catching up to do. So when a man is faced with his wife's disappointment, anger, or criticism, he's so overwhelmed by the

age 50 is relatively low, a measurable percentage of marriages do dissolve at this point.

Yet even if your marriage has been on the rocks for years, signing those divorce papers hurts because of what they represent: the death of your dream to spend a lifetime with this person. Just as you would grieve the death of a loved one, you need to mourn the loss of the marriage. This process can take years. That's why you shouldn't hesitate to seek professional help as you go through the painful loss of your marriage.

The first months after the split are often the toughest. "I remember going to bed and not even undressing," recalls Beth Jenny, a teacher from Macungie, Pennsylvania, whose 20-year

situation that he tries to end it any way he can. He either walks out of the room or tries to change the subject. When he's forced to sit down and talk about it, he becomes quiet, he doesn't maintain eye contact, and the muscles in his face become tense. We're not sure, but we think he might be so distressed that he can't listen very well to what she's saying.

It is also possible that men tune out because they typically feel compelled to fix everything. It's likely that a man feels overwhelmed by a sense of helplessness when faced with his wife's emotions, which aren't something he can swoop in and fix like a leaky kitchen faucet.

Even though women don't get as overwhelmed by their emotions, it's difficult for anyone to solve complex problems in this state. The best thing to do is to take a 15-minute break to cool down and then come back to the table when you're both calmer.

Expert consulted
Sybil Carrere, Ph.D.
Research scientist
Department of psychology
University of Washington
Seattle

marriage ended in divorce. "I ate half of a bagel every day for 3 or 4 weeks. I was so scared, I couldn't stomach anything else."

"Give yourself permission to be sad for a period of time," says Catherine Chambliss, Ph.D., professor of psychology and department chair at Ursinus College in Collegeville, Pennsylvania. "If you pressure yourself to bounce back immediately, you're apt to become depressed when you fail to meet that expectation."

And write down your fears—first as you're contemplating, then as you're actually going through the divorce. Simply clarifying your worries can help you feel more in control and put you in a much better position to do some

problem solving, Dr. Chambliss says. You'll also find that most of your concerns relate to the losses that come with divorce. A common fear of many women, for example, is loss of financial security. If this made it onto your list of anxieties, brainstorm ways to relieve the burden. Can you cut back on spending? How about setting a budget? Are you eligible for child or spousal support?

These are some other common losses you may experience.

Loss of companionship. When you're divorced, there's no longer a "regular" someone to have dinner with, or talk about your day with. That can leave you feeling lonely and isolated. "Before the divorce, my only close relationship was with my husband," Jenny said. "Afterward, I refound some of my women friends. There were many nights they would come over with a bottle of wine, or we would go to the movies or lunch together." That means structuring your time so you're not just coming home from work and collapsing in front of the TV. You'll also feel less isolated if you get involved in group activities. Jenny, for example, led a singles group at her church and joined Parents Without Partners.

Loss of control over your kids. You want primary custody. So does he. You want to spend Christmas with the kids. So does he. To regain a sense of control, get your custody arrangement in writing. That way, there's no guessing where the kids are staying this weekend. Having a legal agreement also protects your rights, says Megan E. Watson, a Philadelphia attorney who practices family law. If your ex doesn't stick with your agreement, he could be found in contempt of court. But without a legal agreement, you have no way of enforcing your custody arrangement, she says. You may also want to check out divorce support groups or talk with friends who have gone through the same thing so you can see how others have dealt with similar problems. Let yourself acknowledge that this is a frightening process.

Loss of self-esteem. Maybe you felt it was your job to sustain the marriage, and now that it's dead, it's your fault. "People assume that if the whole fails, it must be because the parts are deficient," Dr. Chambliss says.

Get over it. "I was trying to figure out why he left me and I immediately thought of my looks," says Jenny. "Am I that horrible looking? What if no one else ever finds me pretty?" Stop over-generalizing, says Dr. Chambliss. Your ex-husband is not the only man on this planet, nor does he dictate what every man finds attractive.

If you're worried about your looks, take charge. Granted, you're never going to be 5 feet 11 inches tall if you're petite, but you can wear heels to look taller. You can exercise and eat right to lose weight. A new haircut, some stylish clothes, and before you know it, you'll actually be that self-assured woman staring back at you in the mirror. Above all, do what makes you feel good because then you'll build confidence in yourself. Treat yourself to those wacky earrings or that wild nail polish you've been coveting. Go after that college degree you put on hold. Start that small business you've always wanted to. Realize that you *can* capitalize on the skills it takes to run a home and manage a family.

Loss of identity. You've been checking off that "married" box for so long, you may not

---

REAL-LIFE SCENARIO
Her Coworkers Think She's a Witch

Marilyn, 43, is an editor in a large publishing firm. If she spent most of her day in front of her computer alone, she'd be doing a great job. But Marilyn has to interact with dozens of people throughout the company each day: writers who write the books, artists who design them, researchers who fact-check them, and copy editors who edit them. Not to mention that the marketing department constantly demands new ideas, different titles, promotional copy . . . some days, she can barely hear herself think.

So Marilyn is always running from one meeting to another, barking out orders to her secretary (and even her peers). She never takes time to stop and chat, to say hello, or to ask how a coworker is feeling. She takes over meetings, insisting that her ideas take precedence, belittling others. And she's the first person to turn on you if it benefits her. It's gotten to the point that writers beg not to work with her because they just can't stand her abuse. Now her job is in jeopardy. Not because she can't do the work—she does a great job at that—but because no one wants to work with her. What should Marilyn do?

Most of us learn how to read cues from other people. We know when we've made them mad or hurt their feelings, and we figure out how to avoid doing it in the future. But somehow Marilyn hasn't picked up on those cues. She may have done fine in lower-level positions, but now that she's a manager, she has a responsibility to get along with her coworkers.

There's no quick fix for her problem, especially since she probably doesn't realize she's doing anything wrong. With

---

know how to define yourself now that you're single again. "I was always 'the minister's wife,'" says Jenny, whose ex-husband is a pastor. "I didn't have any identity for myself."

To find out who you really are, you need to reconnect with yourself and your dreams. "I decided I didn't want to be a victim and I was going to learn something from all of this," Jenny says. "I went back to school, started doing some writing and more reading, and began listening to

her job in jeopardy, however, it's really important that she acknowledge that she needs to change and get constructive criticism from people who aren't afraid to give it to her—in group therapy.

She can find a licensed psychologist or certified social worker who will team her with five to eight other people in therapy. The group setting will allow her therapist to see how Marilyn responds to other people. As others talk about their problems, she'll probably react to them the same way she reacts to her coworkers: by snapping at them, interrupting, and taking over the conversation.

The only difference between the therapy group and her meetings at work will be that the people in her group won't be afraid to tell her when she crosses the line and how it makes them feel when she interrupts them. Suddenly, she'll have a consensus: The people in her group will confirm what her coworkers think, and she'll know what she does that pushes people away.

Once she's ready to change, she can use group therapy to practice being more sensitive to other people's feelings and even act out typical office scenes.

How long it takes before she changes depends on Marilyn's motivation. With her job on the line, she's probably inclined to change more quickly. Once her coworkers like her more, they'll be not only happier but more productive.

Expert consulted
Mindy R. Schiffman, Ph.D.
Clinical psychologist
New York City

the kind of music I liked—all hobbies I wanted to do before, but couldn't because I was too busy being a minister's wife."

Making Your Job Work for You

One reason for the high divorce rate, experts speculate, is that nearly 60 percent of today's women work outside the home. That financial freedom gives us the wherewithal to leave if we're unhappy in our marriage. But what if we're unhappy at work? These days, we're just as likely to leave.

In some ways, the glass ceiling of the past has been replaced by the revolving door of the present. "There is no such thing as a permanent job anymore," says Mary Sickel, a master certified career and personal coach from Lakeville, Minnesota. We're changing careers—not just jobs—five to seven times in our lives.

One reason for the wandering workforce is that we're unhappy. Eighty percent of us, in fact, are dissatisfied in our current jobs, says Sandy Anderson, Ph.D., a certified job and career transition coach in Carlsbad, California, and author of *Women in Career and Life Transitions*.

The key to unlocking job satisfaction is simple: Experts say you should match your job to your needs and values. You may want to try the following tips.

Remember your needs. We're so busy with the day-to-day details of life that we're often disconnected from what's important to us. To rediscover your priorities, it's critical to set up a program of self-care, says Katharine Halpin, an executive coach based in Phoenix. "It's where all the answers come from."

First, exercise for at least 30 minutes each day. Not only does exercise give us mental clarity, it also helps relieve stress. "I find that the quality of my decisions is directly related to how much exercise I get," Halpin says.

Second, "brain dump." Basically, this is writing out daily to-do lists. Jot down everything you have to do, from finishing that report and dropping off the dry cleaning to picking up the kids after soccer practice. This exercise clears out all the stuff that's swirling around in your head, says Halpin.

Third, set aside "think time" each day to get your thoughts down on paper. Use this time to focus on meeting the challenges at your current job. How can you be more efficient? How can you get your department moving in a new direction? Write down any solutions that pop into your head, no matter how silly they seem. "Getting these ideas down on paper is what's going to make them more useful," Halpin says. It helps you get a clearer picture because you have to clarify your ideas before you can write them down. Soon you'll probably find you're more productive, you come up with better ideas, and you approach old problems with a new perspective.

If you're looking for a new job, use the "think time" for reflection. Keep a journal in which you tackle soul-searching questions: What do I feel success is? Is it a paycheck? Is it making a contribution? What kind of job schedule suits me best? How much money do I need to make? Do I mind a long commute? What kind of work environment do I prefer? What did I like and not like about my previous job? Answering these questions will help you get in touch with your core values, so you know what to look for in your next job.

Take time off. Whether you quit your job, were fired, or were laid off, you're bound to be going through a mountain range of emotions. "My boss came into my office one day at 4:00 P.M. and said, 'The company's having some financial trouble and we have to let you go. How about leaving right now?'" recalls Nancy Moffett of Coopersburg, Pennsylvania, who was laid off from her market-managing job in 1995. "I felt

---

ARE YOU IN BALANCE?

Becoming emotionally balanced doesn't happen overnight. It could take weeks, months, or even years. Knowing where you are now and evaluating yourself again in the future will help you track your progress and continue in the right direction. Answer yes or no to every question.

1. My journal is full of my own reflections of my emotions: anger, anxiety, joy, and happiness.
2. It's too hard to squeeze in time for friends between my job, husband, kids, and house.
3. Whenever I get mad at someone, I stand up straight, look him in the eye, and speak in a strong, clear voice.
4. I try to live up to my picture of the ideal woman: She's successful at her job and a perfect mother, keeps an immaculate house, and watches all her sons' soccer games.
5. I give myself an hour of relaxation time every day to read a book, sip some tea, or listen to music.
6. I find it hard to talk about my anxiety, jealousy, and loneliness, even with close friends.
7. To connect with other women, I have joined a book club or another group that I enjoy.
8. Sometimes I feel out of control when it comes to shopping, eating, drinking alcohol, or spending time on the Internet.

---

betrayed because I had put so much of myself into this job. I remember driving home and crying, thinking, 'Oh my God, what am I going to do now?'"

"You really need to take some time off so you can work through your feelings before jumping into another job," Halpin says. These feelings may range from anger to grief. This also prevents you from getting another job just like the one you left. She suggests taking at least 60 to 90 days before starting your job search. If you've been laid off, try to negotiate a minimum of 6 months' severance pay and benefits. Can't afford to take that much time off? Get a low-stress temporary or part-time job to tide you over.

9. When I'm stressed, I schedule a massage or take a long bath.

10. I'm too much of a perfectionist to take creative risks, such as starting to paint, draw, or write.

11. I've written my own vision statement for the next 5 years, and I use it daily to keep me on track.

12. My anxiety sends me to chocolate in the middle of the afternoon.

13. Going for walks, even short ones, helps me relieve stress.

14. I'm lucky if I get 6 hours of sleep every night.

Even-numbered questions: Give yourself one point for every "no" answer.

Odd-numbered questions: Give yourself one point for every "yes" answer.

If you scored:

11–14: You're well on your way to emotional health.

6–10: You're getting there.

1–5: You still have a long journey ahead. Reread this book over the next few weeks and make a list of actions you can take to become more emotionally balanced. Then tackle one a week until they become second nature to you.

Put your personality into your resumé. List more than your job skills and experience. If you like working in groups, describe yourself as a team player. Good at making decisions? Say you're decisive. If you don't know how to describe yourself, ask a friend or coworker to name your top three gifts, Sickel suggests.

Assess the company's culture. You want a work environment that fits your needs. So ask probing questions in your job interview. If you work best as part of a team, for example, and the company says they tried teams but they didn't work, there's a clue that this may not be the place for you. If you work best in a calm, structured environment with little chaos and they

kept you waiting 40 minutes for your interview, consider the implications.

Find outside interests. Expecting your job to meet all of your needs just sets you up for disappointment and discontent, Sickel says. It's up to you to meet the needs your job doesn't. If your clerical post allows little room for creativity, sign up for a pottery class. Wish your desk job was more active? Take dance lessons or join a walking club.

Job Change: Navigating New Waters with Ease

Like marriage, a new job is cause for celebration. Someone *likes* you. Someone *needs* you. You can't wait to get started. Break out the champagne!

So why are you feeling so stressed out?

"Even under the best of circumstances, a job change is a major life stress, especially if you're uprooting a family and moving across the country," says Lynne McClure, Ph.D., a management consultant in Phoenix. And now that one in five working women earn more than their husbands, it's increasingly women who are prompting the move.

"A job change can be very stressful for dual-career families," says Dr. McClure. "But sometimes it's the healthiest thing you can do." Low pay, lack of recognition, and a boss you don't get along with are all good reasons to make a change for the better. The downside: You're leaving behind friends, familiar surroundings, and an established routine for an uncertain future. To ease the transition, follow this expert advice.

Grieve for what you're leaving behind. In one sense, a job change is not unlike a divorce or the loss of a loved one. "Even if you hated your

---

LOCATION, LOCATION, LOCATION

Fewer crowds and wider streets might not be the only reasons to move to the suburbs. A study by the Centers for Disease Control and Prevention found that people who live in cities and rural areas are 25 percent more likely to experience negative moods, such as feeling depressed, upset, lonely, abandoned, bored, or restless, than people who live in the suburbs.

Although where we live isn't hugely predictive of our mood (how much education we have, our ethnicity, and our gender are even stronger predictors), there is evidence that choosing Fifth Avenue, along with all its traffic, crowds, and stress, brings us down, says Bruce S. Jonas, Ph.D., author of the study and a behavioral scientist in Hyattsville, Maryland.

Living far from a city in the rural mountains, though, also makes us a little more moody, probably because resources such as libraries, fitness centers, and community groups are lacking.

The suburbs, he suggests, offer a balance of the two, with museums, theaters, malls, and gyms close by, along with less crowded neighborhoods and parks.

Don't rent a moving van just yet, though. "Wherever you go, you'll find happy people and sad people," says Dr. Jonas.

---

new procedures in bite-size chunks. So be clear about which tasks you're supposed to tackle first. "Don't expect to accomplish it all in a day," adds Dr. Reinhold. "It's going to take some time."

Scope out the social scene. As you settle into a new routine, remember what your mother told you in grade school: Pick your friends carefully. You're known by your associates. "You don't know the politics, so tread lightly," says Marilyn Manning, Ph.D., a management consultant in Mountain View, California. "You could be befriended by the 'difficult' person, so don't identify yourself with any group too soon."

As a newcomer, try to associate with a variety of people: Eat lunch in different areas of the cafeteria, for example, or volunteer for such extracurricular activities as the United Way committee, suggests Dr. Manning.

---

old job, there's a grieving process involved," Dr. McClure says. "Part of you has to grieve for the parts of the job that you'll miss. If you don't, it will eventually catch up with you, like all unfinished grieving."

Give yourself permission to worry. When starting a new job, many workers worry that they won't make a good impression if they can't waltz in and do the job perfectly. "It's natural to have misgivings about changing jobs," says Barbara Reinhold, Ed.D., director of the career development office at Smith College in Northampton, Massachusetts.

Ask for clear direction. Even if the job is the same as your old one, you'll still have to learn

Making the Most of Menopause

It's the seventh-inning stretch in the game of life. To our mothers, menopause marked the beginning of the end, the doorstep to old age. To us, it often represents the beginning of a whole new chapter in our lives, the opportunity to once again remake ourselves.

But into what?

"When it comes to facing menopause, the generations of women before us left no road maps," says Stephanie DeGraff Bender, a licensed clinical psychologist, clinical director of Full Circle Women's Health in Boulder, Colorado, and author of *The Power of Perimenopause.*

They handled the "change" silently, privately, perhaps taking Valium to get through unsettling symptoms and emotions.

We've decided to do it differently. "Women are blazing new trails," Bender says. Here's the modern-day, emotionally healthy way to face the big "M."

Seek out support. It's as if you're setting off on a voyage over rough seas of hot flashes and fatigue. You can't possibly navigate the waters on your own. So pick your crewmates. "We need to constantly be in contact with other women who are going through this same process," Bender says. They validate our experiences, enabling us to realize that our strange symptoms and mixed emotions are normal. We may even learn different ways to cope.

Gather information. Hit the library, the bookstore, and the Internet. Don't limit yourself. Realizing that there is a vast array of information out there will help you feel less afraid and gain a sense of control. You'll also find unique, positive ways to move through this period of your life.

Take stock of your symptoms. They're different for every woman. So write down your symptoms and concerns, then turn your personal inventory into a plan of action. If your main complaint is insomnia, check in with yourself. Is it caffeine? Anxiety? Then brainstorm ways to help yourself sleep better. For possible solutions, tap into your support system and the information you've gathered. Your plan of action will give you a sense of security, Bender says. "It's like when you get on a cruise ship. It's not that you

ALL IN THE GENES?

Why do we get butterflies in our stomachs and what purpose do they serve?

When we're nervous, our bodies think we're in danger. Our hearts send blood from our stomachs to our brains and muscles so we have enough energy to fight or run away, and our digestion slows down, along with other maintenance functions. The movement of blood away from the stomach sometimes creates a feeling of nausea, or "butterflies."

The sensation isn't always consistent. Sometimes we'll feel it when we're just a little nervous (when we're getting ready for a party, for example), and other times we won't feel anything. In truly dangerous situations, we'll be too concerned about the man following us on the street or the bear in front of us in the woods to notice what's going on in our stomachs.

Expert consulted
Kelly Woolaway-Bickel
Senior clinic coordinator
Anxiety and Stress Disorders Clinic
Ohio State University
Columbus

want to use those lifeboats, but you want to know where they are."

Cut through cultural messages. Along with the insomnia and forgetfulness, menopause is a very emotionally charged time in our lives. Suddenly, it's not that we don't *want* to have more children, it's that we *can't* have more children. It's also a sign that the clock is ticking inexorably in only one direction. That's particularly hard to take in today's youth-and-beauty-obsessed culture. "One woman said to me, 'I know in my head that I don't have to have a chiseled face and a 21-year-old figure, but in my heart . . . ,'" says Bender. Write down your feelings and ask yourself where they're coming from.

Then you can say, "I know the source of this message—our youth and beauty culture—and I'm no longer going to buy into it." Take this opportunity to step back and celebrate all you've accomplished and the woman you've become. "You couldn't have done all those things at age 25," Bender says. "That's why we call them life's lessons."

Dealing with a Diagnosis

One lesson we'd rather not learn is the lesson of illness and pain. Whether it strikes us or someone else in our lives, it leaves us feeling angry, insecure, out of control, and terrified.

"When the doctor told me I had multiple sclerosis, I was in shock," says Sandi Lloyd, 38, of Allentown, Pennsylvania, who learned she had multiple sclerosis in 1994. After a second doctor confirmed the diagnosis, the anger set in. "For a week, I cried and cursed and asked, 'Why is this happening to me?'" Lloyd says. "I had a very spirited 1-year-old daughter and I wanted to be physically active in every aspect of this new life. But because I was so exhausted all the time, I felt I was robbed of my ability to be the kind of mother I wanted to be. It seemed cruel and unfair."

Then there were the fears that someday she wouldn't be able to take care of herself, and that she may have passed a susceptibility to multiple sclerosis on to her daughter.

We're also afraid people will treat us differently. We don't want to be pitied, be seen as weak, or have our illness become our identity. We fear being labeled "the cancer patient" or

EMOTIONAL INTELLIGENCE

"I think, therefore I am," said 17th-century French philosopher René Descartes.

Ever since we first wielded number-two pencils, we've been taught the same thing: Intelligence means memorizing multiplication tables, acing history tests, and beating our arch-nemesis in the class spelling bee.

Our friends that rang the phone off the hook, however, were seen as an impediment to getting our homework done.

Not anymore. Our emotions are finally getting the respect they deserve. Your grades and SAT scores may have gotten you into college, but working well with other people is probably what will get you promoted in the workplace.

Emotions are an integral part of the decisions we make. They even existed in the primitive human brain before the rational part, the neocortex, grew around it. Our brains developed into a tapestry of emotional strands and rational strands, which means emotions have power over all brain functions.

Being emotionally intelligent means recognizing our feelings as signals that we have a problem, then rationally thinking of a solution. Once we know our own feelings, we notice them in other people, too.

The first step is to recognize how we feel when crisis strikes, says Susan Heitler, Ph.D., a clinical psychologist in Denver and author of *From Conflict to Resolution*. Your 7-year-old son refuses to put his jacket on before you both leave to

"the AIDS patient," says Debi Frankle, a licensed psychotherapist and grief counselor in Calabasas, California.

One way we deal with all these emotions is with the big "D": denial. "My brother, who died of skin cancer, walked around with this huge spot on his leg for 6 months saying it was nothing," Frankle says. We often won't face the reality of our illness because we think there's

go shopping. Ignoring your anger, you try to reason with him. The longer he refuses, the madder you get, until you explode, "You're such a brat!"

Becoming more emotionally intelligent means using the first glimmer of emotion as a clue to step away and think rationally about a solution. You could say to yourself, "I'm starting to get mad and we're getting into a power struggle. It's late afternoon, he's probably hungry, and he says no to everything when he's hungry."

Instead of yelling, you go into the kitchen for some crackers, grab his jacket, and say, "I'll race you to the car." At the car, you give him his snack. He's satisfied and he puts on his jacket. You're both winners.

It's important to step away from the situation, because emotions travel fast while the rational parts of our brains work more slowly, Dr. Heitler says. Anger, frustration, or anxiety should be a yellow traffic signal that tells us to slow down and think about an effective solution. When we try to smother the emotion, the signal becomes louder and louder, until it's a blazing neon sign that says, "You're frustrated and you have to do something about it."

The signal comes in a different way for everyone. Some women feel their stomachs tighten; others hear a negative voice in their head saying things like "He's a terrible kid." Learn the unique way that you experience your emotions and then take a moment to think rationally. Once you do that, you'll be able to guess and react to how the people around you feel and find a successful solution.

fears about your illness can make it seem less frightening. "I shared a lot of my anger with my family and close friends," Lloyd says. "I truly believe sharing the weight of all that anger with them helped me endure it and eventually let it go."

It's better to face each emotion as it comes, Frankle says, and to be open and honest with yourself and others about what you're feeling. If you can't find the support at home, turn to an outside support group or therapist, she adds. In the long run, opening up will have beneficial results because you will have connected with others: You won't be alone when you realize that other people have similar feelings or have been in similar situations.

Study your disease. "When I was diagnosed with MS, everything I knew was based on the devastating decline of well-known celebrities with the disease," Lloyd says. Since then, she's done her homework, gathering information only from reliable sources. Now she acts as a gatekeeper for her family and friends. "They've come to rely on me for information," Lloyd says. "They'll call me and say, 'Have you heard that drinking too much cola can cause MS?' And I can nip that in the bud right off the bat." Contact the foundation or organization that is associated with your illness to find more information. The organization may even be able to put your family in contact with support groups to help them cope with your illness as well.

nothing we can do. Plus, we feel terrified and helpless against it. But even if your condition is untreatable and you feel afraid, you *can* take steps to feel better both emotionally and physically when you're ready to maximize your quality of life.

Share your feelings. Bottling up your emotions keeps you from working through them. Even though it may be difficult, sharing your

Help yourself heal. Ask your doctor what things you can do on your own that may improve your condition. If you come across any

WOMEN ASK WHY

Why do I have such a hard time giving up friendships that I've outgrown?

Our friends do everything from going shoe shopping with us to providing a sensitive ear when we're stressed about our jobs, our kids, or our men.

But the more we add to our life with marriage, children, and work, the less time we have for many of them. Because we're afraid of hurting their feelings or being impolite, we feel guilty when we don't return their phone calls quickly enough or when we cancel lunch plans.

With the exception of those few people with whom we form lifelong friendships, it's likely that most friends will become less important in our lives. Friendships are built around being in a similar stage of life. You bonded with her because you both had young children or you worked together or you were neighbors. But once the kids moved out, you changed jobs, or she moved, the two of you grew apart.

Once a friend gets signals that you don't have the time to put into the friendship anymore, she usually steps away and gives you room. Unlike romantic relationships, friendships aren't exclusive. They carry an unwritten rule that other obligations such as family come before them.

If a friend just doesn't understand that you've grown apart, be honest with her. Say to her, "I wish I had the time to get together more often, but I just don't."

Expert consulted
Linda Sapadin, Ph.D.
Clinical psychologist
Valley Stream, New York
Author of It's About Time!

self-help tips in your research, run them by your doctor. Sometimes exercising or taking vitamins or herbs, for example, can help you feel better.

Bust stress. Stress can compromise your immune system, so when you're faced with an illness, you need to recognize stressful patterns or habits in your life and find ways to work around them. Take a walk, rent a funny movie, meditate, listen to music—whatever works for you. This way, you won't feel that your illness is getting the best of you, says Frankle.

"My true love is creative writing," Lloyd says. "It's an incredible stress reliever that has helped me tackle some difficult feelings."

Adjust your attitude. Once you've faced reality and begun to accept your illness, try to be as positive as you can about it. "I feel like my illness has been a gift in so many ways," Lloyd says. "Not only has it made me and the people around me more sensitive to others with disabilities, it also has put the things that are important in my life into focus." Be mindful of your daily activities, and give yourself permission to soak up even the smallest details, from the way the light shimmers through a rain-soaked window to the pleasant ache in your muscles after a day of gardening.

Volunteer. Helping others gives you a different perspective and makes you feel that you're not the patient all the time, Frankle says. When you're sick, you may feel as if you have nothing to offer anymore. Volunteering can show you how vital and needed you still are.

Back off. If someone you love is the one who's sick, honor the way they choose to handle it. "My husband felt very strongly about maintaining a positive attitude throughout his illness. For that reason, he never wanted to talk about the possibility of his dying or to read any negative information or statistics I came across," says Kathy Adams, of Center Valley, Pennsylvania, whose husband died at age 43 of breast cancer. "I agreed that it was really important to remain positive, so even though I knew in my heart he was dying, I never spoke to him about it." This worked for Adams and her husband.

Another approach is to say, "I'm really scared you're going to die. Is it okay if we talk about that?" You may be surprised by the answer. Some people don't bring up their illness or fears because they don't want to upset you, Frankle says. When given the chance, they may talk openly about their feelings. But if not, be sure to get the help you need to deal with their illness.

FIND THE OPTIMIST WITHIN

Are you convinced that your health will suffer unless you become an incurable optimist who goes around with a smile on your face and a song in your heart?

That's what such apostles of positivism as Norman Vincent Peale, author of *The Power of Positive Thinking*, would have you believe. For decades, they've been preaching that positive thinking will save you from disease, disability, and an early grave.

That's not necessarily so, says Susan Robinson-Whelen, Ph.D., a researcher at the Center of Excellence on Healthy Aging with Disabilities at the Houston VA Medical Center.

Dr. Robinson-Whelen is coauthor of a study that examined how optimism and pessimism affected the health of 224 middle-age and older adults—mostly women—over a period of several years. She found that embracing optimism isn't as strongly associated as you might think with high levels of self-reported health and low levels of stress and anxiety.

What's more important, the study suggests, is avoiding pessimism. In other words, you don't have to always expect the best. Just don't always expect the worst.

Coping with the Loss of a Loved One

Eventually, you're going to have to deal with death. And here's where an old friend comes in handy. Charlie Brown's eternal lament, "Good grief!" could teach us all a valuable lesson: While grief feels lousy when we're going through it, it's necessary if we're going to move on.

Grief is difficult to work through because it isn't a single emotion. It's a tossed salad of feelings ranging from anger, sorrow, and regret to guilt and even relief. "You feel like a piece of you is missing, like there's a hole that can never be filled," says Eadie Barrie, a development officer for the Indiana Historical Society, whose 74-year-old mother died suddenly in 1990.

John James, founder of the Grief Recovery Institute in Los Angeles, once described grief as reaching out for someone who was there before and realizing they're no longer there. "I can't tell you how many times I picked up the phone to call my mom. It was always such a smack to realize I couldn't call her," Barrie says.

We all deal with that feeling of emptiness differently. Some of us cry enough to water a cornfield. Others become workaholics. Still others can't stop asking why. The problem is, none of these coping methods really work, says Frankle. "We haven't been taught the skills in our society to complete the loss and effectively move on," she says.

Here are some of those lessons.

Translate the messages. In the first few days after the death, we're bombarded with comforting words. As well-meaning as our

INNER-SPACE EXPLORERS

Who were Meyer and Sullivan?

By understanding the role of our environment and our personal relationships in the development of our personalities, early 20th-century psychiatrists Harry Stack Sullivan and Adolf Meyer shifted psychology's focus from the symptoms to the person, helping change attitudes toward psychiatric patients and advancing "moral treatment" in hospitals.

Sullivan, who was born in Norwich, New York, in 1892, said interactions with others, particularly with our parents when we are children, are a major factor in the development of our personalities. He treated anxiety and disorders such as schizophrenia by looking at his patients' relationships with their parents. Because he thought mistrust was the key to his patients' conditions, he treated them with respect and asked his staff to do the same.

Meyer, who was born in Switzerland in 1866 and emigrated to the United States in 1892, also thought a patient's background was crucial to treatment, so he created life charts, which are now standardized case histories. He also cofounded the mental hygiene movement, which helped improve conditions of psychiatric care, and integrated social work into his treatments. In the first efforts in psychiatric social work, his wife, Mary, visited patients' families.

friends are, they fill our heads with unhelpful, and sometimes even harmful, messages. Recognizing the reality is one step to grieving effectively. These are some examples.

❧ You'll (remarry, have another child, make a new friend). It's a nice idea, says Frankle, but people can't be replaced. If your husband of 20 years dies, you can't go buy a new one at the corner store.

❧ You need to be strong. "When my mother passed away, I felt I had to be strong for my brother and sisters because I'm the oldest," Barrie says. "When my son was killed at age 30 by a drunk driver, I again tried to be strong because I thought if I let myself fall apart, I'd never be able to put the pieces back together." The truth is, there's no reason for us to be strong, Frankle says, if being strong forces us to deny our feelings. Crying, yelling, pounding a pillow—these are all healthy ways of expressing emotion. If we do these things, we're not falling apart. We're grieving.

❧ Just stay busy and you'll feel better. Some people take this advice and begin a whirlwind of activity when a loved one dies, just to keep their minds off their pain. But that just keeps them from grieving, says Frankle. In order to move on, you need to face your feelings, she says. If you don't face them now, they're bound to come knocking weeks or even years later. This doesn't mean that you have to stop your life to grieve, however. On the contrary, Barrie stayed active when her mother died so that she *could* grieve. "First, I planned Mom's service down to every last detail, which meant picking out each flower one by one. When that was over, I took consolation in doing things my mother had taught me—I used her recipes to bake pies, bread, pasta. This allowed me to think about her, which in turn allowed me to grieve more proactively."

❧ At least he's not in pain anymore. Or the converse: At least she didn't suffer. Maybe not, but you're suffering. "When I found out something had happened to Mom, I was scared for me and how I would possibly cope without her," says Barrie. Acknowledge that your emotional pain needs to be dealt with.

❧ You just need some time by yourself. Isolation is the worst thing for someone who's grieving, Frankle says. You churn up all the things you wish had been different with that person, and you go over them again and again in your head, which leaves you more depressed, more anxious, and more cut off from those who can help you.

➤ Time will heal your pain. One problem with this message is that you're hurting now. The other problem is that it just isn't true. "When you're dealing with a loss, it's not time but what you do with that time that helps you heal," Frankle says. If you're avoiding your emotions by clocking 12-hour days at the office, you're not taking the time to work through your feelings.

Take care of unfinished business. Death not only takes away someone we love, it also leaves behind regrets. To move past the pain of the "if onlys" and "I wish I hads," you need to complete your relationship with the person who has died, Frankle says. That means working through all of the unresolved issues you have with that person. It's a six-step process.

➤ Count your losses. Make a time line of your life and write down all the losses you've experienced over the years. It will help you see how ineffectively you've dealt with them. So forget about how you've coped in the past; it hasn't worked. Now get ready to try a new process that will help you move on.

➤ Review your relationship. Draw a line across the middle of a piece of paper. Now think back to your first memory of the person who died. If it was a really positive event, put it at the top of the paper. Horrible? Write it below the line. Review your entire relationship, plotting each memory on the paper. This helps you get at the unresolved issues you need to work through to move beyond your pain. And it allows you to "talk" about the person you've lost.

➤ Say you're sorry. Make a list of all the things you need to make amends for and things you wish you had done differently. Getting these down on paper helps you let go of the guilt you feel.

➤ Forgive without forgetting. Write down all the things you need to forgive the person for. When you look at your relationship graph, these are usually the things that fall below the line. "Forgiving means you have a resentment you don't want to carry anymore. You're the one who's left with it, and you want to let it go," Frankle says. This step is often difficult for us to do, she says, because we're afraid if we forgive the person, we'll forget them. Not true. Our resentments are where much of the pain of the relationship comes from. Letting go of the pain opens us up to a new, more positive connection.

➤ Say the unsaid. Jot down all the things you wish you had told the person. These things should be positive. If they're not, you need to go back to your "I'm sorry" and "I forgive you" lists. Include things you're grateful for, things you appreciated them for, and things you learned from them.

➤ Say goodbye. Write a goodbye letter. Use the three lists you just made as the body of your letter. Start by saying, "Dear Mom, I have some things to tell you. I'm sorry for . . . ," and that's your sorry list. Then copy down the things you forgive her for and what you wish you had told her. The most important and most difficult part is the end. "That's where you say goodbye to the pain and to the physical relationship that you no longer have with the person," Frankle says. That's not to say you won't feel sad on the person's birthday or a special anniversary, but if you feel resentment, you have to go back and do the process again, Frankle says. You may need to repeat it a few times over the years before you've worked through all your unresolved issues. But like the joy that follows the pain of childbirth, the peace and love that ensue cannot be matched.

Index

Underscored page references indicate boxed text.